CONTENTS

MEMOIR OF GEORGE HERBERT..........................

THE POETRY OF GEORGE HERBERT

  I. THE TEMPLE.

     1. THE CHURCH-PORCH. 14
     2. SUPERLIMINARE. 27
     3. THE ALTAR. 27
     4. THE SACRIFICE. 27
     5. THE THANKSGIVING. 35
     6. THE REPRISALL. 36
     7. THE AGONIE. 36
     8. THE SINNER. 37
     9. GOOD FRIDAY. 37
     10. REDEMPTION. 38
     11. SEPULCHRE. 38
     12. EASTER. 39
     13. EASTER-WINGS. 41
     14. HOLY BAPTISME. 42
     15. HOLY BAPTISME. 42
     16. NATURE. 43
     17. SINNE. 43
     18. AFFLICTION. 44
     19. REPENTANCE. 45
     20. FAITH. 46
     21. PRAYER. 48
     22. THE HOLY COMMUNION. 48
     23. ANTIPHON. 49
     24. LOVE. 50
     25. THE TEMPER. 51
     26. THE TEMPER. 51
     27. JORDAN. 52
     28. EMPLOYMENT. 52
     29. THE HOLY SCRIPTURES. 53
     30. WHITSUNDAY. 54
     31. GRACE. 55
     32. PRAISE. 55
     33. AFFLICTION. 56
     34. MATTENS. 56
     35. SINNE. 57
     36. EVEN-SONG. 57
     37. CHURCH-MONUMENTS. 58
     38. CHURCH-MUSICK. 59
     39. CHURCH-LOCK AND KEY. 59

40. THE CHURCH-FLOORE. 60
41. THE WINDOWS. 60
42. TRINITIE SUNDAY. 61
43. CONTENT. 61
44. THE QULDDITIE. 62
45. HUMILITIE. 62
46. FRAILTIE. 63
47. CONSTANCES. 64
48. AFFLICTION. 65
49. THE STARRE. 65
50. SUNDAY. 66
51. AVARICE. 68
52. ANA-GRAM 68
53. TO ALL ANGELS AND SAINTS. 68
54. EMPLOYMENT. 69
55. DENIALL. 70
56. CHRISTMAS. 71
57. UNGRATEFULNESSE. 72
58. SIGHS AND GRONES. 73
59. THE WORLD. 74
60. COLOSS. iii. 3. 74
61. VANITIE. 75
62. LENT. 75
63. VERTUE. 77
64. THE PEARL. 77
65. AFFLICTION. 78
66. MAN. 79
67. ANTIPHON. 81
68. UNKINDNESSE. 81
69. LIFE. 82
70. SUBMISSION 83
71. JUSTICE. 83
72. CHARMS AND KNOTS. 84
73. AFFLICTION. 84
74. MORTIFICATION. 85
75. DECAY. 86
76. MISERIE. 87
77. JORDAN. 89
78. PRAYER. 89
79. OBEDIENCE. 90
80. CONSCIENCE. 91
81. SION. 92
82. HOME. 92
83. THE BRITISH CHURCH. 94
84. THE QUIP. 95
85. VANITIE. 96
86. THE DAWNING. 96
87. JESU 97

THE COMPLETE WORKS OF GEORGE HERBERT

A Digireads.com Book
Digireads.com Publishing

The Complete Works of George Herbert
By George Herbert
ISBN 10: 1-4209-4792-3
ISBN 13: 978-1-4209-4792-2

This edition copyright © 2013

Please visit *www.digireads.com*

88. BUSINESSE.	97
89. DIALOGUE.	98
90. DULNESSE.	99
91. LOVE-JOY.	100
92. PROVIDENCE.	100
93. HOPE.	105
94. SINNE'S ROUND.	105
95. TIME.	105
96. GRATEFULNESSE.	106
97. PEACE.	107
98. CONFESSION.	108
99. GEDDINESSE.	109
100. THE BUNCH OF GRAPES.	110
101. LOVE UNKNOWN.	111
102. MAN'S MEDLEY.	112
103. THE STORM.	113
104. PARADISE.	114
105. THE METHOD.	114
106. DIVINITIE.	115
107. EPHES. IV. 30.	116
108. THE FAMILIE.	117
109. THE SIZE.	118
110. ARTILLERIE.	119
111. CHURCH-RENTS AND SCHISMES.	120
112. JUSTICE.	121
113. THE PILGRIMAGE.	121
114. THE HOLDFAST.	122
115. COMPLAINING.	123
116. THE DISCHARGE.	123
117. PRAISE.	125
118. AN OFFERING.	125
119. LONGING.	127
120. THE BAG.	129
121. THE JEWS.	130
122. THE COLLAR.	131
123. THE GLIMPSE.	131
124. ASSURANCE.	132
125. THE CALL.	133
126. CLASPING OF HANDS.	134
127. PRAISE.	134
128. JOSEPH'S COAT.	135
129. THE PULLEY.	136
130. THE PRIESTHOOD.	136
131. THE SEARCH.	137
132. GRIEF.	139
133. THE CROSSE.	140
134. THE FLOWER.	141
135. DOTAGE.	142

136. THE SONNE...143
137. A TRUE HYMNE...143
138. THE ANSWER...144
139. A DIALOGUE-ANTHEM..144
140. THE WATER-COURSE...144
141. SELF-CONDEMNATION..145
142. BITTER-SWEET..145
143. THE GLANCE..146
144. THE TWENTY-THIRD PSALME..146
145. MARIE MAGDALENE..147
146. AARON..148
147. THE ODOUR..148
148. THE FOIL..149
149. THE FORERUNNERS...149
150. THE ROSE...150
151. DISCIPLINE..151
152. THE INVITATION..152
153. THE BANQUET..153
154. THE POSIE..155
155. A PARODIE...155
156. THE ELIXER...156
157. A WREATH...157
158. DEATH..157
159. DOOMS-DAY..158
160. JUDGEMENT..158
161. HEAVEN...159
162. LOVE...159

II. THE CHURCH MILITANT...161

JACULA PRUDENTUM;..168

THE PROSE OF GEORGE HERBERT

A PRIEST TO THE TEMPLE;...194

THE AUTHOR TO THE READER..194
CHAPTER I. OF A PASTOR..195
CHAPTER II. THEIR DIVERSITIES..195
CHAPTER III. THE PARSON'S LIFE..196
CHAPTER IV. THE PARSON'S KNOWLEDGE...196
CHAPTER V. THE PARSON'S ACCESSORY KNOWLEDGES....................197
CHAPTER VI. THE PARSON PRAYING...198
CHAPTER VII. THE PARSON PREACHING...199
CHAPTER VIII. THE PARSON ON SUNDAYS...200
CHAPTER IX. THE PARSON'S STATE OF LIFE..201
CHAPTER X. THE PARSON IN HIS HOUSE...202
CHAPTER XI. THE PARSON'S COURTESY...205

- CHAPTER XII. THE PARSON'S CHARITY. 205
- CHAPTER XIII. THE PARSON'S CHURCH. 206
- CHAPTER XIV. THE PARSON IN CIRCUIT. 207
- CHAPTER XV. THE PARSON COMFORTING. 208
- CHAPTER XVI. THE PARSON A FATHER. 208
- CHAPTER XVII. THE PARSON IN JOURNEY. 209
- CHAPTER XVIII. THE PARSON IN SENTINEL. 209
- CHAPTER XIX. THE PARSON IN REFERENCE. 210
- CHAPTER XX. THE PARSON IN GOD'S STEAD. 211
- CHAPTER XXI. THE PARSON'S CATECHISING. 211
- CHAPTER XXII. THE PARSON IN SACRAMENTS. 213
- CHAPTER XXIII. THE PARSON'S COMPLETENESS. 214
- CHAPTER XXIV. THE PARSON'S ARGUING. 215
- CHAPTER XXV. THE PARSON PUNISHING. 216
- CHAPTER XXVI. THE PARSON'S EYE. 216
- CHAPTER XXVII. THE PARSON IN MIRTH. 218
- CHAPTER XXVIII. THE PARSON IN CONTEMPT. 219
- CHAPTER XXIX. THE PARSON WITH HIS CHURCH WARDENS. 219
- CHAPTER XXX. THE PARSON'S CONSIDERATION OF PROVIDENCE. ...220
- CHAPTER XXXI. THE PARSON IN LIBERTY. 221
- CHAPTER XXXII. THE PARSON'S SURVEYS. 222
- CHAPTER XXXIII. THE PARSON'S LIBRARY. 224
- CHAPTER XXXIV. THE PARSON'S DEXTERITY IN APPLYING OF REMEDIES. 225
- CHAPTER XXXV. THE PARSON'S CONDESCENDING. 227
- CHAPTER XXXVI. THE PARSON BLESSING. 227
- CHAPTER XXXVII. CONCERNING DETRACTION. 228
- THE AUTHOR'S PRAYER BEFORE SERMON. 229
- PRAYER AFTER SERMON. 230

LETTERS OF GEORGE HERBERT. 231

THE ORATION OF MASTER GEORGE HERBERT 237

PREFACE AND NOTES TO THE DIVINE CONSIDERATIONS OF JOHN VALDESSO. 238

NOTES TO THE DIVINE CONSIDERATIONS. 239

A TREATISE OF TEMPERANCE AND SOBRIETY 244

MEMOIR OF GEORGE HERBERT

George Herbert was born in Montgomery Castle, Shropshire, on the 3d of April 1593. His father, Richard Herbert of Blakehall, was descended of a younger branch of the family of Pembroke. His mother was Magdalen Newport, the youngest daughter of Sir Richard Newport of High Arkall, in the county of Salop. Donne, who knew her well, has, in one of his finest poems, the "Autumnal Beauty," commemorated her noble qualities and her majestic person. Izaak Walton tells us, that as "the happy mother of seven sons and three daughters," she would often thank God that He had given her "Job's number and Job's distribution." When her fifth son, George, was four years old, her husband died. After the lapse of a few years, she removed to Oxford, to superintend the education of her youngest son, Edward, afterwards the celebrated Lord Herbert of Cherbury, author of the once famous book, *De Veritate prout distinguitur de Revelatione.*

George, in the meantime, whose childhood had been spent, as Walton says, "in a sweet content, under the eye and care of a prudent mother, and the tuition of a chaplain," had been removed to Westminster School, then under the presidency of Mr. Ireland. During the three years he remained at Westminster, he is said to have attained to considerable proficiency in classical, and especially in Greek learning. About the year 1608 he was entered of Trinity College, Cambridge, where he enjoyed the almost paternal care of Dr. Nevil, then Dean of Canterbury and Master of the College. His name appears on the Register of Scholars under date 6th May 1609. At Cambridge he seems to have distinguished himself greatly. In 1611 he took his Bachelor's degree; within two years thereafter he was chosen a Fellow; he became Master of Arts in 1615; and on the 21st October 1619, on the resignation of Sir Francis Nethersole, he was elected to the distinguished post of Public Orator to the University.

Walton has described this portion of Herbert's career with fine feeling and much beauty of expression. "As he grew older," he says, "so he grew in learning, and more and more in favour both with God and man: insomuch that, in this morning of that short day of his life, he seemed to be marked out for virtue, and to become the care of Heaven; for God still kept his soul in so holy a frame, that he may, and ought to be a pattern of virtue to all posterity, and especially to his brethren of the clergy." During all the time he was at College, continues the fine old gossip, "all, or the greatest diversion from his study, was the practice of music, in which he became a great master; and of which he would say, that it did relieve his drooping spirits, compose his distracted thoughts, and raise his weary soul so far above earth, that it gave him an earnest of the joys of heaven before he possessed them."

By his elevation to the office of Public Orator, which he held for eight years, Herbert was on the highway to court preferment. His predecessors, Naunton and Nethersole, had attained respectively to the dignities of Secretary of State and principal Secretary to the Queen of Bohemia. His *debût* in his new capacity was a successful one. James I had presented to the University a copy of his book, *Basilicon Doron,* and it was Herbert's duty to acknowledge the honour. In a Latin letter, still extant, written with an elegance not unworthy of Milton or Buchanan, he intermingled with compliments to the King expressions "so full of conceits," and so adapted to James's taste, that the gratified monarch was pleased to pronounce the writer "the jewel of the University."

To the University itself the King at length came, where it was Herbert's duty, as often as James could spare time from his sports at Newmarket and Royston, to welcome him with "gratulations and the applauses of an orator," which "he performed so well, that he still grew more and more into the King's favour."[1] It was during these progresses that Herbert became acquainted with Lord Bacon and Bishop Andrews—an acquaintance that ripened into an intimacy which only ceased with the poet's death. With Sir Henry Wotton, also, he was on terms of close friendship; and Donne esteemed him so highly, that on his deathbed he bequeathed to the son of the "Lady Magdalen" a seal, bearing the figure of Christ crucified on an anchor, and the motto, "*Crux mihi anchora.*"

Herbert seems at this period to have been exceedingly solicitous for Court preferment, and with this view to have become an assiduous student of foreign languages. But his hopes were blasted by the death of James, who had, however, previously bestowed upon his favourite a sinecure, once the property of Sir Philip Sydney. With the profits arising from his post, which were valued at £120 a-year, an annuity which he enjoyed from his family, and the income he derived from his College and his Oratorship, Herbert was enabled to gratify what Walton calls his genteel humour for clothes and court-like company. How long he resided in London is not known. But shortly after the King's death he retired into Kent, "where he lived very privately, and was such a lover of solitariness as was judged to impair his health nore than his study had done. In this time of retirement he had many conflicts with himself, whether he should return to the painted pleasures of a court-life, or betake himself to the study of divinity, and enter into sacred orders, to which his dear mother had often persuaded him. These were such conflicts as they only can know that have endured them; for ambitious desires and the outward glory of this world are not easily laid aside; but at last God inclined him to put on a resolution to serve at his altar."[2]

It was on his return to London that this resolution was first announced. The date of his ordination is unknown; but Walton discovered, from the records of Lincoln, that the prebend of Layton Ecclesia, in that diocese, was conferred upon him by Bishop Williams in the summer of 1626. At the period of his appointment, the parish church of Layton was in so dilapidated a condition that the parishioners could not meet in it for public worship. Herbert's first step was to undertake its restoration, and "he lived," says Walton, "to see it so wainscotted as to be exceeded by none."

In 1627 he lost his mother, who, in the twelfth year of her widowhood, had married the brother and heir of the Earl of Danby. For years before her death she seems to have suffered much; but she had a tender consoler in her son. "For the afflictions of the body, dear madam," he wrote, in a letter still extant, "remember the holy martyrs of God, how they have been burned by thousands, and have endured such other tortures as the very mention of them might beget amazement; but their fiery trials have had an end; and yours, which, praised be God, are less, are not like to continue long. I beseech you, let such thoughts as these moderate your present fear and sorrow; and know, that if any of yours should prove a Goliah-like trouble, yet you may say with David, 'That God, who delivered me out of the paws of the lion and bear, will also deliver me out of the hands of this uncircumcised Philistine.' Lastly, for those afflictions of the soul; consider that God intends that to be as a sacred temple for Himself to dwell in, and will not allow any room there for such an inmate as grief, or allow that any sadness shall be his competitor. And,

---

[1] Walton's Life of Herbert.
[2] Walton's Life of Herbert.

above all, if any care of future things molest you, remember those admirable words of the Psalmist,—'Cast thy care on the Lord, and he shall nourish thee.'"[3]

Two years later, when Herbert was in his thirty-ninth year, he was himself seized with quotidian ague, and for change of air removed to Woodford, in Essex, where his brother, Sir Henry Herbert, and some other friends were residing. At Woodford he remained about a year, and by "forbearing drink, and not eating any meat," he cured himself of his disorder, although a tendency to consumption now began to manifest itself. To counteract this tendency, he removed to Dauntsey in Wiltshire, a seat of the Earl of Danby. There, by a spare diet, moderate exercise, and abstinence from study, his health apparently improved. He therefore, in compliance with the long-expressed wishes of his mother, determined to marry and enter on the priesthood. The story of his courtship is curious. There resided near Dauntsey a gentleman named Danvers, a near kinsman of Herbert's friend Lord Danby. Mr. Danvers had a family of nine daughters, and had often and publicly expressed a wish that Herbert would marry one of them, "but rather his daughter Jane than any other, because his daughter Jane was his favourite daughter." "And he had often said the same to Mr. Herbert himself; and that if he could like her for a wife, and she him for a husband, Jane should have a double blessing: and Mr. Danvers had so often said the like to Jane, and so much commended Mr. Herbert to her, that Jane became so much a Platonic as to fall in love with Mr. Herbert unseen." "This," adds Walton, from whom we have been quoting, "was a fair preparation for a marriage; but alas! her father died before Mr. Herbert's retirement to Dauntsey: yet some friends to both parties procured their meeting; at which time a mutual affection entered into both of their hearts, as a conqueror enters into a surprised city: and love having got such possession, governed, and made there such laws and resolutions, as neither party was able to resist; insomuch that she changed her name into Herbert the third day after this first interview." The marriage proved eminently happy; for, as Walton beautifully says, "the Eternal Lover of mankind made them happy in each other's mutual and equal affections and compliance; indeed, so happy, that there never was any opposition betwixt them, unless it were a contest which should most incline to a compliance with the other's desires. And though this begot, and continued in them, such a mutual love, and joy, and content, as was no way defective; yet this mutual content, and love, and joy, did receive a daily augmentation by such daily obligingness to each other, as still added new affluences to the former fulness of these divine souls, as was only improvable in heaven, where they now enjoy it."

About three months after the marriage, the rectory of Bemerton, in Wiltshire, fell vacant through the elevation of the incumbent, Dr. Curll, to the see of Bath and Wells. Through the influence of the Earl of Pembroke with the King, the living was offered to Herbert. Not without much prayer and fasting did he at last accept it. "And in this time of considering he endured, as he would often say, such spiritual conflicts as none can think but only those that have endured them."[4]

At length, principally through the interposition of Laud, then Bishop of London, Herbert was prevailed upon to lay his presentation before the Bishop of Salisbury, who at once gave him institution. Walton tells an interesting story in connection with the induction. Being shut up in the church to toll the bell, as the law then required, he staid so much longer than the ordinary time that his friends became anxious, and one of them, Mr.

---

[3] Psalm iv. 22.
[4] Walton's Life of Herbert.

Woodnot, looking in at the church window, saw him lie prostrate on the ground before the altar. Not for some time was it known that he was then setting rules for the government of his life, and making a vow to keep them.

And now commenced the most interesting period of Herbert's life. The care of his parish became the engrossing topic of his thoughts. From repairing the parish church and rebuilding the parsonage house, he turned away to give rules to himself and his parishioners, "for their Christian carriage both to God and man." How he laboured in his vocation, and how his labours were so blest, that, while the better class of his parishioners, and many of the neighbouring gentry, were attending on his daily ministrations in the church, "some of the meaner sort did so love him, that they would let their plough rest when Mr. Herbert's saints'-bell rung to prayers, that they might also offer their devotions to God with him,"—we read in the quaint but eloquent page of Walton. Herbert's chief if not sole recreation was music, "in which heavenly art," says his affectionate biographer, "he was a most excellent master, and did himself compose many divine hymns and anthems, which he set and sung to his lute or viol; and though he was a lover of retiredness, yet his love to music was such, that he went usually twice every week, on certain appointed days, to the cathedral church in Salisbury; and at his return would say, that his time spent in prayer and cathedral music elevated his soul, and was his heaven upon earth. But before his return thence to Bemerton, he would usually sing and play his part at an appointed private music-meeting; and to justify this practice, he would often say, 'Religion does not banish mirth, but only moderates and sets rules to it.'"

At length, after a residence at Bemerton of about two years, his health became so much impaired that he was forced to confine himself for the most part to the house. But still, in spite of his increasing weakness, he continued as formerly to read prayers in public twice a-day, sometimes at home and sometimes in the church which immediately adjoined. "In one of which times of his reading, his wife observed him to read in pain, and told him so, and that it wasted his spirits, and weakened him; and he confessed it did, but said his life could not be better spent than in the service of his master Jesus, who had done and suffered so much for him. "But," said he, "I will not be wilful; for though I find my spirit be willing, yet I find my flesh is weak; and therefore Mr. Bostock[5] shall be appointed to read prayers for me to-morrow; and I will now be only a hearer of them, till this mortal shall put on immortality.' And Mr. Bostock," says Walton, "did the next day undertake and continue this happy employment, till Mr. Herbert's death."

A few weeks before his death, Herbert was visited by his friend Mr. Duncon, afterwards rector of Friar Barnet in Middlesex. To him, at parting, the dying man delivered *The Temple,* with instructions to place it in the hands of their common friend Nicholas Farrer, the "Protestant Monk" of Little Gidding, saying, as he did so, "Sir, I pray you deliver this little book to my dear brother Farrer, and tell him he shall find in it a picture of the many spiritual conflicts that have passed betwixt God and my soul, before I could subject mine to the will of Jesus my master; in whose service I have now found perfect freedom. Desire him to read it; and then, if he can think it may turn to the advantage of any dejected poor soul, let it be made public; if not, let him burn it; for I and it are the least of God's mercies." "Thus meanly," adds Walton, who reports the words, "did this humble man think of this excellent book, of which Mr. Farrer would say, there was in it the picture of a divine soul in every page; and that the whole book was such a harmony of holy passions, as would enrich the world with pleasure and piety."

---

[5] Mr. Bostock was Herbert's curate in the neighbouring church of Fugglestone.

The closing scene of this good man's life cannot be better told than in the language of Walton. He had now become very "restless," says Izaak, "and his soul seemed to be weary of her earthly tabernacle, and this uneasiness became so visible, that his wife, his three nieces, and Mr. Woodnot, stood constantly about his bed, beholding him with sorrow, and an unwillingness to lose the sight of him, whom they could not hope to see much longer. . . . . And when he looked up, and saw his wife and nieces weeping to an extremity, he charged them, if they loved him, to withdraw into the next room, and there pray every one alone for him; for nothing but their lamentations could make his death uncomfortable. To which request their sighs and tears would not suffer them to make any reply; but they yielded him a sad obedience, leaving only with him Mr. Woodnot and Mr. Bostock. Immediately after they had left him, he said to Mr. Bostock, 'Pray, sir, open that door, then look into that cabinet, in which you may easily find my last will, and give it into my hand:' which being done, Mr. Herbert delivered it into the hand of Mr. Woodnot, and said, 'My old friend, I here deliver you my last will, in which you will find that I have made you sole executor for the good of my wife and nieces; and I desire you to show kindness to them, as they shall need it. I do not desire you to be just, for I know you will be so for your own sake; but I charge you, by the religion of our friendship, to be careful of them.' And having obtained Mr. Woodnot's promise to be so, he said, 'I am now ready to die.' After which words, he said, 'Lord, forsake me not, now my strength faileth me; but grant me mercy for the merits of my Jesus. And now, Lord—Lord, now receive my soul!' And with these words he breathed forth his divine soul, without any apparent disturbance, Mr. Woodnot and Mr. Bostock attending his last breath, and closing his eyes."

So died George Herbert. Let our last hope be that of his artless and affectionate biographer—"If God shall be so pleased, may I be so happy as to die like him!"

The Temple was published at Cambridge shortly after its anther's death, with a preface by Nicholas Farrer. It immediately became popular—to such an extent, indeed, that when Walton published his lives, upwards of twenty thousand copies had been sold. Cowley alone enjoyed a greater popularity. But while the works of Cowley are now half forgotten, those of Herbert are still highly esteemed and widely read. And they are worthy of the distinction. *The Temple* may be disfigured by conceits which may sometimes displease us, and by obscurities which may seem to partake of the mysticism of the later Schoolmen. But our displeasure bears no proportion to the delight with which we contemplate the richness of his fancy and the idiomatio beauties of his language; while the deep devotion with which the poem is instinct warrants us in believing, with Henry Vaughan, that the "holy life and verse" of Herbert did much to divert that "foul and overflowing stream" of impurity by which the literature of Eng-, land was then inundated.

>'More sweet than odours caught by him who sails
>Near spicy shores of Araby the blest,
>A thousand times more exquisitely meet,
>The freight of holy feeling which we meet,
>In thoughtful moments, wafted by the gale
>From fields where good man walk, or bowers wherein they rest.'
>   WORDSWORTH."

THE POETRY OF GEORGE HERBERT

I. THE TEMPLE.

THE DEDICATION.

Lord, my first fruits present themselves to thee;
Yet not mine neither: for from thee they came,
And must return. Accept of them and me,
And make us strive, who shall sing best thy name.
    Turn their eyes hither, who shall make a gain
    Theirs, who shall hurt themselves or me, refrain.

1. THE CHURCH-PORCH.

Perirrhanterium.

THOU, whose sweet youth and early hopes inhance
Thy rate and price, and mark thee for a treasure,
Hearken unto a Verser, who may chance
Ryme thee to good, and make a bait of pleasure:
    A verse may finde him who a sermon flies,
    And turn delight into a sacrifice.

Beware of lust; it doth pollute and foul
Whom God in baptisme washt with his own blood:
It blots thy lesson written in thy soul;
The holy lines cannot be understood.
    How dare those eyes upon a Bible look,
    Much lesse towards God, whose lust is all their book!

Abstain wholly, or wed. Thy bounteous Lord
Allows thee choise of paths: take no by-wayes;
But gladly welcome what he doth afford;
Not grudging, that thy lust hath bounds and staies.
    Continence hath his joy: weigh both; and so
    If rottennesse have more, let Heaven go.

If God had laid all common, certainly
Man would have been th' incloser: but since now
God hath impal'd us, on the contrarie
Man breaks the fence, and every ground will plough.
    O what were man, might he himself misplace!
    Sure to be crosse he would shift feet and face.

Drink not the third glasse, which thou canst not tame,
When once it is within thee; but before
Mayst rule it, as thou list: and poure the shame,
Which it would poure on thee, upon the floore.
    It is most just to throw that on the ground,
      Which would throw me there, if I keep the round.

He that is drunken, may his mother kill
Bigge with his sister: he hath lost the reins,
Is outlaw'd by himself: all kinde of ill
Did with his liquor slide into his veins.
    The drunkard forfets Man, and doth devest
      All worldly right, save what he hath by beast.

Shall I, to please anothers wine-sprung minde,
Lose all mine own? God hath giv'n me a measure
Short of his canne, and bodie; must I finde
A pain in that, wherein he findes a pleasure?
    Stay at the third glasse: if thou lose thy hold,
      Then thou art modest, and the wine grows bold.

If reason move not Gallants, quit the room;
(All in a shipwrack shiit their severall way)
Let not a common ruine thee intombe:
Be not a beast in courtesie, but stay,
    Stay at the third cup, or forego the place.
      Wine above all things doth God's stamp deface.

Yet, if thou sinne in wine or wantonnesse,
Boast not thereof; nor make thy shame thy glorie.
Frailtie gets pardon by submissivenesse;
But he that boasts, shuts that out of his storie:
    He makes flat warre with God, and doth defie
      With his poore clod of earth the spacious sky.

Take not his name, who made thy mouth, in vain:
It gets thee nothing, and hath no excuse.
Lust and wine plead a pleasure, avarice gain:
But the cheap swearer through his open sluce
    Lets his soul runne for nought, as little fearing:
      Were I an *Epicure,* I could bate swearing.

When thou dost tell another's jest, therein
Omit the oathes, which true wit cannot need:
Pick out of tales the mirth, but not the sinne.
He pares his apple, that will cleanly feed.
    Play not away the vertue of that name,
    Which is thy best stake, when griefs make thee tame.

The cheapest sinnes most dearly punisht are;
Because to shun them also is so cheap:
For we have wit to mark them, and to spare.
O crumble not away thy soul's fair heap.
    If thou wilt die, the gates of hell are broad:
    Pride and full Sinnes have made the way a road.

Lie not; but let thy heart be true to God,
Thy mouth to it, thy actions to them both:
Cowards tell lies, and those that fear the rod;
The stormie working soul spits lies and froth.
    Dare to be true. Nothing can need a ly:
    A fault, which needs it most, grows two thereby.

Flie idlenesse, which yet thou canst not flie
By dressing, mistressing, and complement.
If those take up thy day, the sunne will crie
Against thee; for his light was onely lent.
    God gave thy soul brave wings; put not those feathers
    Into a bed, to sleep out all ill weathers.

Art thou a Magistrate? then be severe:
If studious; copie fair what time hath blurr'd;
Redeem truth from his jawes: if souldier,
Chase brave employments with a naked sword
    Throughout the world. Fool not; for all may have,
    If they dare try, a glorious life, or grave.

O England! full of sinne, but most of sloth;
Spit out thy flegme, and fill thy breast with glorie:
Thy Gentrie bleats, as if thy native cloth
Transfuse'd a sheepishnesse into thy storie:
    Not that they all are so; but that the most
    Are gone to grasse, and in the pasture lost.

This losse springs chiefly from our education. [sonne:
Some till their ground, but let weeds choke their
Some mark a partridge, never their childes fashion:
Some ship them over, and the thing is done.
    Studie this art, make it thy great designe;
    And if God's image move thee not, let thine.

Some great estates provide, but do not breed
A mast'ring minde; so both are lost thereby:
Or els they breed them tender, make them need
All that they leave: this is flat povertie.
    For he, that needs five thousand pound to live
    Is full as poore as he, that needs but five.

The way to make thy sonne rich, is to fill
His minde with rest, before his trunk with riches:
For wealth without contentment, climbes a hill,
To feel those tempests, which fly over ditches.
    But if thy sonne can make ten pound his measure,
    Then all thou addest may be call'd his treasure.

When thou dost purpose ought, (within thy power)
Be sure to doe it, though it be but small:
Constancie knits the bones, and makes us stowre,
When wanton pleasures becken us to thrall.
    Who breaks his own bond, forfeiteth himself:
    What nature made a ship, he makes a shelf.

Doe all things like a man, not sneakingly:
Think the king sees thee still; for his King does.
Simpring is but a lay-hypocrisie:
Give it a corner, and the clue undoes.
    Who fears to do ill, sets himself to task:
    Who fears to do well, sure should wear a mask.

Look to thy mouth: diseases enter there.
Thou hast two sconses, if thy stomach call;
Carve, or discourse; do not a famine fear.
Who carves, is kind to two; who talks, to all.
    Look on meat, think it dirt, then eat a bit;
    And say withall, Earth to earth I commit.

Slight those who say amidst their sickly healths,
Thou liv'st by rule. What doth not so, but man?
Houses are built by rule, and common-wealths.
Entice the trusty sunne, if that you can,
    From his Ecliptick line; becken the skie.
    Who lives by rule then, keeps good companie.

Who keeps no guard upon himself, is slack,
And rots to nothing at the next great thaw.
Man is a shop of rules, a well-truss'd pack,
Whose every parcell under-writes a law.
    Lose not thyself, nor give thy humours way:
    God gave them to thee under lock and key.

By all means use sometimes to be alone.
Salute thy self: see what thy soul doth wear.
Dare to look in thy chest; for 'tis thine own:
And tumble up and down what thou find'st there.
    Who cannot rest till he good fellows finde,
    He breaks up house, turns out of doores his minde.

Be thriftie, but not covetous: therefore give
Thy need, thine honour, and thy friend his due.
Never was scraper brave man. Get to live;
Then live, and use it: else, it is not true
    That thou hast gotten. Surely use alone
    Makes money not a contemptible stone.

Never exceed thy income. Youth may make
Ev'n with the yeare: but age, if it will hit,
Shoots a bow short, and lessens still his stake,
As the day lessens, and his life with it.
    Thy children, kindred, friends upon thee call;
    Before thy journey fairly part with all.

Yet in thy thriving still misdoubt some evil;
Lest gaining gain on thee, and make thee dimme
To all things els. Wealth is the conjurer's devil;
Whom when he thinks he hath, the devil hath him.
    Gold thou mayst safely touch; but if it stick
    Unto thy hands, it woundeth to the quick.

What skills it, if a bag of stones or gold
About thy neck do drown thee? raise thy head;
Take starres for money; starres not to be told
By any art, yet to be purchased.
    None is so wastefull as the scraping dame:
    She loseth three for one; her soul, rest, fame.

By no means runne in debt; take thine own measure:
Who cannot live on twentie pound a yeare,
Cannot on fourtie: he's a man of pleasure,
A kinde of thing that's for itself too deere.
    The curious unthrift makes his cloth too wide,
    And spares himself, but would his taylor chide.

Spend not on hopes. They that by pleading clothes
Do fortunes seek, when worth and service fail,
Would have their tale beleeved fox their oathes,
And are like empty vessels under sail.
    Old courtiers know this; therefore set out so,
    As all the day thou mayst hold out to go.

In clothes, cheap handsomnesse doth bear the bell.
Wisdome's a trimmer thing, than shop e're gave.
Say not then, This with that lace will do well;
But, This with my discretion will be brave.
    Much curiousnesse is a perpetual wooing,
    Nothing with labour, folly long a doing.

Play not for gain, but sport. Who playes for more,
Than he can lose with pleasure, stakes his heart:
Perhaps his wives too, and whom she hath bore:
Servants and churches also play their part.
    Onely a herauld, who that way doth passe,
    Findes his crackt name at length in the church-glasse.

If yet thou love game at so deere a rate,
Learn this, that hath old gamesters deerely cost:
Dost lose? rise up: dost winne? rise in that state.
Who strive to sit out losing hands, are lost.
    Game is a civil gunpowder, in peace
    Blowing up houses with their whole increase.

In conversation boldnesse now bears sway.
But know, that nothing can so foolish be,
As empty boldnesse: therefore first assay
To stuffe thy minde with solid braverie;
  Then march on gallant: get substantiall worth:
  Boldnesse guilds finely, and will set it forth.

Be sweet to all. Is thy complexion sowre?
Then keep such companie; make them thy allay:
Get a sharp wife, a servant that will lowre.
A stumbler stumbles least in rugged way.
  Command thyself in chief. He life's warre knows,
  Whom all his passions follow, as he goes.

Catch not at quarrels. He that dares not speak
Plainly and home, is coward of the two.
Think not thy fame at ev'ry twitch will break:
By great deeds shew, that thou canst little do;
  And do them not: that shall thy wisdome be;
  And change thy temperance into braverie.

If that thy fame with ev'ry toy be pos'd,
'Tis a thinne web, which poysonous fancies make;
But the great souldiers honour was compos'd
Of thicker stuffe, which would endure a shake.
  Wisdome picks friends; civilitie playes the rest.
  A toy shunn'd cleanly passeth with the best.

Laugh not too much: the wittie man laughs least:
For wit is newes only to ignorance.
Lesse at thine own things laugh; lest in the jest
Thy person share, and the conceit advance.
  Make not thy sport, abuses: for the fly,
  That feeds on dung, is coloured thereby.

Pick out of mirth, like stones out of thy ground,
Profanenesse, filthinesse, abusivenesse.
These are the scumme, with which course wits abound
The fine may spare these well, yet not go lesse.
  All things are bigge with jest: nothing that's plain
  But may be wittie, if thou hast the vein.

Wit's an unruly engine, wildly striking
Sometimes a friend, sometimes the engineer:
Hast thou the knack? pamper it not with liking:
But if thou want it, buy it not too deere.
    Many affecting wit beyond their power,
    Have got to be a deare fool for an houre.

A sad wise valour is the brave complexion,
That leads the van, and swallows up the cities.
The gigler is a milk-maid, whom infection,
Or a fir'd beacon frighteth from his ditties.
    Then he's the sport: the mirth then in him rests,
    And the sad man is cock of all his jests.

Towards great persons use respective boldnesse:
That temper gives them theirs, and yet doth take
Nothing from thine: in service, care, or coldnesse
Doth ratably thy fortunes marre or make.
    Feed no man in his sinnes: for adulation
    Doth make thee parcell-devil in damnation.

Envie not greatnesse: for thou mak'st thereby
Thyself the worse, and so the distance greater.
Be not thine own worm: yet such jealousie,
As hurts not others, but may make thee better.
    Is a good spurre. Correct thy passion's spite;
    Then may the beasts draw thee to happy light.

When basenesse is exalted, do not bate
The place its honour, for the person's sake.
The shrine is that which thou dost venerate;
And not the beast, that bears it on his back.
    I care not though the cloth of state should be
    Not of rich arras, but mean tapestrie.

Thy friend put in thy bosome: wear his eies
Still in thy heart, that he may see what's there.
If cause require, thou art his sacrifice;
Thy drops of bloud must pay down all his fear;
    But love is lost; the way of friendship's gone;
    Though *David* had his *Jonathan, Christ* his *John.*

Yet be not surety, if thou be a father.
Love is a personall debt. I cannot give
My children's right, nor ought be take it; rather
Both friends should die, than hinder them to live.
    Fathers first enter bonds to nature's ends;
    And are her sureties, ere they are a friend's.

If thou be single, all thy goods and ground
Submit to love; but yet not more then all.
Give one estate, as one life. None is bound
To work for two, who brought himself to thrall.
    God made me one man; love makes me no more,
    Till labour come, and make my weaknesse score.

In thy discourse, if thou desire to please:
All such is courteous, usefull, new, or wittie:
Usefulnesse comes by labour, wit by ease;
Courtesie grows in court; news in the citie.
    Get a good stock of these, then draw the card;
    That suites him best, of whom thy speech is heard.

Entice all neatly to what they know best;
For so thou dost thy self and him a pleasure:
(But a proud ignorance will lose his rest,
Rather than shew his cards) steal from his treasure
    What to ask further. Doubts well-rais'd do lock
    The speaker to thee, and preserve thy stock.

If thou be Master-gunner, spend not all
That thou canst speak, at once but husband it,
And give men turns of speech: do not forestall
By lavishnesse thine own, and others wit,
    As if thou mad'st thy will. A civil guest
    Will no more talk all, than eat all the feast.

Be calm in arguing: for fiercenesse makes
Errour a fault and truth discourtesie.
Why should I feel another man's mistakes
More, than his sicknesses or povertie?
    In love I should: but anger is not love,
    Nor wisdome neither; therefore gently move.

Calmnesse is great advantage: he that lets
Another chafe, may warm him at his fire:
Mark all his wandrings, and enjoy his frets;
As cunningfencers suffer heat to tire.
    Truth dwels not in the clouds: the bow that's there
    Doth often aim at, never hit the sphere.

Mark what another sayes: for many are
Full of themselves, and answer their own notion.
Take all into thee; then with equall care
Ballance each dramme of reason, like a potion.
    If truth be with thy friend, be with them both
    Share in the conquest, and confesse a troth.

Be useful where thou livest, that they may
Both want, and wish thy pleasing presence still.
Kindnesse, good parts, great places are the way
To compasse this. Finde out men's wants and will,
    And meet them there. All worldly joyes go lesse
    To the one joy of doing kindnesses.

Pitch thy behaviour low, thy projects high;
So shalt thou humble and magnanimous be:
Sink not in spirit: who aimeth at the sky
Shoots higher much than he that means a tree.
    A grain of glorie mixt with humblenesse
    Cures both a fever and lethargicknesse.

Let thy minde still be bent, still plotting where,
And when, and how the businesse may be done.
Slacknesse breeds worms; but the sure traveller,
Though he alight sometimes, still goeth on.
Active and stirring spirits live alone:
Write on the others, Here lies such a one.

Slight not the smallest losse, whether it be
In love or honour; take account of all:
Shine like the sunne in every corner: see
Whether thy stock of credit swell, or fall.
    Who say, I care not, those I give for lost;
    And to instruct them, 'twill not quit the cost.

Scorn no man's love, though of a mean degree
(Love is a present for a mightie king,)
Much lesse make any one thine enemie.
As gunnes destroy, so may a little sling.
    The cunning workman never doth refuse
    The meanest tool, that he may chance to use.

All forrain wisdome doth amount to this,
To take all that is given; whether wealth,
Or love, or language; nothing comes amisse:
A good digestion turneth all to health:
    And then as farre as fair behaviour may,
    Strike off all scores; none are so cleare as they.

Keep all thy native good, and naturalize
All forrain of that name; but scorn their ill:
Embrace their activenesse, not vanities.
Who follows all things, forfeiteth his will.
    If thou observest strangers in each fit,
    In time they'l runne thee out of ail thy wit.

Affect in things about thee cleanlinesse,
That all may gladly board thee, as a flowre.
Slovens take up their stock of noisomenesse
Beforehand, and anticipate their last houre.
    Let thy mindes sweetness have his operation
    Upon thy body, clothes, and habitation.

In Almes regard thy means, and others merit.
Think heav'n a better bargain, then to give
Onely thy single market-money for it.
Joyn hands with God to make a man to live.
    Give to all something; to a good poore man,
    Till thou change names, and be where he began.

Man is God's image; but a poore man is
Christ's stamp to boot: both images regard.
God reckons for him, counts the favour his:
Write, So much giv'n to God; thou shalt be heard.
    Let thy almes go before, and keep heav'n's gate
    Open for thee; or both may come too late.

Restore to God his due in tithe and time:
A tithe purloin'd cankers the whole estate.
Sundaies observe: think when the bells do chime,
'Tis angel's musick; therefore come not late.
    God then deals blessings: If a king did so,
    Who would not haste, nay give, to see the show?

Twice on the day his due is understood;
For all the week thy food so oft he gave thee.
Thy cheere is mended; bate not of the food,
Because 'tis better, and perhaps may save thee.
    Thwart not th' Almighty God: O be not crosse.
    Fast when thou wilt; but then 'tis gain, not losse.

Though private prayer be a brave designe,
Yet publick hath more promises, more love:
And love's a weight to hearts, to eies a signe.
We all are but cold suitours; let us move
    Where it is warmest. Leave thy six and seven;
    Pray with the most: for where most pray, is heaven.

When once thy foot enters the church, be bare.
God is more there, then thou: for thou art there
Onely by his permission. Then beware,
And make thyself all reverence and fear.
    Kneeling ne're spoil'd silk stocking: quit thy state.
    All equall are within the churches gate.

Resort to sermons, but to prayers most:
Praying's the end of preaching. O be drest;
Stay not for th' other pin: why thou hast lost
A joy for it worth worlds. Thus hell doth jest
    Away thy blessings, and extreamly flout thee,
    Thy clothes being fast, but thy soul loose about thee.

In time of service seal up both thine eies,
And send them to thine heart; that spying sinne,
They may weep out the stains by them did rise:
Those doores being shut, all by the eare comes in.
    Who marks in church-time other symmetrie,
    Makes all their beautie his deformitie.

Let vain or busie thoughts have there no part:
Bring not thy plough, thy plots, thy pleasures thither.
Christ purg'd his temple; so must thou thy heart.
All worldly thoughts are but theeves met together
    To couzin thee. Look to thy actions well;
    For churches either are our heav'n or hell.

Judge not the preacher; for he is thy Judge:
If thou mislike him, thou conceiv'st him not.
God calleth preaching folly. Do not grudge
To pick out treasures from an earthen pot.
    The worst speaks something good: if all want sense,
    God takes a text, and preacheth patience.

He that gets patience, and the blessing which
Preachers conclude with, hath not lost his pains.
He that by being at church escapes the ditch,
Which he might fall in by companions, gains.
    He that loves God's abode, and to combine
    With saints on earth, shall one day with them shine

Jest not at preacher's language, or expression:
How know'st thou, but thy sinnes made him miscarrie?
Then turn thy faults and his into confession:
God sent him, whatsoe're he be: O tarry,
    And love him for his Master: his condition,
    Though it be ill, makes him no ill Physician.

None shall in hell such bitter pangs endure
As those, who mock at God's way of salvation.
Whom oil and balsames kill, what salve can cure?
They drink with greedinesse a full damnation.
    The Jews refused thunder; and we, folly.
    Though God do hedge us in, yet who is holy?

Summe up at night, what thou hast done by day;
And in the morning, what thou hast to do.
Dresse and undresse thy soul: mark the decay
And growth of it: if with thy watch, that too
    Be down, then winde up both, since we shall be
    Most surely judg'd, make thy accounts agree.

In brief, acquit thee bravely; play the man.
Look not on pleasures as they come, but go.
Defer not the least vertue: life's poore span
Make not an ell, by trifling in thy wo.
    If thou do ill, the joy fades, not the pains:
    If well; the pain doth fade, the joy remains.

2. SUPERLIMINARE.

Thou, whom the former precepts have
Sprinkled and taught, how to behave
Thy self in church; approach, and taste
The churches mysticall repast.

Avoid profanenesse; come not here:
Nothing but holy, pure, and cleare,
Or that which groneth to be so,
May at his perill further go.

3. THE ALTAR.

    A broken ALTAR, Lord, thy servant reares,
    Made of a heart, and cemented with teares:
      Whose parts are as thy hand did frame;
      No workman's tool hath touch'd the same.
          A HEART alone
          Is such a stone,
          As nothing but
          Thy pow'r doth cut.
          Wherefore each part
          Of my hard heart
          Meets in this frame,
          To praise thy name:
      That, if I chance to hold my peace,
      These stones to praise thee may not cease.
      O let thy blessed SACRIFICE be mine,
      And sanctifie this ALTAR to be thine.

4. THE SACRIFICE.

Oh all ye, who passe by, whose eyes and minde
To worldly things are sharp, but to me blinde;
To me, who took eyes that I might you finde:
          Was ever grief like mine?

The Princes of my people make a head
Against their Maker: they do wish me dead,
Who cannot wish, except I give them bread:
                    Was ever grief like mine?

Without me each one, who doth now me brave,
Had to this day been an Egyptian slave.
They use that power against me, which I gave:
                    Was ever grief like mine?

Mine own Apostle, who the bag did beare,
Though he had all I had, did not forbeare
To sell me also, and to put me there:
                    Was ever grief like mine?

For thirtie pence he did my death devise,
Who at three hundred did the ointment prize,
Not half so sweet as my sweet sacrifice:
                    Was ever grief like mine?

Therefore my soul melts, and my heart's deare treasure
Drops bloud (the only beads) my words to measure:
O let this cup passe, if it be thy pleasure:
                    Was ever grief like mine?

These drops being temper'd with a sinner's tears,
A Balsome are for both the Hemispheres,
Curing all wounds, but mine; all, but my fears.
                    Was ever grief like mine?

Yet my Disciples sleep: I cannot gain
One houre of watching; but their drowsie brain
Comforts not me, and doth my doctrine stain:
                    Was ever grief like mine?

Arise, arise; they come. Look how they runne!
Alas! what haste they make to be undone!
How with their lanterns do they seek the sunne!
                    Was ever grief like mine?

With clubs and staves they seek me, as a thief,
Who am the way of truth, the true relief,
Most true to those who are my greatest grief:
                    Was ever grief like mine?

Judas, dost thou betray me with a kisse?
Canst thou finde hell about my lips? and misse
Of life, just at the gates of life and blisse?
                Was ever grief like mine?

See, they lay hold on me, not with the hands
Of faith, but furie; yet at their commands
I suffer binding, who have loos'd their bands:
                Was ever grief like mine?

All my Disciples flie; fear puts a barre
Betwixt my friends and me. They leave the starre,
That brought the wise men of the East from farre:
                Was ever grief like mine?

Thea from one ruler to another bound
They leade me: urging, that it was not found
What I taught: Comments would the text confound.
                Was ever grief like mine?

The Priests and rulers all false witnesse seek
'Gainst him, who seeks not life, but is the meek
And readie Paschal Lambe of this great week:
                Was ever grief like mine?

Then they accuse me of great blasphemie,
That I did thrust into the Deitie,
Who never thought that any robberie:
                Was ever grief like mine?

Some said, that I the Temple to the floore
In three days raz'd, and raised as before.
Why, he that built the world can do much more:
                Was ever grief like mine?

Then they condemne me all with that same breath,
Which I do give them daily, unto death.
Thus *Adam* my first breathing rendereth:
                Was ever grief like mine?

They binde, and leade me unto *Herod:* he
Sends me to *Pilate.* This makes them agree;
But yet their friendship is my enmitie.
                Was ever grief like mine?

Herod and all his bands do set me light,
Who teach all hands to warre, fingers to fight,
And onely am the Lord of hosts and might.
                    Was ever grief like mine?

Herod in judgment sits, while I do stand;
Examines me with a censorious hand:
I him obey, who all things else command:
                    Was ever grief like mine?

The *Jews* accuse me with despitefulnesse;
And vying malice with my gentlenesse,
Pick quarrels with their onely happinesse:
                    Was ever grief like mine?

I answer nothing, but with patience prove
If stonie hearts will melt with gentle love.
But who does hawk at eagles with a dove?
                    Was ever grief like mine?

My silence rather doth augment their crie;
My dove doth back into my bosome flie,
Because the raging waters still are high:
                    Was ever grief like mine?

Hark how they cry aloud still, *Crucifie:*
It is not fit he live a day, they crie,
Who cannot live lesse than eternally:
                    Was ever grief like mine?

Pilate a stranger holdeth off; but they,
Mine own deare people, cry, *Away, away,*
With noises confused frighting the day:
                    Was ever grief like mine?

Yet still they shout, and crie, and stop their eares,
Putting my life among their sinnes and feares,
And therefore wish *my bloud on them and theirs:*
                    Was ever grief like mine?

See how spite cankers things. These words aright
Used, and wished, are the whole world's light:
But honey is their gall, brightnesse their night:
                    Was ever grief like mine?

They choose a murderer, and all agree
In him to do themselves a courtesie;
For it was their own cause who killed me:
                Was ever grief like mine?

And a seditious murderer he was:
But I the Prince of Peace; peace that doth passe
All understanding, more than heav'n doth glasse:
                Was ever grief like mine?

Why, Cesar is their onely king, not I:
He clave the stonie rock, when they were drie;
But surely not their hearts, as I will trie:
                Was ever grief like mine?

Ah! how they scourge me! yet my tendernesse
Doubles each lash: and yet their bitternesse
Windes up my grief to a mysteriousnesse:
                Was ever grief like mine?

They buffet me, and box me as they list,
Who grasp the earth and heaven with my fist,
And never yet, whom I would punish, miss'd:
                Was ever grief like mine?

Behold, they spit on me in scornfull wise;
Who by my spittle gave the blinde man eies,
Leaving his blindnesse to mine enemies:
                Was ever grief like mine?

My face they cover, though it be divine.
As *Moses* face was vailed, so is mine,
Lest on their double-dark souls either shine:
                Was ever grief like mine?

Servants and abjects flout me; they are wittie:
Now prophesie who strikes thee, is their dittie.
So they in me denie themselves all pitie:
                Was ever grief like mine?

And now I am deliver'd unto death,
Which each one cals for so with utmost breath,
That he before me well-nigh suflereth:
                Was ever grief like mine?

Weep not, deare friends, since I for both have wept
When all my tears were bloud, the while you slept:
Your tears for your own fortunes should be kept:
                Was ever grief like mine?

The souldiers lead me to the common hall;
There they deride me, they abuse me all:
Yet for twelve heav'nly legions I could call:
                Was ever grief like mine?

Then with a scarlet robe they me aray;
Which shews my bloud to be the onely way
And cordiall left to repair man's decay:
                Was ever grief like mine?

Then on my head a crown of thorns I wear;
For these are all the grapes *Sion* doth bear,
Though I my vine planted and watred there:
                Was ever grief like mine?

So sits the earth's great curse in *Adam's* fall
Upon my head; so I remove it all
From th' earth unto my brows, and bear the thrall:
                Was ever grief like mine?

Then with the reed they gave to me before,
They strike my head, the rock from whence all store
Of heav'nly blessings issue evermore:
                Was ever grief like mine?

They bow their knees to me, and cry, *Hail king:*
What ever scoffes or scornfulnesse can bring,
I am the floore, the sink, where they it fling:
                Was ever grief like mine?

Yet since man's scepters are as frail as reeds,
And thorny all their crowns, bloudie their weeds;
I, who am Truth, turn into truth their deeds:
                Was ever grief like mine?

The souldiers also spit upon that face
Which Angels did desire to have the grace,
And Prophets once to see, but found no place:
                Was ever grief like mine?

Thus trimmed forth they bring me to the rout,
Who *Crucifie him,* crie with one strong shout.
God holds his peace at man, and man cries out:
                    Was ever grief like mine?

They leade me in once more, and putting then
Mine own clothes on, they leade me out agen.
Whom devils flie, thus is he toss'd of men:
                    Was ever grief like mine?

And now wearie of sport, glad to ingrosse
All spite in one, counting my life their losse,
They carrie me to my most bitter crosse:
                    Was ever grief like mine?

My crosse I bear my self, untill I faint:
Then Simon bears it for me by constraint,
The decreed burden of each mortall Saint:
                    Was ever grief like mine?

O all ye who passe by, behold and see:
Man stole the fruit, but I must climbe the tree;
The tree of life to all, but onely me:
                    Was ever grief like mine?

Lo, here I hang, charg'd with a world of sinne,
The greater world o' th' two; for that came in
By words, but this by sorrow I must win:
                    Was ever grief like mine?

Such sorrow, as if sinful man could feel,
Or feel his part, he would not cease to kneel,
Till all were melted, though he were all steel.
                    Was ever grief like mine?

But, *O my God, my God!* why leav'st thou me,
The sonne, in whom thou dost delight to be?
My God, my Go———
                    Never was grief like mine!

Shame tears my soul, my bodie many a wound;
Sharp nails pierce this, but sharper that confound;
Reproches, which are free, while I am bound:
                    Was ever grief like mine?

Now heal thyself, Physician; now come down.
Alas! I did so, when I left my crown
And father's smile for you, to feel his frown:
                    Was ever grief like mine?

In healing not myself, there doth consist
All that salvation, which ye now resist;
Your safetie in my sicknesse doth subsist:
                    Was ever grief like mine?

Betwixt two theeves I spend my utmost breath,
As he that for some robberie suffereth,
Alas! what have I stollen from you? death:
                    Was ever grief like mine?

A king my title is, prefixt on high;
Yet by my subjects am condemn'd to die
A servile death in servile companie:
                      Was ever grief like mine?

They gave me vineger mingled with gall,
But more with malice: yet, when they did call,
With manna, angel's food, I fed them all:
                    Was ever grief like mine?

They part my garments, and by lot dispose
My coat, the type of love, which once cur'd those
Who sought for help, never malicious foes:
                    Was ever grief like mine?

Nay, after death their spite shall further go;
For they will pierce my side, I full well know;
That as sinne came, so sacraments might flow:
                    Was ever grief like mine?

But now I die; now all is finished.
My wo, man's weal: and now I bow my head:
Onely let others say, when I am dead,
                    Never was grief like mine!

5. THE THANKSGIVING.

OH King of grief! (a title strange, yet true,
        To thee of all kings onely due)
Oh King of wounds! how shall I grieve for thee,
        Who in all grief preventest me?
Shall I weep bloud? why, thou hast wept such store,
        That all thy body was one doore.
Shall I be scourged, flouted, boxed, sold?
        'Tis but to tell the tale is told.
My God, my God, why dost thou part from me?
        Was such a grief as cannot be.
Shall I then sing, skipping, thy dolefull storie,
        And side with thy triumphant glorie?
Shall thy strokes be my stroking? thorns, my flower?
        Thy rod, my posie? crosse, my bower?
But how then shall I imitate thee, and
        Copie thy fair, though bloudie hand?
Surely I will revenge me on thy love,
        And trie who shall victorious prove.
If thou dost give me wealth; I will restore
        All back unto thee by the poore.
If thou dost give me honour; men shall see,
        The honour doth belong to thee.
I will not marry; or, if she be mine,
        She and her children shall be thine.
My bosome friend, if he blaspheme thy name,
        I will tear thence his love and fame.
One half of me being gone, the rest I give
        Unto some Chapell), die or live.
As for thy passion—But of that anon,
        When with the other I have done.
For thy predestination, I'll contrive,
        That three years hence, if I survive,
I'll build a spittle, or mend common waves,
        But mend mine own without delayes.
Then I will use the works of thy creation,
        As if I us'd them but for fashion.
The world and I will quarrell; and the yeare
        Shall not perceive, that I am here.
My musick shall finde thee, and ev'ry string
        Shall have his attribute to sing;
That all together may accord in thee,
        And prove one God, one harmonie.
If thou shalt give me wit, it shall appeare,
        If thou hast giv'n it me, 'tis here.
Nay, I will reade thy booke, and never move

    Till I have found therein thy love;
  Thy art of love, which I'll turn back on thee,
     Oh my deare Saviour, Victorie!
  Then for thy passion—I will do for that—
     Alas, my God, I know not what.

6. THE REPRISALL.

    I HAVE consider'd it, and finde
  There is no dealing with thy mighty passion:
  For though I die for thee, I am behinde;
    My sinnes deserve the condemnation.

    O make me innocent, that I
  May give a disentangled state and free;
  And yet thy wounds still my attempts defie,
    For by thy death I die for thee.

    Ah! was it not enough that thou
  By thy eternall glorie didst outgo me?
  Couldst thou not grief's sad conquests me allow,
    But in all vict'ries overthrow me?

    Yet by confession will I come
  Into the conquest. Though I can do nought
  Against thee, in thee I will overcome
    The man, who once against thee fought.

7. THE AGONIE.

    PHILOSOPHERS have measur'd mountains,
  Fathom'd the depths of seas, of states, and kings,
  Walk'd with a staffe to heav'n, and traced fountains:
    But there are two vast, spacious things,
  The which to measure it doth more behove:
  Yet few there are that found them; Sinne and Love.

    Who would know Sinne, let him repair
  Unto mount Olivet; there shall he see
  A man so wrung with pains, that all his hair,
    His skinne, his garments bloudie be.
  Sinne is that presse and vice, which forceth pain
  To hunt his cruell food through ev'ry vein.

       Who knows not Love, let him assay,
And taste that juice, which on the crosse a pike
Did set again abroach; then let him say
       If ever he did taste the like.
Love in that liquour sweet and most divine,
Which my God feels as bloud; but I, as wine.

8. THE SINNER.

LORD, how I am all ague, when I seek
What I have treasured in my memorie!
      Since, if my soul make even with the week,
Each seventh note by right is due to thee.
I finde there quarries of pil'd vanities,
       But shreds of holinesse, that dare not venture
       To shew their face, since crosse to thy decrees:
There the circumference earth is, heav'n the centre.
In so much dregs the quintessence is small:
       The spirit and good extract of my heart
       Comes to about the many hundreth part.
Yet, Lord, restore thine image, heare my call:
       And though my hard heart scarce to thee can grone,
       Remember that thou once didst write in stone.

9. GOOD FRIDAY.

     O MY chief good,
How shall I measure out thy bloud?
How shall I count what thee befell,
      And each grief tell?

     Shall I thy woes
Number according to thy foes?
Or, since one starre shew'd thy first breath,
      Shall all thy death?

     Or shall each leaf,
Which falls in autumne, score a grief?
Or cannot leaves, but fruit, be signe,
      Of the true vine?

     Then let each houre
Of my whole life one grief devoure;
That thy distresse through all may runne,
      And be my sunne.

   Or rather let
My severall sinnes their sorrows get;
That as each beast his cure doth know,
    Each sinne may so.

Since bloud is fittest, Lord, to write
Thy sorrows in, and bloudie fight;
My heart hath store; write there, where in
One box doth lie both ink and sinne:

That when sinne spies so many foes,
Thy whips, thy nails, thy wounds, thy woes,
All come to lodge there, sinne may say,
No room for me, and flie away.

Sinne being gone, oh fill the place,
And keep possession with thy grace;
Lest sinne take courage and return,
And all the writings blot or burn.

10. REDEMPTION.

HAVING been tenant long to a rich Lord,
   Not thriving, I resolved to be bold,
   And make a suit unto him, to afford
A new small-rented lease, and cancell th' old.

In heaven at his manour I him sought:
   They told me there, that he was lately gone
   About some land, which he had dearly bought
Long since on earth, to take possession.

I straight return'd, and knowing his great birth,
   Sought him accordingly in great resorts;
   In cities, theatres, gardens, parks, and courts:
At length I heard a ragged noise and mirth

   Of theeves and murderers: there I him espied,
   Who straight, *Your suit is granted,* said, and died.

11. SEPULCHRE.

O BLESSED bodie! whither art thou thrown?
No lodging for thee, but a cold hard stone?
So many hearts on earth, and yet not one
       Receive thee?

Sure there is room within our hearts good store;
For they can lodge transgressions by the score:
Thousand of toyes dwell there, yet out of doore
                    They leave thee.

But that which shews them large, shews them unfit.
Whatever sinne did this pure rock commit,
Which holds thee now? Who hath indited it
                    Of murder?

Where our hard hearts have took up stones to brain thee,
And missing this, most falsely did arraigne thee;
Onely these stones in quiet entertain thee,
                    And order.

And as of old, the law by heav'nly art,
Was writ in stone; so thou, which also art
The letter of the word, find'st no fit heart
                    To hold thee.

Yet do we still persist as we began,
And so should perish, but that nothing can,
Though it be cold, hard, foul, from loving man
                    Withhold thee.

12. EASTER.

RISE heart; thy Lord is risen. Sing his praise
                    Without delays,
Who takes thee by the hand, that thou likewise
                    With him mayst rise:
That, as his death calcined thee to dust,
His life may make thee gold, and much more just.

Awake, my lute, and struggle for thy part
                    With all thy art.
The crosse taught all wood to resound his name
                    Who bore the same
His stretched sinews taught all strings, what key
Is best to celebrate this most high day.

Consort both heart and lute, and twist a song
                    Pleasant and long:
Or since all musick is but three parts vied,
                    And multiplied;
O let thy blessed Spirit bear a part,
And make up our defects with his sweet art.

I got me flowers to straw thy way;
I got me boughs off many a tree:
But thou wast up by break of day,
And brought'st thy sweets along with thee.

The Sunne arising in the East,
Though he give light, and th' East perfume;
If they should offer to contest
With thy arising, they presume.

Can there be any day but this,
Though many sunnes to shine endeavour?
We count three hundred, but we misse:
There is but one, and that one ever.

13. EASTER-WINGS.

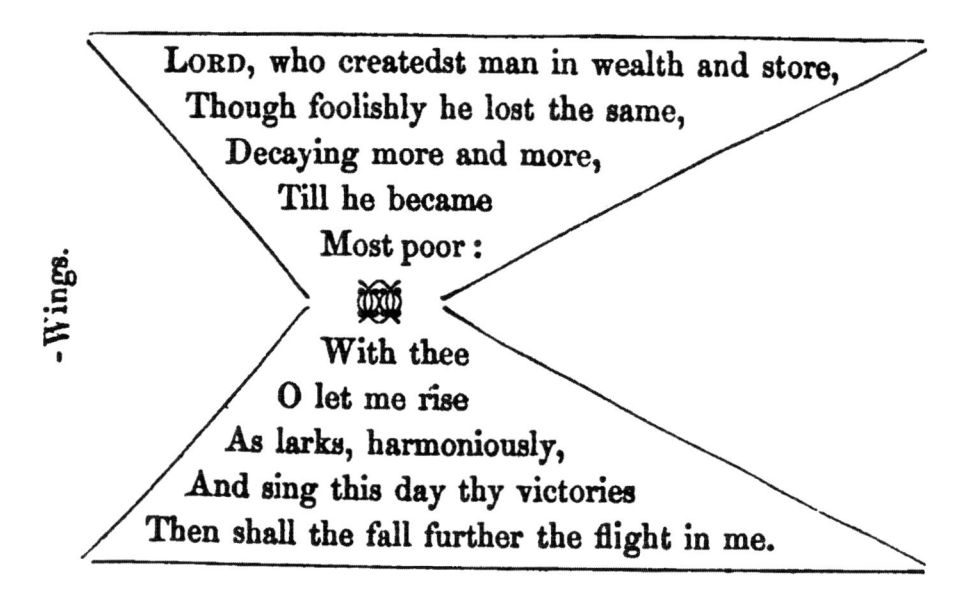

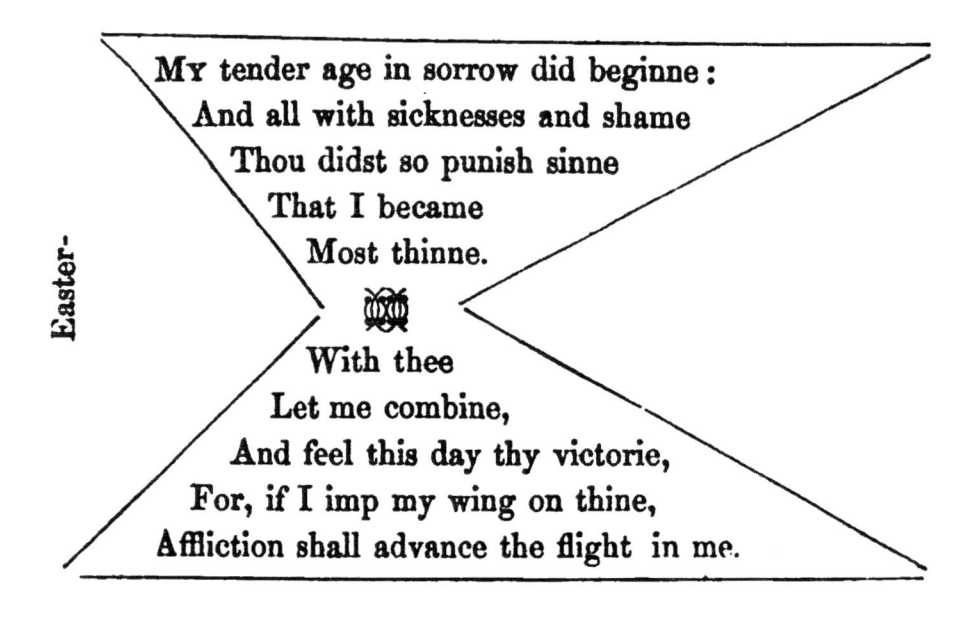

Lord, who createdst man in wealth and store,
  Though foolishly he lost the same,
    Decaying more and more,
      Till he became
        Most poor :
        With thee
      O let me rise
    As larks, harmoniously,
  And sing this day thy victories
Then shall the fall further the flight in me.

My tender age in sorrow did beginne :
  And all with sicknesses and shame
    Thou didst so punish sinne
      That I became
        Most thinne.
        With thee
      Let me combine,
    And feel this day thy victorie,
  For, if I imp my wing on thine,
Affliction shall advance the flight in me.

14. HOLY BAPTISME.

As he that sees a dark and shadie grove,
    Stayes not, but looks beyond it on the skie;
    So when I view my sinnes, mine eyes remove
More backward still, and to that water file,

Which is above the heav'ns, whose spring and rent
    Is in my dear Redeemer's pierced side.
    O blessed streams! either ye do prevent
And stop our sinnes from growing thick and wide,

Or else give tears to drown them, as they grow.
    In you Redemption measures all my time,
    And spreads the plaister equall to the crime:
You taught the book of life my name, that so,

    Whatever future sinnes should me miscall,
    Your first acquaintance might discredit all.

15. HOLY BAPTISME.

    SINCE, Lord, to thee
    A narrow way and little gate
Is all the passage, on my infancie
    Thou didst lay hold, and antedate
    My faith in me.

    O let me still
    Write thee great God, and me a childe:
Let me be soft and supple to thy will,
    Small to myself, to others milde,
    Behither ill.

    Although by stealth
    My flesh get on; yet let her sister
My soul bid nothing, but preserve her wealth:
    The growth of flesh is but a blister;
    Childhood is health.

16. NATURE.

FULL of rebellion, I would die,
Or fight, or travell, or denie
That thou hast ought to do with me.
                 O tame my heart;
                It is thy highest art
To captivate strong holds to thee.

If thou shalt let this venome lurk,
And in suggestions fume and work,
My soul will turn to bubbles straight,
                 And thence by kinde
                Vanish into a winde,
Making thy workmanship deceit.

O smooth my' rugged heart, and there
Engrave thy rev'rend law and fear;
Or make a new one, since the old
                 Is saplesse grown,
                And a much fitter stone
To hide my dust, then thee to hold.

17. SINNE.

LORD, with what care hast thou begirt us round!
        Parents first season us: then schoolmasters
        Deliver us to laws; they send us bound
To rules of reason, holy messengers,

Pulpits and sundayes, sorrow dogging sinne,
        Afflictions sorted, anguish of all sizes,
        Fine nets and stratagems to catch us in,
Bibles laid open, millions of surprises,

Blessings beforehand, tyes of gratefulnesse,
        The sound of glorie ringing in our eares;
        Without, our shame; within, our consciences;
Angels and grace, eternall hopes and fears.

        Yet all these fences and their whole aray.
        One cunning bosome-sinne blows quite away.

18. AFFLICTION.

WHEN first thou didst entice to thee my heart,
          I thought the service brave:
So many joyes I writ down for my part,
          Besides what I might have
Out of my stock of naturall delights,
Augmented with thy gracious benefits.

I looked on thy furniture so fine,
          And made it fine to me;
Thy glorious household-stuffe did me entwine,
          And 'tice me unto thee.
Such starres I counted mine: both heav'n and earth
Payd me my wages in a world of mirth.

What pleasures could I want, whose King I served,
          Where joyes my fellows were?
Thus argu'd into hopes, my thoughts reserved
          No place for grief or fear;
Therefore my sudden soul caught at the place,
And made her youth and fiercenesse seek thy face:

At first thou gav'st me milk and sweetnesses;
          I had my wish and way:
My dayes were straw'd with flow'rs and happinesse;
          There was no moneth but May.
But with my yeares sorrow did twist and grow,
And made a partie unawares for wo.

My flesh began unto my soul in pain,
          Sicknesses cleave my bones,
Consuming agues dwell in ev'ry vein,
          And tune my breath to grones:
Sorrow was all my soul; I scarce beleeved,
Till grief did tell me roundly, that I lived.

When I got health, thou took'st away my life,
          And more; for my friends die:
My mirth and edge was lost; a blunted knife
          Was of more use then I.
Thus thinne and lean without a fence or friend,
I was blown through with ev'ry storm and winde.

Whereas my birth and spirit rather took
                The way that takes the town;
Thou didst betray me to a lingring book,
                And wrap me in a gown.
I was entangled in the world of strife,
Before I had the power to change my life.

Yet, for I threatened oft the siege to raise,
                Not simpring all mine age,
Thou often didst with academick praise
                Melt and dissolve my rage.
I took thy sweetened pill, till I came neare;
I could not go away, nor persevere.

Yet lest perchance I should too happie be
                In my unhappinesse
Turning my purge to food, thou throwest me
                Into more sicknesses.
Thus doth thy power cross-bias me, not making
Thine own gift good, yet me from my ways taking.

Now I am here, what thou wilt do with me
                None of my books will show:
I reade, and sigh, and wish I were a tree;
                For sure then I should grow
To fruit or shade: at least some bird would trust
Her household to me, and I should be just.

Yet, though thou troublest me, I must be meek;
                In weaknesse must be stout.
Well, I will change the service, and go seek
                Some other master out.
Ah my deare God! though I am clean forgot,
Let me not love thee, if I love thee not.

19. REPENTANCE.

LORD, I confesse my sinne is great;
Great is my sinne. Oh! gently treat
With thy quick flow'r, thy momentarie bloom;
                Whose life still pressing
                Is one undressing,
  A steadie aiming at a tombe.

Man's age is two houres work, or three;
Each day doth round about us see.
Thus are we to delights: but we are all
    To sorrows old,
    If life be told
From what life feeleth, Adam's fall.

Oh let thy height of mercie then
Compassionate short-breathed men,
Cut me not off for my most foul transgression:
    I do confesse
    My foolishnesse;
My God, accept of my confession.

Sweeten at length this bitter bowl,
Which thou hast pour'd into my soul;
Thy wormwood turn to health, windes to fair weather,
    For if thou stay,
    I and this day,
As we did rise we die together.

When thou for sinne rebukest man,
Forthwith he waxeth wo and wan:
Bitternesse fills our bowels; all our hearts
    Pine, and decay,
    And drop away,
And carrie with them th' other parts.

But thou wilt sinne and grief destroy;
That so the broken bones may joy,
And tune together in a well-set song,
    Full of his praises
    Who dead men raises.
Fractures well cur'd make us more strong.

20. FAITH.

LORD, how couldst thou so much appease
Thy wrath for sinne, as when man's sight was dimme,
And could see little, to regard his ease,
 And bring by Faith all things to him?

Hungrie I was, and had no meat:
I did conceit a most delicious feast;
I had it straight, and did as truly eat,
 As ever did a welcome guest.

There is a rare outlandish root,
Which when I could not get, I thought it here:
That apprehension cur'd so well my foot,
    That I can walk to heav'n well neare.

I owed thousands and much more:
I did believe that I did nothing owe,
And liv'd accordingly; my creditor
    Beleeves so too, and lets me go.

Faith makes me any thing, or all
That I beleeve is in the sacred storie:
And where sinne placeth me in Adam's fall.
    Faith sets me higher in his glorie.

If I go lower in the book,
What can be lower than the common manger?
Faith puts me there with Him, who sweetly took
    Our flesh and frailtie, death and danger.

If blisse had lien in art or strength,
None but the wise or strong had gained it:
Where now by Faith all arms are of a length;
    One size doth all conditions fit.

A peasant may beleeve as much
As a great clerk, and reach the highest stature.
Thus dost thou make proud knowledge bend and
    While grace fills up uneven nature. [crouch,

When creatures had no reall light
Inherent in them, thou didst make the sunne,
Impute a lustre, and allow them bright:
    And in this show, what Christ hath done.

That which before was darkned clean
With bushie groves, pricking the looker's eie,
Vanisht away, when Faith did change the scene:
    And then appeared a glorious skie.

What though my bodie run to dust?
Faith cleaves unto it, counting ev'ry grain,
With an exact and most particular trust,
    Reserving all for flesh again.

21. PRAYER.

PRAYER, the church's banquet, angel's age,
    God's breath in man returning to his birth,
    The soul in paraphrase, heart in pilgrimage,
The Christian plummet sounding heav'n and earth;

Engine against th' Almightie, sinner's towre,
    Reversed thunder, Christ-side-piercing spear,
    The six daies' world-transposing in an houre,
A kinde of tune, which all things heare and fear;

Softnesse, and peace, and joy, and love, and blisse,
    Exalted manna, gladnesse of the best,
    Heaven in ordinarie, man well drest,
The milkie way, the bird of Paradise,

    Church-bels beyond the stars heard, the soul's bloud,
    The land of spices, something understood.

22. THE HOLY COMMUNION.

NOT in rich furniture, or fine array,
    Nor in a wedge of gold,
    Thou, who from me wast sold,
    To me dost now thyself convey;
For so thou should'st without me still have been,
    Leaving within me sinne:

But by the way of nourishment and strength,
    Thou creep'st into my breast;
    Making thy way my rest,
    And thy small quantities my length;
Which spread their forces into every part,
    Meeting sinnes force and art.

Yet can these not get over to my soul,
    Leaping the wall that parts
    Our souls and fleshly hearts;
    But as th' outworks, they may controll
My rebel-flesh, and carrying thy name,
    Affright both sinne and shame.

Onely thy grace, which with these elements comes,
      Knoweth the ready way,
      And hath the privie key,
    Op'ning the soul's most subtile rooms:
While those to spirits refin'd, at doore attend
      Despatches from their friend.

Give me my captive soul, or take
      My body also thither.
Another lift like this will make
      Them both to be together.

Before that sinne turn'd flesh to stone,
      And all our lump to leaven;
A fervent sigh might well have blown
      Our innocent earth to heaven.

For sure when Adam did not know
      To sinne, or sinne to smother;
He might to heav'n from Paradise go,
      As from one room t' another.

Thou hast restor'd us to this ease
      By this thy heav'nly bloud,
Which I can go to, when I please,
      And leave th' earth to their food.

23. ANTIPHON.

Cho. LET all the world in ev'ry corner sing,
      My God and King,

    Vers. The heav'ns are not too high,
      His praise may thither flie:
      The earth is not too low,
      His praises there may grow.

Cho. Let all the world in ev'ry corner sing,
      My God and King.

    Vers. The church with psalms must shout,
      No doore can keep them out:
      But above all, the heart
      Must bear the longest part.

Cho. Let all the world in ev'ry corner sing,
    My God and King.

24. LOVE.

1.

IMMORTAL LOVE, authour of this great frame,
    Sprung from that beautie which can never fade;
    How hath man parcel'd out thy glorious name,
And thrown it on that dust which thou hast made,

While mortall love doth all the title gain!
    Which siding with invention, they together
    Bear all the sway, possessing heart and brain,
(Thy workmanship) and give thee share in neither.

Wit fancies beautie, beautie raiseth wit:
    The world is theirs; they two play out the game,
    Thou standing by: and though thy glorious name
Wrought our deliverance from the infernall pit,

    Who sings thy praise? onely a skarf or glove
    Doth warm our hands, and make them write of love.

2.

Immortal Heat, O let thy greater flame
    Attract the lesser to it: let those fires
    Which shall consume the world, first make it tame,
And kindle in our hearts such true desires,

As may consume our lusts, and make thee way.
    Then shall our hearts pant thee; then shall our
    All her invention on thine altar lay, [brain
And there in hymnes send back thy fire again:

Our eies shall see thee, which before saw dust;
    Dust blown by wit, till that they both were blinde:
    Thou shalt recover all thy goods in kinde,
Who wert disseized by usurping lust:

    All knees shall bow to thee; all wits shall rise,
    And praise him who did make and mend our eies.

25. THE TEMPER.

How should I praise thee, Lord! how should my rymes
    Gladly engrave thy love in steel,
    If what my soul doth feel sometimes,
        My soul might ever feel!

Although there were some fourtie heav'ns, or more,
    Sometimes I peere above them all;
    Sometimes I hardly reach a score,
        Sometimes to hell I fall.

O rack me not to such a vast extent;
    Those distances belong to thee:
    The world's too little for thy tent,
        A grave too big for me.

Wilt thou meet arms with man, that thou dost stretch
    A crumme of dust from heav'n to hell?
    Will great God measure with a wretch?
        Shall he thy stature spell?

O let me, when thy roof my soul hath hid,
    O let me roost and nestle there:
    Then of a sinner thou art rid
        And I of hope and fear.

Yet take thy way; for sure thy way is best:
    Stretch or contract me thy poore debter:
    This is but tuning of my breast,
        To make the musick better.

Whether I flie with angels, fall with dust,
    Thy hands made both, and I am there.
    Thy power and love, my love and trust,
        Make one place ev'ry where.

26. THE TEMPER.

IT cannot be. Where is that mightie joy,
    Which just now took up all my heart?
    Lord! if thou must needs use thy dart,
Save that, and me; or sin for both destroy.

The grosser world stands to thy word and art;
    But thy diviner world of grace
    Thou suddenly doth raise and race,
And ev'ry day a new Creatour art.

O fix thy chair of grace, that all my powers
    May also fix their reverence:
    For when thou dost depart from hence,
They grow unruly, and sit in thy bowers.

Scatter, or binde them all to bend to thee:
    Though elements change, and heaven move;
    Let not thy higher court remove,
But keep a standing majestie in me.

27. JORDAN.

WHO sayes that fictions onely and false hair
Become a verse? Is there in truth no beautie?
Is all good structure in a winding stair?
May no lines passe, except they do their dutie
    Not to a true, but painted chair?

Is it not verse, except enchanted groves
And sudden arbours shadow coarse-spunne lines?
Must purling streams refresh a lover's loves?
Must all be vail'd, while he that reades, divines,
    Catching the sense at two removes?

Shepherds are honest people; let them sing:
Riddle who list, for me, and pull for prime:
I envie no man's nightingale or spring;
Nor let them punish me with losse of ryme,
    Who plainly say, *My God, My King.*

28. EMPLOYMENT.

    IF as a flowre doth spread and die,
    Thou wouldst extend me to some good,
Before I were by frost's extremitie
        Nipt in the bud;

    The sweetnesse and the praise were thine;
    But the extension and the room,
Which in thy garland I should fill, were mine
        At thy great doom.

>   For as thou dost impart thy grace,
>   The greater shall our glorie be.
> The measure of our joyes is in this place,
>   The stuffe with thee.
>
>   Let me not languish then, and spend
>   A life as barren to thy praise
> As is the dust, to which that life doth tend,
>   But with delaies.
>
>   All things are busie; only I
>   Neither bring hony with the bees,
> Nor flowres to make that, nor the husbandrie
>   To water these.
>
>   I am no link of thy great chain,
>   But all my companie is a weed.
> Lord, place me in thy consort; give one strain
>   To my poore reed.

29. THE HOLY SCRIPTURES.

OH Book! infinite sweetnesse! let my heart
    Suck ev'ry letter, and a hony gain,
    Precious for any grief in any part;
To cleare the breast, to mollifie all pain.

Thou art all health, health thriving, till it make
    A full eternitie: thou art a masse
    Of strange delights, where we may wish and take.
Ladies, look here; this is the thankful! glasse,

That mends the looker's eyes: this is the well
    That washes what it shows. Who can indeare
    Thy praise too much? thou art Heav'n's lidger here,
Working against the states of death and hell.

    Thou art joyes handsell: heav'n lies flat in thee,
    Subject to ev'ry mounters bended knee.

2.

Oh that I knew how all thy lights combine,
    And the configurations of their glorie!
    Seeing not only how each verse doth shine,
But all the constellations of the storie.

This verse marks that, and both do make a motion
    Unto a third, that ten leaves off doth lie:
    Then as dispersed herbs do watch a potion,
These three make up some Christian's destinie.

Such are thy secrets, which my life makes good,
    And comments on thee: for in ev'ry thing
    Thy words do finde me out, and parallels bring,
And in another make me understood.

    Starres are poore books, and oftentimes do misse;
    This book of starres lights to eternall blisse.

30. WHITSUNDAY.

LISTEN, sweet Dove, unto my song,
    And spread thy golden wings in me;
    Hatching my tender heart so long,
Till it get wing, and file away with thee.

Where is that fire which once descended
    On thy Apostles? thou didst then
    Keep open house, richly attended,
Feasting all comers by twelve chosen men.

Such glorious gifts thou didst bestow,
    That th' earth did like a heav'n appeare:
    The starres were coming down to know
If they might mend their wages, and serve here.

The sunne, which once did shine alone,
    Hung down his head, and wisht for night,
    When he beheld twelve sunnes for one
Going about the world, and giving light.

But since those pipes of gold, which brought
    That cordiall water to our ground,
    Were cut and martyr'd by the fault
Of those who did themselves through their side wound.

Thou shutt'st the doore, and keep'st within;
    Scarce a good joy creeps through the chink:
    And if the braves of conqu'ring sinne
Did not excite thee, we should wholly sink.

Lord, though we change, thou art the same;
The same sweet God of love and light:
Restore this day, for thy great name,
Unto his ancient and miraculous right.

31. GRACE.

My stock lies dead, and no increase
Doth my dull husbandrie improve:
O let thy graces without cease
        Drop from above I

If still the sunne should hide his face,
Thy house would but a dungeon prove,
Thy works night's captives; O let grace
        Drop from above!

The dew doth ev'ry morning fall;
And shall the dew outstrip thy dove?
The dew, for which grasse cannot call,
        Drop from above.

Death is still working like a mole,
And digs my grave at each remove:
Let grace work too, and on my soul
        Drop from above.

Sinne is still hammering my heart
Unto a hardnesse, void of love:
Let suppling grace, to crosse his art,
        Drop from above.

O come! for thou dost know the way.
Or if to me thou wilt not move,
Remove me, where I need not say—
        Drop from above.

32. PRAISE.

To write a verse or two is all the praise,
        That I can raise;
Mend my estate in any wayes,
        Thou shalt have more.

I go to Church; help me to wings, and I
        Will thither flie;
   Or, if I mount unto the skie,
        I will do more.

Man is all weaknesse; there is no such thing
        As Prince or King:
   His arm is short; yet with a sling
        He may do more.

A herb destill'd, and drunk, may dwell next doore,
        On the same floore,
           To a brave soul: Exalt the poore,
   They can do more.

O raise me then! poore bees, that work all day,
        Sting my delay,
   Who have a work, as well as they,
        And much, much more.

33. AFFLICTION.

        KILL me not ev'ry day,
Thou Lord of life; since thy one death for me
        Is more than all my deaths can be,
        Though I in broken pay
Die over each hour of Methusalem's stay.

        If all men's tear were let
Into one common sewer, sea, and brine;
        What were they all, compar'd to thine?
        Wherein if they were set,
They would discolour thy most bloudy sweat.

        Thou art my grief alone,
Thou, Lord, conceal it not: and as thou art
        All my delight, so all my smart:
        Thy crosse took up in one,
By way of imprest, all my future mone.

34. MATTENS.

        I cannot ope mine eyes,
        But thou art ready there to catch
        My morning-soul and sacrifice:
Then we must needs for that day make a match.

My God, what is a heart?
Silver, or gold, or precious stone,
Or starre, or rainbow, or a part
Of all these things, or all of them in one?

My God, what is a heart,
That thou shouldst it so eye, and wooe,
Powring upon it all thy art,
As if that thou hadst nothing els to do?

Indeed man's whole estate
Amounts (and richly) to serve thee:
He did not heav'n and earth create,
Yet studies them, not him by whom they be.

Teach me thy love to know;
That this new light, which now I see,
May both the work and workman show:
Then by a sunne-beam I will climbe to thee.

35. SINNE.

O THAT I could a sinne once see!
We paint the devil foul, yet he
Hath some good in him, all agree.
Sinne is flat opposite to th' Almighty, seeing
It wants the good of *vertue,* and of *being.*

But God more care of us hath had,
If apparitions make us sad,
By sight of sinne we should grow mad.
Yet as in sleep we see foul death, and live;
So devils are our sinnes in perspective.

36. EVEN-SONG.

BLEST be the God of love,
Who gave me eyes, and light, and power this day,
Both to be busie, and to play.
But much more blest be God above,

Who gave me sight alone,
Which to himself he did denie:
For when he sees my waies, I dy:
But I have got his Sonne, and he hath none.

       What have I brought thee home
      For this thy love? have I discharg'd the debt
        Which this day's favour did beget?
I ranne; but all I brought, was fome.

       Thy diet, care, and cost
      Do end in bubbles, balls of winde;
       Of winde to thee whom I have crost,
But balls of wilde-fire to my troubled minde.

       Yet still thou goest on,
      And now with darknesse closest wearie eyes,
       Saying to man, *It doth suffice:*
Henceforth repose: your work is done.

       Thus in thy ebony box
      Thou dost inclose us, till the day
       Put our amendment in our way,
And give new wheels to our disorder'd clocks.

       I muse, which shows more love,
      The day or night; that is the gale, this th' harbour;
       That is the walk, and this the arbour;
Or that the garden, this the grove.

       My God, thou art all love.
      Not one poore minute 'scapes thy breast,
       But brings a favour from above;
And in this love, more than in bed, I rest.

37. CHURCH-MONUMENTS.

WHILE that my soul repairs to her devotion,
Here I entombe my flesh, that it betimes
May take acquaintance of this heap of dust;
To which the blast of death's incessant motion,
Fed with the exhalation of our crimes,
Drives all at last. Therefore I gladly trust

My bodie to this school, that it may learn
To spell his elements, and finde hb birth
Written in dustie heraldrie and lines;
Which dissolution sure doth best discern,
Comparing dust with dust, and earth with earth.
These laugh at Jeat, and Marble put for signes,

To sever the good fellowship of dust,
And spoil the meeting. What shall point out them,
When they shall bow, and kneel, and fall down flat
To kisse those heaps, which now they have in trust?
Deare flesh, while I do pray, learn here thy stemme

And true descent; that when thou shalt grow fat,
And wanton in thy cravings, thou mayst know,
That flesh is but the glasse, which holds the dust
That measures all our time; which also shall
Be crumbled into dust. Mark here below,
How tame these ashes are, how free from lust,
That thou mayst fit thyself against thy fall.

38. CHURCH-MUSICK.

SWEETEST of sweets, I thank you: when displeasure
        Did through my bodie wound my minde,
You took me thence; and in your house of pleasure
        A daintie lodging me assign'd.

Now I in you without a bodie move,
        Rising and falling with your wings:
We both together sweetly live and love,
        Yet say sometimes, *God help poore Kings*.

Comfort, I'll die; for if you poste from me,
        Sure I shall do so and much more:
But if I travell in your companie,
        You know the way to heaven's doore.

39. CHURCH-LOCK AND KEY.

I KNOW it is my sinne, which locks thine eares,
        And bindes thy hands!
Out-crying my requests, drowning my tears;
Or else the chilnesse of my faint demands.
But as cold hands are angrie with the fire,
        And mend it still;
So I do lay the want of my desire,
Not on my sinnes, or coldnesse, bat thy will.

Yet heare, O God, onely for his blood's sake,
        Which pleads for me:
For though sinnes plead too, yet like stones they make
His bloud's sweet current much more loud to be.

40. THE CHURCH-FLOORE.

MARK you the floore? that square and speckled stone,
        Which looks so firm and strong,
              Is *Patience:*

And th' other black and grave, where with each one
        Is checker'd all along,
              Humilitie:

The gentle rising, which on either hand
        Leads to the quire above,
              Is *Confidence:*

But the sweet cement, which in one sure band
        Ties the whole frame, is *Love*
              And *Charitie.*

    Hither sometimes Sinne steals, and stains
        The marble's neat and curious veins:
But all is cleansed when the marble weeps.
        Sometimes Death, puffing at the doore,
        Blows all the dust about the floore:
But while he thinks to spoil the room, he sweeps.
        Blest be the *Architect,* whose art
        Could build so strong in a weak heart.

41. THE WINDOWS.

LORD, how can man preach thy eternall word?
      He is a brittle crazie glasse:
Yet in thy temple thou dost him afford
      This glorious and transcendent place,
      To be a window, through thy grace.

But when thou dost anneal in glasse thy storie,
      Making thy life to shine within
The holy preacher's, then the light and glorie
      More rev'rend grows, and more doth win;
      Which else shows watrish, bleak, and thin.

Doctrine and life, colours and light, in one
      When they combine and mingle, bring
A strong regard and aw: but speech alone
      Doth vanish like a flaring thing,
      And in the eare, not conscience ring.

42. TRINITIE SUNDAY.

LORD, who hast formed me out of mud,
    And hast redeemed me through thy bloud,
    And sanctified me to do good;
Purge all my sinnes done heretofore;
    For I confesse my heavie score,
    And I will strive to sinne no more.

Enrich my heart, mouth, hands in me,
    With faith, with hope, with charitie;
    That I may runne, rise, rest with thee.

43. CONTENT.

PEACE mutt'ring thoughts, and do not grudge to keep
    Within the walls of your own breast.
Who cannot on his own bed sweetly sleep,
    Can on another's hardly rest.

Gad not abroad at ev'ry quest and call
    Of an untrained hope or passion.
To court each place or fortune that doth fall,
    Is wantonnesse in contemplation.

Mark how the fire in flints doth quiet lie,
    Content and warm t' it self alone:
But when it would appeare to other's eye,
    Without a knock it never shone.

Give me the pliant mind, whose gentle measure
    Complies and suits with all estates;
Which can let loose to a crown, and yet with pleasure
    Take up within a cloister's gates.

This soul doth span the world, and hang content
    From either pole unto the centre:
Where in each room of the well-furnisht tent
    He lies warm, and without adventure.

The brags of life are but a nine days[1] wonder:
    And after death the fumes that spring
From private bodies, make as big a thunder
    As those which rise from a huge king.

Onely thy chronicle is lost: and yet
    Better by worms be all once spent,
Than to have hellish moths still gnaw and fret
    Thy name in books, which may not rent.

When all thy deeds, whose brunt thou feel'st alone,
    Are chaw'd by others' pens and tongue,
And as their wit is, their digestion,
    Thy nourisht fame is weak or strong.

Then cease discoursing soul, till thine own ground;
    Do not thyself or friends importune.
He that by seeking hath himself once found,
    Hath ever found a happie fortune.

44. THE QULDDITIE.

MY God, a verse is not a crown;
No point of honour, or gay suit,
No hawk, or banquet, or renown,
Nor a good sword, nor yet a lute:

It cannot vault, or dance, or play;
It never was in *France* or *Spain;*
Nor can it entertain the day
With a great stable or demain.

It is no office, art, or news;
Nor the Exchange, or busie Hall:
But it is that which while I use,
I am with thee, and *Most take all.*

45. HUMILITIE.

I SAW the Vertues sitting hand in hand
In sev'rall ranks upon an azure throne,
Where all the beasts and fowls, by their command,
Presented tokens of submission.
Humilitie, who sat the lowest there
        To execute their call,
When by the beasts the presents tendred were,
        Gave them about to all.

The angrie Lion did present his paw,
Which by consent was giv'n to Mansuetude.
The fearfull Hare her eares, which by their law
Humilitie did reach to Fortitude.
The jealous Turkie brought his corall-chain,
                That went to Temperance.
On Justice was bestow'd the Fox's brain,
                Kill'd in the way by chance.

At length the Crow, bringing the Peacock's plume,
For he would not) as they beheld the grace
Of that brave gift, each one began to fume.
And challenge it, as proper to his place,
Till they fell out; which when the beasts espied,
                They leapt upon the throne;

And if the Fox had liv'd to rule their side,
                They had depos'd each one.

Humilitie, who held the plume, at this
Did weep so fast, that the tears trickling down
Spoil'd all the train: then saying, *Here it is*
For which ye wrangle, made them turn their frown
Against the beasts: so jointly bandying,
                They drive them soon away;
And then amerc'd them, double gifts to bring
                At the next Session-day.

46. FRAILTIE.

LORD, in my silence how do I despise
                What upon trust
Is styled *honour, riches, or fair eyes;*
                But *is fair dust!*
    I surname them *guilded clay,*
    Deare earth, fine grasse or hay;
In all, I think my foot doth ever tread
                Upon their head.

But when I view abroad both regiments,
                The world's, and thine;
Thine clad with simplenesse, and sad events;
                The other fine,
    Full of glorie and gay weeds,
    Brave language, braver deeds:
That which was dust before, doth quickly rise,
                And prick mine eyes.

O brook not this, lest if what even now
                My foot did tread,
Affront those joyes, wherewith thou didst endow,
                And long since wed
  My poore soul, ev'n sick of love;
    It may a Babel prove,
Commodious to conquer heav'n and thee
                Planted in me.

47. CONSTANCES.

WHO is the honest man?
He that doth still and strongly good pursue,
To God, his neighbour, and himself most true:
            Whom neither force nor fawning can
Unpinne, or wrench from giving all their due.

            Whose honestie is not
So loose or easie, that a ruffling winde
Can blow away, or glittering look it blinde:
            Who rides his sure and even trot,
While the world now rides by, now lags behinde.

            Who, when great trials come,
Nor seeks, nor shunnes them; but doth calmly stay,
Till he the thing and the example weigh:
            All being brought into a summe,
What place or person calls for, he doth pay.

            Whom none can work or wooe,
To use in any tiling a trick or sleight;
For above all things he abhorres deceit:
            His words and works and fashion too
All of a piece, and all are cleare and straight.

            Who never melts or thaws
At close tentations: when the day is done,
His goodnesse sets not, but in dark can runne:
            The sunne to others writeth laws,
And is their vertue; Vertue is his Sunne.

            Who, when he is to treat
With sick folks, women, those whom passions sway,
Allows for that, and keeps his constant way:
            Whom others' faults do not defeat;
But though men fail him, yet his part doth play.

   Whom nothing can procure,
When the wide world runnes bias, from his will
To writhe his limbes, and share, not mend the ill.
   This is the Mark-man, safe and sure,
Who still is right, and prayes to be so still.

48. AFFLICTION.

MY heart did heave, and there came forth, *O God!*
By that I knew that thou wast in the grief,
To guide and govern it to my relief,
   Making a scepter of the rod:
     Hadst thou not had thy part,
Sure the unruly sigh had broke my heart.

But since thy breath gave me both life and shape,
Thou knowst my tallies; and when there's assign'd
So much breath to a sigh, what's then behinde?
   Or if some yeares with it escape,
     The sigh then onely is
A gale to bring me sooner to my blisse.

Thy life on earth was grief, and thou art still
Constant unto it, making it to be
A point of honour, now to grieve in me,
   And in thy members suffer ill.
     They who lament one crosse,
Thou dying dayly, praise thee to thy losse.

49. THE STARRE.

BRIGHT spark, shot from a brighter place,
 Where beams surround my Saviour's face,
   Canst thou be any where
    So well as there?

Yet, if thou wilt from thence depart,
 Take a bad lodging in my heart;
   For thou canst make a debter,
    And make it better.

First with thy fire-work burn to dust
 Folly, and worse than folly, lust:
   Then with thy light refine,
    And make it shine.

So disengag'd from sinne and sicknesse,
　　Touch it with thy celestiall quicknesse
　　　　That it may hang and move
　　　　　　After thy love.

Then with our trinitie of light,
　　Motion, and heat, let's take our flight
　　　　Unto the place where thou
　　　　　　Before didst bow.

Get me a standing there, and place
　　Among the beams, which crown the face
　　　　Of him, who dy'd to part
　　　　　　Sinne and my heart:

That so among the rest I may
　　Glitter, and curle, and winde as they:
　　　　That winding is their fashion
　　　　　　Of adoration.

Sure thou wilt joy, by gaining me
　　To flie home like a laden bee
　　　　Unto that hive of beams
　　　　　　And garland-streams.

　　　　　　50. SUNDAY.

　　　　O DAY most calm, most bright,
The fruit of this, the next world's bud,
Th' indorsement of supreme delight,
Writ by a friend, and with his bloud;
The couch of time; cares balm and bay;
The week were dark, but for thy light:
　　　　Thy torch doth show the way.

　　　　The other dayes and thou
Make up one man; whose face thou art,
Knocking at heaven with thy brow:
The worky-daies are the back-part;
The burden of the week lies there,
Making the whole to stoup and bow,
　　　　Till thy release appeare.

        Man had straight forward gone
To endlesse death; but thou dost pull
And turn us round to look on one,
Whom, if we were not very dull,
We could not choose but look on still;
Since there is no place so alone
            The which he doth not fill.

        Sundaies the pillars are,
On which heav'n's palace arched lies:
The other dayes fill up the spare
And hollow room with vanities.
They are the fruitfull beds and borders
In God's rich garden: that is bare
            Which parts their ranks and orders.

        The Sundaies of man's life,
Thredded together on Time's string,
Make bracelets to adorn the wife
Of the eternall glorious King.
On Sunday heaven's gate stands ope;
Blessings are plentifull and rife,
            More plentifull then hope.

        This day my Saviour rose,
And did inclose this light for his:
That, as each beast his manger knows,
Man might not of his fodder misse.
Christ hath took in this piece of ground,
And made a garden there for those
            Who want herbs for their wound.

        The rest of our Creation
Our great Redeemer did remove
With the same shake, which at his passion
Did th' earth and all things with it move.
As Samson bore the doores away,
Christ's hands, though nailed, wrought our salvation,
            And did unhinge that day.

        The brightnesse of that daye
We sullied by our foul offence:
Wherefore that robe we cast away,
Having a new at his expense,
Whose drops of bloud paid the full price,
That was requir'd to make us gay,
            And fit for Paradise.

        Thou art a day of mirth:
And where the week-dayes trail on ground,
    Thy flight is higher, as thy birth:
      O let me take thee at the bound,
Leaping with thee from sev'n to sev'n,
Till that we both, being toss'd from earth,
        Flie hand in hand to heav'n!

51. AVARICE.

MONEY, thou bane of blisse, and source of wo,
    Whence com'st thou, that thou art so fresh and fine?
    I know thy parentage is base and low:
Man found thee poore and dirtie in a mine.

Surely thou didst so little contribute
    To this great kingdome, which thou now hast got,
That he was fain, when thou wert destitute,
    To digge thee out of thy dark cave and grot.

Then forcing thee, by fire he made thee bright:
    Nay, thou hast got the face of man; for we
Have with our stamp and seal transferr'd our right:
    Thou art the man, and man but drosse to thee.

Man calleth thee his wealth, who made thee rich;
And while he digs out thee, falls in the ditch.

52. ANA-GRAM

Ana- { **MARY** / **ARMY** } *gram.*

How well her name an *Army* doth present,
In whom the *Lord of hosts* did pitch his tent!

53. TO ALL ANGELS AND SAINTS.

OH glorious spirits, who after all your bands
See the smooth face of God, without a frown,
        Or strict commands;

Where ev'ry one is king, and hath his crown,
If not upon his head, yet in his hands:

Not out of envy or maliciousnesse
Do I forbear to crave your speciall aid.
                I would addresse

My vows to thee most gladly, blessed Maid,
And Mother of my God, in my distresse:

Thou art the holy mine, whence came the gold,
The great restorative for all decay
                In young and old;

Thou art the cabinet where the jewell lay:
Chiefly to thee would I my soul unfold.

But now, (alas!) I dare not; for our King,
Whom we do all joyntly adore and praise,
                Bids no such thing:

And where his pleasure no injunction layes,
('Tis your own case) ye never move a wing.

All worship is prerogative, and a flower
Of his rich crown, from whom lyes no appeal
                At the last houre:

Therefore we dare not from his garland steal,
To makea posie for inferiour power.

Although then others court you, if ye know
What's done on earth, we shall not fare the worse,
                Who do not so;

Since we are ever ready to disburse,
If any one our Master's hand can show.

54. EMPLOYMENT.

HE that is weary, let him sit.
                My soul would stirre
And tread in courtesies and wit,
                Quitting the furre
To cold complexions needing it.

Man is no starre, but a quick coal
                Of mortall fire:
Who blows it not, nor doth controll
                A faint desire,
Lets his own ashes choke his soul

When th' elements did for place contest
                With him, whose will
Ordain'd the highest to be best:
                The earth sat still,
And by the others is opprest.

Life is a businesse, not good cheer;
                Ever in warres.
The sunne still shineth there or here,
                Whereas the starres
Watch an advantage to appeare.

Oh that I were an orenge-tree,
                That busie plant!
Then should I ever laden be,
                And never want
Some fruit for him that dressed me.

But we are still too young or old;
                The man is gone,
Before we do our wares unfold:
                So we freeze on,
Until the grave increase our cold.

55. DENIALL.

WHEN my devotions could not pierce
            Thy silent eares;
Then was my heart broken, as was my verse;
            My breast was full of fears
            And disorder,

My bent thoughts, like a brittle bow,
            Did flie asunder:
Each took his way; some would to pleasures go,
            Some to the warres and thunder
            Of alarms.

As good go any where, they say,
   As to benumme
Both knees and heart, in crying night and day,
   Come, come, my God, O come,
   But no hearing.

O thou that shouldst give dust a tongue
   To cry to thee,
And then not hear it crying! all day long
   My heart was in my knee,
   But no hearing.

Therefore my soul lay out of sight,
   Untun'd, unstrung:
My feeble spirit, unable to look right,
   Like a nipt blossome, hung
   Discontented.

O cheer and tune my heartlesse breast,
   Deferre no time;
That so thy favours granting my request,
   They and my minde may chime,
   And mend my ryme.

56. CHRISTMAS.

ALL after pleasures as I rid one day,
 My horse and I, both tir'd, bodie and minde,
 With full crie of affections, quite astray;
I took up in the next inne I could finde.

There when I came, whom found I but my deare,
 My dearest Lord, expecting till the grief
 Of pleasures brought me to him, readie there
To be all passengers' most sweet relief?

O Thou, whose glorious, yet contracted light,
 Wrapt in night's mantle, stole into a manger;
 Since my dark soul and brutish is thy right,
To Man of all beasts be not thou a stranger:

Furnish and deck my soul, that thou mayst have
A better lodging, then a rack, or grave.

THE shepherds sing; and shall I silent be?
        My God no hymne for thee?
My soul's a shepherd too: a flock it feeds
        Of thoughts, and words, and deeds.
The pasture is thy word; the streams, thy grace
        Enriching all the place.
Shepherd and flock shall sing, and all my powers
        Out-sing the day-light houres.
Then we will chide the sunne for letting night
        Take up his place and right:
We sing one common Lord; wherefore he should
        Himself the candle hold.
I will go searching, till I finde a sunne
        Shall stay, till we have done;
A willing shiner, that shall shine as gladly,
        As frost nipt sunnes look sadly.
Then we will sing, and shine all our own day,
        And one another pay:
His beams shall cheer my breast, and both so twine,
Till ev'n his beams sing, and my musick shine.

57. UNGRATEFULNESSE.

LORD, with what bountie and rare clemencie
    Hast thou redeem'd us from the grave!
        If thou hadst let us runne,
    Gladly had man ador'd the sunne,
        And thought his god most brave;
Where now we shall be better gods then he.

Thou hast but two rare cabinets full of treasure,
    The *Trinitie,* and *Incarnation:*
        Thou hast unlockt them both,
    And made them jewels to betroth
        The work of thy creation
Unto thyself in everlasting pleasure.

The statelier cabinet is the *Trinitie,*
    Whose sparkling light access denies:
        Therefore thou dost not show
    This fully to us, till death blow
        The dust into our eyes;
For by that powder thou wilt make us see.

But all thy sweets are packt up in the other;
    Thy mercies thither flock and flow;
        That as the first affrights,
      This may allure us with delights;
        Because this box we know;
For we have all of us just such another.

But man is close, reserv'd, and dark to thee;
    When thou demandest but a heart,
        He cavils instantly.
    In his poor cabinet of bone
        Sinnes have their box apart,
Defrauding thee, who gavest two for one.

58. SIGHS AND GRONES.

        O Do not use me
After my sinnes! look not on my desert,
But on thy glorie! then thou wilt reform,
And not refuse me: for thou onely art
The mightie God, but I a sillie worm:
        O do not bruise me!

        O do not urge me!
For what account can thy ill steward make?
I have abus'd thy stock, destroy'd thy woods,
Suckt all thy magazens: my head did ake,
Till it found out how to consume thy goods:
        O do not scourge me!

        O do not blind me!
I have deserv'd that an Egyptian night
Should thicken all my powers; because my lust
Hath still sow'd fig-leaves to exclude thy light:
But I am frailtie, and already dust:
        O do not grinde me!

        O do not fill me
With the turn'd viall of thy bitter wrath!
For thou hast other vessels full of bloud,
A part whereof my Saviour emptied hath,
Ev'n unto death: since he died for my good,
        O do not kill me!

>   But O reprieve me I
> For thou hast *life* and *death* at thy command;
> Thou art both *Judge* and *Saviour, feast* and *rod,*
> *Cordiall* and *corrosive*: put not thy hand
> Into the bitter box; but O my God,
>   My God, relieve me!

59. THE WORLD.

LOVE built a stately house: where *Fortune* came:
And spinning phansies, she was heard to say,
That her fine cobwebs did support the (frame,
Whereas they were supported by the same:
But *Wisdome* quickly swept them all away.

Then *Pleasure* came, who liking not the fashion,
Began to make *Balcones, Terraces,*
Till she had weakned all by alteration:
But rev'rend *laws,* and many a *proclamation*
Reformed all at length with menaces.

Then enter'd *Sinne,* and with that Sycomore,
Whose leaves first sheltred man from drought and
Working and winding slily evermore, [dew,
The inward walls and Sommers cleft and tore:
But *Grace* shor'd these, and cut that as it grew.

Then *Sinne* combined with *Death* in a firm band,
To rase the building to the very floore:
Which they effected, none could them withstand;
But *Love* and *Grace* took *Glorie* by the hand,
And built a braver Palace than before.

60. COLOSS. iii. 3.

Our life is hid with Christ in God.

My words and thoughts do both express this notion.
That *Life* hath with the sun a double motion.
The first *Is* straight, and our diurnall friend;
The other *Hid,* and doth obliquely bend.
One life is wrapt *In* flesh, and tends to earth:
The other winds towards *Him,* whose happie birth
Taught me to live here so, *That* still one eye
Should aim and shoot at that which *Is* on high;
Quitting with daily labour all *My* pleasure,
To gain at harvest an eternall *Treasure.*

61. VANITIE.

THE fleet Astronomer can bore
And thred the spheres with his quick-piercing minde:
He views their stations, walks from doore to doore,
    Surveys, as if he had design'd
To make a purchase there: he sees their dances,
    And knoweth long before,
Both their full-ey'd aspects, and secret glances.

    The nimble Diver with his side
Cuts through the working waves, that he may fetch
His dearely-earned pearl, which God did hide
    On purpose from the ventrous wretch;
That he might save his life, and also hers,
    Who with excessive pride
Her own destruction and his danger wears.

    The subtil Chymick can devest
And strip the creature naked, till he finde
The callow principles within their nest:
    There he imparts to them his minde,
Admitted to their bed-chamber, before
    They appeare trim and drest
To ordinarie suitours at the doore.

    What hath not man sought out and found,
But his deare God? who yet his glorious law
Embosomes in us, mellowing the ground
    With showres and frosts, with love and aw;
So that we need not say, Where's this command?
    Poore man! thou searchest round
To finde out *death,* but missest *life* at hand.

62. LENT.

WELCOME, deare feast of Lent: who loves not thee,
He loves not Temperance, or Authoritie,
    But is compos'd of passion.
The Scriptures bid us *fast*; the Church says, *now:*
Give to thy Mother what thou wouldst allow
    To ev'ry Corporation.

The humble soul compos'd of love and fear,
Begins at home, and layes the burden there,
      When doctrines disagree:
He sayes, in things which use hath justly got,
I am a scandall to the Church, and not
      The Church is so to me.

True Christians should be glad of an occasion
To use their temperance, seeking no evasion,
      When good is seasonable;
Unlesse Authoritie, which should increase
The obligation in us, make it lesse,
      And Power it self disable.

Besides the cleannesse of sweet abstinence,.
Quick thoughts and motions at a small expense,
      A face not fearing light:
Whereas in fulnesse there are sluttish fumes,
Sowre exhalations, and dishonest rheumes,
      Revenging the delight.

Then those same pendant profits, which the spring
And Easter intimate, enlarge the thing,
      And goodnesse of the deed.
Neither ought other men's abuse of Lent
Spoil the good use; lest by that argument
      We forfeit all our Creed,

It's true, we cannot reach Christ's forti'th day;
Yet to go part of that religious way
      Is better than to rest:
We cannot reach our Saviour's puritie;
Yet are we bid, "*Be holy ev'n as he.*"
      In both let's do our best.

Who goeth in the way which Christ hath gone,
Is much more sure to meet with him, than one
      That travelleth by-wayes.
Perhaps my God, though he be farre before,
May turn, and take me by the hand, and more,
      May strengthen my decayes.

Yet, Lord, instruct us to improve our fast
By starving sinne and taking such repast
        As may our faults controll:
That ev'ry man may revell at his doore,
Not in his parlour; banquetting the poore,
        And among those his soul.

63. VERTUE.

SWEET day, so cool, so calm, so bright,
The bridall of the earth and skie:
The dew shall weep thy fall to-night;
        For thou must die.

Sweet rose, whose hue angrie and brave
Bids the rash gazer wipe his eye,
Thy root is ever in its grave,
        And thou must die.

Sweet spring, full of sweet dayes and roses,
A box where sweets compacted lie,
My musick shows ye have your closes,
        And all must die.

Onely a sweet and vertuous soul,
Like season'd timber, never gives;
But though the whole world turn to coal,
        Then chiefly lives.

64. THE PEARL.

Matt. XIII.

I KNOW the wayes of learning; both the head
And pipes that feed the presse, and make it runne;
What reason hath from nature borrowed,
Or of itself, like a good huswife, spunne
In laws and policie; what the starres conspire,
What willing nature speaks, what forc'd by fire;
Both th' old discoveries, and the new-found seas,
The stock and surplus, cause and historie:
All these stand open, or I have the keyes:
        Yet I love thee.

I know the wayes of honour, what maintains
The quick returns of courtesie and wit:
In vies of favours whether partie gains,
When glorie swells the heart, and moldeth it
To all expressions both of hand and eye,
Which on the world a true-love-knot may tie,
And bear the bundle, wheresoe're it goes:
How many drammes of spirit there must be
To sell my life unto my friends or foes:
    Yet I love thee.

I know the wayes of pleasure, the sweet strains,
The lullings and the relishes of it;
The propositions of hot bloud and brains;
What mirth and musick mean; what love and wit
Have done these twentie hundred yeares, and more:
I know the projects of unbridled store:
My stuffe is flesh, not brasse; my senses live,
And grumble oft, that they have more in me
Than he that curbs them, being but one to five:
    Yet I love thee.

I know all these, and have them in my hand:
Therefore not sealed, but with open eyes
I flie to thee, and fully understand
Both the main sale, and the commodities;
And at what rate and price I have thy love;
With all the circumstances that may move:
Yet through the labyrinths, not my groveling wit,
But thy silk twist let down from heav'n to me,
Did both conduct and teach me, how by it
    To climb to thee.

65. AFFLICTION.

BROKEN in pieces all asunder,
   Lord, hunt me not,
   A thing forgot,
Once a poore creature, now a wonder,
   A wonder tortur'd in the space
   Betwixt this world and that of grace.

My thoughts are all a case of knives,
               Wounding my heart
               With scatter'd smart;
As watring pots give flowers their lives.
        Nothing their furie can controll,
        While they do wound and prick my soul.

All my attendants are at strife
               Quitting their place
               Unto my face:
Nothing performs the task of life:
        The elements are let loose to fight,
        And while I live, trie out their right.

Oh help, my God! let not their plot
               Kill them and me,
               And also thee,
Who art my life: dissolve the knot,
        As the snnne scatters by his light
        All the rebellions of the night.

Then shall those powers, which work for grief,
               Enter thy pay,
               And day by day
Labour thy praise, and my relief;
        With care and courage building me,
        Till I reach heav'n, and much more thee.

66. MAN.

        MY God, I heard this day,
That none doth build a stately habitation
        But he that means to dwell therein.
        What house more stately hath there been,
Or can be, then is Man? to whose creation
        All things are in decay.

        For man is ev'ry thing,
And more: He is a tree, yet bears no fruit;
        A beast, yet is, or should be more:
        Reason and speech we onely bring.
Parrats may thank us, if they are not mute,
        They go upon the score.

        Man is all symmetric,
Full of proportions, one limbe to another,
        And all to all the world besides:
          Each part may call the farthest, brother:
For head with foot hath private amitie,
        And both with moons and tides.

        Nothing hath got so farre,
Bat Man hath caught and kept it, as his prey.
        His eyes dismount the highest starre:
          He is in little all the sphere.
Herbs gladly cure our flesh, because that they
        Finde their acquaintance there.

        For us the windes do blow;
The earth doth rest, heav'n move, and fountains flow.
        Nothing we see, but means our good,
          As our *delight,* or as our *treasure:*
The whole is, either our cupboard of *food,*
        Or cabinet of *pleasure.*

        The starres have us to bed;
Night draws the curtain, which the sunne withdraws:
        Musick and light attend our head.
          All things unto our *flesh* are kinde
In their *descent* and *being*; to our *minde*
        In their *ascent* and *cause.*

        Each thing is full of dutie:
Waters united are our navigation;
        Distinguished, our habitation;
          Below, our drink; above, our meat:
Both are our cleanlinesse. Hath one such beautie?
        Then how are all things neat!

        More servants wait on Man,
Than he'l take notice of: in ev'ry path
        He treads down that which doth befriend him,
          When sicknesse makes him pale and wan.
Oh mightie love! Man is one world, and hath
        Another to attend him.

    Since then, my God, thou hast
So brave a Palace built; O dwell in it,
   That it may dwell with thee at last!
    Till then, afford us so much wit;
That, as the world serves us, we may serve thee,
    And both thy servants be.

67. ANTIPHON.

Chor. PRAISED be the God of love,
    Men. Here below,
    Angels. And here above:
Chor. Who hath dealt his mercies so,
    Ang. To his friend,
    Men. And to his foe;

Chor. That both grace and glorie tend
    Ang. Us of old,
    Men. And us in th' end.
Chor. The great Shepherd of the fold
    Any. Us did make,
    Men. For us was sold.

Chor. He our foes in pieces brake:
    Ang. Him we touch;
    Men. And him we take.
Chor. Wherefore since that he is such,
    Ang. We adore,
    Men. And we do crouch.

Chor. Lord, thy praises should be more.
    Men. We have none,
    Ang. And we no store.
Chor. Praised be the God alone
    Who hath made of two folds one.

68. UNKINDNESSE.

LORD, make me coy and tender to offend:
In friendship, first I think, if that agree,
      Which I intend,
  Unto my friends intent and end.
I would not use a friend, as I use Thee.

If any touch my friend, or his good name,
It is my honour and my love to free
                             His blasted fame
         From the least spot or thought of blame.
I could not use a friend, as I use Thee.

My friend may spit upon my curious floore:
Would he have gold? I lend it instantly;
                             But let the poore,
         And thou within them starve at doore.
I cannot use a friend, as I use Thee,

When that my friend pretendeth to a place,
I quit my interest, and leave it free:
                             But when thy grace
         Sues for my heart, I thee displace;
Nor would I use a friend, as I use Thee.

Yet can a friend what thou hast done fulfill?
O write in brass, *My God upon a tree*
                             His bloud did spill,
         Onely to purchase my good will;
Yet use I not my foes, as I use Thee.

69. LIFE.

I MADE a posie, while the day ran by:
Here will I smell my remnant out, and tie
                             My life within this band.
But time did becken to the flowers, and they
By noon most cunningly did steal away,
                             And wither'd in my hand.

My hand was next to them, and then my heart;
I took, without more thinking, in good part
                             Time's gentle admonition;
Who did so sweetly death's sad taste convey,
Making my minde to smell my fatall day,
                             Yet sugring the suspicion.

Farewell, dear flowers, sweetly your time ye spent,
Fit, while ye lived, for smell or ornament,
                             And after death for cures.
I follow straight without complaints or grief,
Since if my scent be good, I care not, if
                             It be as short as yours.

70. SUBMISSION.

BUT that thou art my wisdome, Lord,
      And both mine eyes are thine,
My minde would be extreamly stirr'd
      For missing my designe.

Were it not better to bestow
      Some place and power on me?

Then should thy praises with me grow,
      And share in my degree.

But when I thus dispute and grieve,
      I do resume my sight;
And pilfring what I once did give,
      Disseize thee of thy right.

How know I, if thou shouldst me raise,
      That I should then raise thee?
Perhaps great places and thy praise
      Do not so well agree.

Wherefore unto my gift I stand;
      I will no more advise:
Onely do thou lend me a hand,
      Since thou hast both mine eyes.

71. JUSTICE.

    I CANNOT skill of these thy ways:
Lord, thou didst make me, yet thou woundest me:
Lord, thou dost wound me, yet thou dost relieve me:
Lord, thou relievest, yet I die by thee:
Lord, thou dost kill me, yet thou dost reprieve me.

    But when I mark my life and praise,
    Thy justice me most fitly payes:
For, *I do praise thee, yet I praise thee not:*
My prayers mean thee, yet my prayers stray:
I would do well, yet sinne the hand hath got:
My soul doth love thee, yet it loves delay.
    I cannot skill of these my ways.

72. CHARMS AND KNOTS.

WHO reade a chapter when they rise,
Shall ne're be troubled with ill eyes.

A poore man's rod, when thou dost ride,
Is both a weapon and a guide.

Who shuts his hand, hath lost his gold:
Who opens it, hath it twice told.

Who goes to bed, and doth not pray,
Maketh two nights to ev'ry day.

Who by aspersions throw a stone
At th' head of others, hit their own.

Who looks on ground with humble eyes,
Findes himself there, and seeks to rise.

When th' hair is sweet through pride or lust,
The powder doth forget the dust.

Take one from ten, and what remains?
Ten still, if sermons go for gains.

In shallow waters heav'n doth show:
But who drinks on, to hell may go.

73. AFFLICTION.

    MY God, I read this day,
That planted Paradise was not so firm
As was and is thy floting Ark; whose stay
And anchor thou art onely, to confirm
        And strengthen it in ev'ry age,
          When waves do rise, and tempests rage.

    At first we liv'd in pleasure;
Thine own delights thou didst to us impart:
When we grew wanton, thou didst use displeasure
To make us thine: yet that we might not part,
        As we at first did board with thee,
          Now thou wouldst taste our miserie.

There is but joy and grief;
If either will convert us, we are thine:
Some Angels us'd the first; if our relief
Take up the second, then thy double line
        And sev'rall baits in either kinde
        Furnish thy table to thy minde.

        Affliction then is ours;
We are the trees, whom shaking fastens more,
While blustring windes destroy the wanton bowres,
And ruffle all their curious knots and store.
        My God, so temper joy and wo,
        That thy bright beams may tame thy bow.

74. MORTIFICATION.

        How soon doth man decay!
When clothes are taken from a chest of sweets
        To swaddle infants, whose young breath
            Scarce knows the way;
        Those clouts are little winding sheets,
Which do consigne and send them unto death.

        When boyes go first to bed,
They step into their voluntarie graves;
        Sleep binds them fast; onely their breath
            Makes them not dead.
        Successive nights, like rolling waves,
Convey them quickly, who are bound for death.

        When youth is frank and free,
And calls for musick, while his veins do swell,
        All day exchanging mirth and breath
            In companie;
        That musick summons to the knell,
Which shall befriend him at the house of death.

        When man grows staid and wise,
Getting a house and home, where he may move
        Within the circle of his breath,
            Schooling his eyes;
        That dumbe inclosure maketh love
Unto the coffin, that attends his death.

    When age grows low and weak,
Marking his grave and thawing ev'ry yeare,
     Till all do melt, and drown his breath
      When he would speak;
    A chair or litter shows the biere,
Which shall convey him to the house of death.

    Man, ere he is aware,
Hath put together a solemnitie,
     And drest his herse, while he has breath
      As yet to spare.
    Yet, Lord, instruct us so to die
That all these dyings may be life in death.

75. DECAY.

SWEET were the dayes, when thou didst lodge with
Struggle with Jacob, sit with Gideon, [Lot,
Advise with Abraham, when thy power could not
Encounter Moses' strong complaints and moan:
    Thy words were then, *Let me alone.*

One might have sought and found thee presently
At some fair oak, or bush, or cave, or well;
Is my God this way? No, they would reply;
He is to Sinai gone, as we heard tell:
    List, ye may heare great Aaron's bell.

But now thou dost thyself immure and close
In some one corner of a feeble heart:
Where yet both Sinne and Satan, thy old foes,
Do pinch and straiten thee, and use much art
    To gain thy thirds and little part.

I see the world grows old, when as the heat
Of thy great love once spread, as in an urn
Doth closet up itself, and still retreat,
Cold sinne still forcing it, till it return
    And calling Justice, all things bum.

76. MISERIE.

LORD, let the Angels praise thy name.
Man is a foolish thing, a foolish thing,
   Folly and Sinne play all his game.
His house still burns; and yet he still doth sing,
      Man is but grasse,
      He knows it, fill the glasse.

   How canst thou brook his foolishnesse?
Why, he'l not lose a cup of drink for thee:
   Bid him but temper his excesse;
Not he: he knows, where he can better be,
      As he will swear,
      Then to serve thee in fear.

What strange pollutions doth he wed,
And make his own? as if none knew, but he.
   No man shall beat into his head
That thou within his curtains drawn canst see:
      They are of cloth,
      Where never yet came moth.

   The best of men, turn but thy hand
For one poore minute, stumble at a pinne:
   They would not have their actions scann'd,
Nor any sorrow tell them that they sinne,
      Though it be small,
      And measure not their fall.

   They quarrell thee, and would give over
The bargain made to serve thee: but thy love
   Holds them unto it, and doth cover
Their follies with the wing of thy milde Dove,
      Not suff'ring those
      Who would, to be thy foes.

   My God, Man cannot praise thy name:
Thou art all brightnesse, perfect puritie:
   The sunne holds down his head for shame,
Dead with eclipses, when we speak of thee.
      How shall infection
      Presume on thy perfection?

       As dirtie hands foul all they touch,
And those things most, which are most pure and fine;
       So our clay hearts, ev'n when we crouch
To sing thy praises, make them lesse divine.
                    Yet either this,
                 Or none thy portion is.

       Man cannot serve thee; let him go
And serve the swine: there, there is his delight:
       He doth not like this vertue, no;
Give him his dirt to wallow in all night;
                    These Preachers make
                 His head to shoot and ake.

       Oh foolish man! where are thine eyes?
How hast thou lost them in a crowd of cares?
       Thou pull'st the rug, and wilt not rise,
No not to purchase the whole pack of starres;
                    There let them shine,
                 Thou must go sleep, or dine.

       The bird that sees a daintie bowre
Made in the tree, where she was wont to sit,
       Wonders and sings, but not his power
Who made the arbour: this exceeds her wit.
                    But Man doth know
                 The spring, whence all things flow:

       And yet as though he knew it not,
His knowledge winks, and lets his humours reigne:
       They make his life a constant blot,
And all the blond of God to run in vain.
                    Ah, wretch I what verse
                 Can thy strange wayes rehearse?

       Indeed at first Man was a treasure,
A box of jewels, shop of rarities,
    A ring, whose posie was, *My pleasure:*
He was a garden in a Paradise:
                    Glorie and grace
                 Did crown his heart and face.

But sinne hath fool'd him. Now he is
A lump of flesh, without a foot or wing
    To raise him to the glimpse of blisse:
A sick toss'd vessel, dashing on each thing;
            Nay, his own shelf:
        My God, I mean myself.

77. JORDAN.

WHEN first my lines of heav'nly joyes made mention,
Such was their lustre, they did so excell,
That I sought out quaint words, and trim invention;
My thoughts began to burnish, sprout, and swell,
Curling with metaphors a plain intention,
Decking the sense, as if it were to sell.

Thousands of notions in my brain did runne,
Off'ring their service, if I were not sped:
I often blotted what I had begunne;
This was not quick enough, and that was dead.
Nothing could seem too rich to clothe the sunne,
Much lesse those joyes which trample on his head.

As flames do work and winde, when they ascend;
So did I weave myself into the sense.
But while I bustled, I might hear a friend
Whisper, *How wide is all this long pretence!*
There is in love a sweetnesse ready penn'a:
Copie out onely that, and save expense.

78. PRAYER.

    OF what an easie quick accesse,
My blessed Lord, art thou! how suddenly
    May our requests thine eare invade!
To shew that state dislikes not easinesse,
If I but lift mine eyes, my suit is made:
Thou canst no more not heare, than thou canst die.

    Of what supreme almightie power
Is thy great arm which spans the east and west,
    And tacks the centre to the sphere!
By it do all things live their measur'd houre:
We cannot ask the thing, which is not there,
Blaming the shallownesse of our request.

      Of what unmeasurable love
Art thou possest, who, when thou couldst not die,
      Wert fain to take our flesh and curse,
And for our sakes in person sinne reprove;
That by destroying that which ty'd thy purse,
Thou mightst make way for liberalitie!

      Since then these three wait on thy throne,
Ease, Power, and *Love;* I value prayer so,
      That were I to leave all but one,
Wealth, fame, endowments, vertues, all should go;
I and deare prayer would together dwell,
And quickly gain, for each inch lost, an ell.

79. OBEDIENCE.

      MY God, if writings may
    Convey a Lordship any way
Whither the buyer and the seller please;
      Let it not thee displease,
If this poore paper do as much as they.

      On it my heart doth bleed
    As many lines, as there doth need
To pass itself and all it hath to thee.
      To which I do agree,
And here present it as my speciall deed.

      If that hereafter Pleasure
    Cavill, and claim her part and measure,
As if this passed with a reservation,
      Or some such words in fashion;
I here exclude the wrangler from thy treasure.

      O let thy sacred will
    All thy delight in me fulfill!
Let me not think an action mine own way,
      But as thy love shall sway,
Resigning up the rudder to thy skill.

      Lord, what is man to thee,
    That thou shouldst minde a rotten tree?
Yet since thou canst not choose but see my actions;
      So great are thy perfections,
Thou mayst as well my actions guide, as see.

　　　　　Besides, thy death and bloud
　　　　Show'd a strange love to all our good:
Thy sorrows were in earnest; no faint proffer,
　　　　　Or superficiall offer
Of what we might not take, or be withstood.

　　　　　Wherefore I all forego:
　　　　To one word onely I say, No:
Where in the deed there was an intimation
　　　　　Of a *gift* or *donation,*
Lord, let it now by way of *purchase* go.

　　　　　He that will passe his land,
　　　　As I have mine, may set his hand
And heart unto this deed, when he hath read;
　　　　　And make the purchase spread
To both our goods, if he to it will stand.

　　　　　How happie were my part,
　　　　If some kinde man would thrust his heart
Into these lines; till in heav'n's court of rolls
　　　　　They were by winged souls
Entred for both, farre above their desert!

　　　　　　80. CONSCIENCE.

　　　　　PEACE pratler, do not lowre:
Not a fair look, but thou dost call it foul:
Not a sweet dish, but thou dost call it sowre:
　　　　　Musick to thee doth howl.
　　　By listning to thy chatting fears
　　　I have both lost mine eyes and eares.

　　　　　Pratler, no more, I say:
My thoughts must work, but like a noiselesse sphere,
Harmonious peace must rock them all the day:
　　　　　No room for pratlers there.
　　　If thou persistest, I will tell thee,
　　　That I have physick to expell thee.

　　　　　And the receit shall be
My Saviour's bloud; whenever at his board
I do but taste it, straight it cleanseth me,
　　　　　And leaves thee not a word;
　　　No, not a tooth or nail to scratch,
　　　And at my actions carp, or catch.

    Yet if thou talkest still,
Besides my physick, know there's some for thee:
Some wood and nails to make a staffe or bill
    For those that trouble me:
   The bloudie cross of my deare Lord
   Is both my physick and my sword.

81. SION.

LORD, with what glorie wast thou serv'd of old,
When Solomon's temple stood and flourished!
   Where most things were of purest gold;
   The wood was all embellished
With flowers and carvings, mysticall and rare:
All show'd the builder's, crav'd the seer's care.

Yet all this glorie, all this pomp and state,
Did not affect thee much, was not thy aim:
   Something there was that sow'd debate:
   Wherefore thou quitt'st thy ancient claim:
And now thy Architecture meets with sinne;
For all thy frame and fabrick is within.

There thou art struggling with a peevish heart,
Which sometimes crosseth thee, thou sometimes it:
   The fight is hard on either part.
   Great God doth fight, he doth submit.
All Solomon's sea of brass and world of stone
Is not so deare to thee as one good grone.

And truly brasse and stones are heavie things,
Tombes for the dead, not temples fit for thee:
   But grones are quick, and full of wings,
   And all their motions upward be;
And ever as they mount, like larks they sing:
The note is sad, yet musick for a king.

82. HOME.

COME, Lord, my head doth burn, my heart is sick,
   While thou dost ever, ever stay:
Thy long deferrings wound me to the quick,
   My spirit gaspeth night and day.
     O shew thy self to me,
     Or take me up to thee!

How canst thou stay, considering the pace
        The bloud did make, which thou didst waste?
When I behold it trickling down thy face,
        I never saw thing make such haste.
              O show thy self, &c.

When man was lost, thy pitie lookt about,
        To see what help in th' earth or skie:
But there was none; at least no help without:
        The help did in thy bosome lie.
              O show thy self to me,
              Or take me up to thee!

There lay thy sonne: and must he leave that nest,
        That hive of sweetnesse, to remove
Thraldome from those, who would not at a feast
        Leave one poor apple for thy love?
              O show thy self, &c

He did, he came: O my Redeemer deare,
        After all this canst thou be strange?
So many yeares baptiz'd, and not appeare;
        As if thy love could fail or change?
              O show thy self, &c.

Yet if thou stayest still, why must I stay?
        My God, what is this world to me?
This world of wo? hence, all ye clouds, away,
        Away; I must get up and see.
              O show thy self, &c

What is this weary world; this meat and drink,
        That chains us by the teeth so fast?
What is this woman-kinde, which I can wink
        Into a blacknesse and distaste?
              O show thy self, &c

With one small sigh thou gav'st me th' other day
        I blasted all the joyes about me:
And scouling on them as they pin'd away,
        Now come again, said I, and flout me.
              O show thy self to me,
              Or take me up to thee!

Nothing but drought and dearth, but bush and brake,
    Which way soe're I look, I see.
Some may dream merrily, but when they wake,
    They dresse themselves and come to thee.
        O show thy self, &c.

We talk of harvests; there are no such things,
    But when we leave our corn and hay:
There is no fruitfull yeare, but that which brings
    The last and lov'd, though dreadfull day.
        O show thy self, &c.

Oh loose this frame, this knot of man untie!
    That my free soul may use her wing,
Which now is pinion'd with mortalitie,
    As an intangled, hamper'd thing.
        O show thy self, &c.

What have I left, that I should stay and grone?
    The most of me to heav'n is fled:
My thoughts and joyes are all packt up and gone,
    And for their old acquaintance plead.
        O show thy self, &c.

Come, dearest Lord, passe not this holy season,
    My flesh and bones and joynts do pray:
And ev'n my verse, when by the ryme and reason
    The word is, *Stay,* says ever, *Come.*
        O show thy self, &c.

83. THE BRITISH CHURCH.

I JOY, deare Mother, when I view
Thy perfect lineaments, and hue
        Both sweet and bright:

Beautie in thee takes up her place,
And dates her letters from thy face,
        When she doth write.

A fine aspect in fit aray,
Neither too mean, nor yet too gay,
        Shows who is best:

Outlandish looks may not compare;
For all they either painted are,
        Or else undrest.

She on the hills, which wantonly
Allureth all in hope to be
                By her preferr'd,

Hath kiss'd so long her painted shrines,
That ev'n her face by kissing shines,
                For her reward.

She in the valley is so shie
Of dressing, that her hair doth lie
                About her eares:

While she avoids her neighbour's pride.
She wholly goes on th' other side,
                And nothing wears.

But, dearest Mother, (what those misse)
The mean thy praise and glorie is,
                And long may be.

Blessed be God, whose love it was
To double-moat thee with his grace,
                And none but thee.

84. THE QUIP.

THE merrie world did on a day
With his train-bands and mates agree
To meet together, where I lay,
And all in sport to geere at me.

First, Beautie crept into a rose;
Which when I pluckt not, Sir, said she,
Tell me, I pray, Whose hands are those?
But thou shalt answer, Lord, for me.

Then Money came, and chinking still,
What tune is this, poore man? said he:
I heard in Musick you had skill:
But thou shalt answer, Lord, for me.

Then came brave Glorie puffing by
In silks that whistled, who but he!
He scarce allow'd me half an eie:
But thou shalt answer, Lord, for me.

Then came quick Wit and Conversation,
And he would needs a comfort be,
And, to be short, make an oration:
But thou shalt answer, Lord, for me.

Yet when the houre of thy designe
To answer these fine things shall come;
Speak not at large, say, I am thine,
And then they have their answer home.

85. VANITIE.

POORE silly soul, whose hope and head lies low;
Whose flat delights on earth do creep and grow:
To whom the starres shine not so fair, as eyes;
Nor solid work, as false embroyderies;
Hark and beware, lest what you now do measure,
And write for sweet, prove a most sowre displeasure.

  O heare betimes, lest thy relenting
    May come too late!
  To purchase heaven for repenting
    Is no hard rate.
  If souls be made of earthly mould,
    Let them love gold;
    If born on high,
  Let them unto their kindred flie:
  For they can never be at rest,
  Till they regain their ancient nest.
Then silly soul take heed; for earthly joy
Is but a bubble, and makes thee a boy.

86. THE DAWNING.

AWAKE sad heart, whom sorrow ever drowns:
  Take up thine eyes, which feed on earth,
Unfold thy forehead gather'd into frowns:
  Thy Saviour comes, and with him mirth:
      Awake, awake;
And with a thankfull heart his comforts take.
  But thou dost still lament, and pine, and crie;
  And feel his death, but not his victorie.

Arise sad heart; if thou dost not withstand,
    Christ's resurrection thine may be:
Do not by hanging down break from the hand,
    Which as it riseth, raiseth thee;
        Arise, arise;
And with his buriall-linen drie thine eyes.
    Christ left his grave-clothes, that we might, when grief
    Draws tears, or bloud, not want an handkerchief.

87. JESU.

JESU is in my heart, his sacred name
Is deeply carved there; but th' other week
A great affliction broke the little frame,
Ev'n all to pieces; which I went to seek:
And first I found the corner where was *J,*
After, where *ES,* and next where *U* was graved.
When I had got these parcels, instantly
I sat me down to spell them, and perceived
That to my broken heart he was I *ease you,*
    And to my whole is *JESU.*

88. BUSINESSE.

CANST be idle? canst thou play,
Foolish soul who sinn'd to day?

Rivers run, and springs each one
Know their home, and get them gone:
Hast thou tears, or hast thou none?

If, poore soul, thou hast no tears;
Would thou hadst no faults or fears!
Who hath these, those ill forbears.

Windes still work: it is their plot,
Be the season cold, or hot:
Hast thou sighs, or hast thou not?

If thou hast no sighs or grones,
Would thou hadst no flesh and bones!
Lesser pains scape greater ones.

But if yet thou idle be,
Foolish soul, Who died for thee?

Who did leave his Father's throne,
To assume thy flesh and bone?
Had he life, or had he none?

If he had not liv'd for thee,
Thou hadst died most wretchedly;
And two deaths had been thy fee.

He so farre thy good did plot,
That his own self he forgot.
Did he die, or did he not?

If he had not died for thee,
Thou hadst liv'd in miserie.
Two lives worse than ten deaths be.

And hath any space of breath
'Twixt his sinnes and Saviour's death?

He that loseth gold, though drosse,
Tells to all he meets, his crosse:
He that sinnes, hath he no losse?

He that findes a silver vein,
Thinks on it, and thinks again:
Brings thy Saviour's death no gain?

Who in heart not ever kneels,
Neither sinne nor Saviour feels.

89. DIALOGUE.

SWEETEST Saviour, if my soul
    Were but worth the having,
Quickly should I then controll
    Any thought of waving.
But when all my care and pains
Cannot give the name of gains
To thy wretch so full of stains;
What delight or hope remains?

What (childe), is the ballance thine,
*   Thine the poise and measure?*
If I say, Thou shalt be mine,
*   Finger not my treasure.*
What the gains in having thee
Do amount to, onely he,
Who for man was sold, can see,
That transferr'd th' accounts to me.

But as I can see no merit,
    Leading to this favour:
So the way to fit me for it,
    Is beyond my savour.
As the reason then is thine;
So the way is none of mine:
I disclaim the whole designe:
Sinne disclaims and I resigne.

That is ally if that I could
*   Get without repining;*
And my clay my creature would
*   Follow my resigning:*
That as I did freely part
With my glorie and desert,
Left all joyes to feel all smart
Ah! no more: thou break'st my heart.

90. DULNESSE.

WHY do I languish thus, drooping and dull,
    As if I were all earth?
O give me quicknesse, that I may with mirth
    Praise thee brim-full I

The wanton lover in a curious strain
    Can praise his fairest fair;
And with quaint metaphors her curled hair
    Curl o'er again:

Thou art my lovelinesse, my life, my light,
    Beautie alone to me:
Thy bloudy death and undeserv'd, makes thee
    Pure red and white.

When all perfections as but one appeare,
        That those thy form doth show,
The very dust where thou dost tread and go
        Makes beauties here;

Where are my lines then? my approaches? views?
        Where are my window-songs?
Lovers are still pretending, and ev'n wrongs
        Sharpen their Muse.

But I am lost in flesh, whose sugred lyes
        Still mock me, and grow bold:
Sure thou didst put a minde there, if I could
        Finde where it lies.

Lord, cleare thy gift, that with a constant wit
        I may but look towards thee:
Look onely; for to *love* thee, who can be,
        What angel fit?

91. LOVE-JOY.

As on a window late I cast mine eye,
I saw a vine drop grapes with *J* and *C*
Anneal'd on every bunch. One standing by
Ask'd what it meant. I (who am never loth
To spend my judgement) said, It seem'd to me
To be the bodie and the letters both
Of *Joy* and *Charitie*; Sir, you have not miss'd,
The man reply'd; It figures *JESUS CHRIST*

92. PROVIDENCE.

O SACRED Providence, who from end to end
Strongly and sweetly movest! shall I write,
And not of thee, through whom my fingers bend
To hold my quill? shall they not do thee right?

Of all the creatures both in sea and land,
Onely to Man thou hast made known thy wayes,
And put the penne alone into his hand,
And made him Secretarie of thy praise.

Beasts fain would sing; birds dittie to their notes;
Trees would be tuning on their native lute
To thy renown: but all their hands and throats
Are brought to Man, while they are lame and mute.

Man is the world's high Priest: he doth present
The sacrifice for all; while they below
Unto the service mutter an assent,
Such as springs use that fall, and windes that blow.

He that to praise and laud thee doth refrain,
Doth not refrain unto himself alone,
But robs a thousand who would praise thee fain;
And doth commit a world of sinne in one.

The beasts say, Eat me; but, if beasts must teach,
The tongue is yours to eat, but mine to praise.
The trees say, Pull me: but the hand you stretch
Is mine to write, as it is yours to raise.

Wherefore, most sacred Spirit, I here present
For me and all my fellows praise to thee:
And just it is that I should pay the rent,
Because the benefit accrues to me.

We all acknowledge both thy power and love
To be exact, transcendent, and divine;
Who dost so strongly and so sweetly move,
While all things have their will, yet none but thine.

For either thy *command* or thy *permission*
Lay hands on all: they are thy *right* and *left:*
The first puts on with speed and expedition;
The other curbs sinnes stealing pace and theft;

Nothing escapes them both: all must appeare,
And be dispos'd and dress'd and tun'd by thee,
Who sweetly temper'st all. If we could heare
Thy skill and art, what musick would it be!

Thou are in small things great, not small in any:
Thy even praise can neither rise, nor fall.
Thou art in all things one, in each thing many:
For thou art infinite in one and all.

Tempests are calm to thee, they know thy hand,
And hold it fast, as children do their fathers,
Which crie and follow. Thou hast made poore sand
Check the proud sea, ev'n when it swells and gathers.

Thy cupboard serves the world: the meat is set,
Where all may reach: no beast but knows his feed.
Birds teach us hawking: fishes have their net:
The great prey on the lesse, they on some weed.

Nothing ingendred doth prevent his meat;
Flies have their table spread, ere they appeare;
Some creatures have in winter what to eat;
Others do sleep, and envie not their cheer.

How finely dost thou times and seasons spin,
And make a twist checkered with night and day!
Which as it lengthens windes, and windes us in,
As bouls go on, but turning all the way.

Each creature hath a wisdome for his good.
The pigeons feed their tender offspring, crying,
When they are callow; but withdraw their food,
When they are fledge, that need may teach them flying.

Bees work for man; and yet they never bruise
Their master's flower, but leave it, having done,
As fair as ever, and as fit to use:
So both the flower doth stay, and honey run.

Sheep eat the grasse, and dung the ground for more:
Trees after bearing drop their leaves for soil:
Springs vent their streams, and by expense get store:
Clouds cool by heat, and baths by cooling boil.

Who hath the vertue to expresse the rare
And curious vertues both of herbs and stones?
Is there an herb for that? O that thy care
Would show a root, that gives expressions!

And if an herb hath power, what hath the starres?
A rose, besides his beautie, is a cure.
Doubtlesse our plagues and plentie, peace and warres,
Are there much surer than our art is sure.

Thou hast hid metals: man may take them thence;
But at his perill: when he digs the place,
He makes a grave; as if the thing had sense,
And threatned man, that he should fill the space.

Ev'n poysons praise thee. Should a thing be lost?
Should creatures want, for want of heed their due?
Since where are poysons, antidotes are most;
The help stands close, and keeps the fear in view.

The sea, which seems to stop the traveller,
Is by a ship the speedier passage made.
The windes, who think they rule the mariner,
Are rul'd by him, and taught to serve his trade.

And as thy house is full, so I adore
Thy curious art in marshalling thy goods.
The hills with health abound, the vales with store;
The South with marble; North with furres and woods.

Hard things are glorious; easie things good cheap;
The common all men have; that which is rare,
Men therefore seek to have, and care to keep.
The healthy frosts with summer-fruits compare.

Light without winde is glasse: warm without weight
Is wooll and furres: cool without closenesse, shade:
Speed without pains, a horse: tall without height,
A servile hawk: low without losse, a spade.

All countries have enough to serve their need:
If they seek fine things, thou dost make them run
For their offence; and then dost turn their speed
To be commerce and trade from sunne to sunne.

Nothing wears clothes, but Man; nothing doth need
But he to wear them. Nothing useth fire,
But Man alone, to show his heav'nly breed:
And onely he hath fuell in desire.

When th' earth was dry, thou mad'st a sea of wet:
When that lay gather'd, thou didst broach the moun-
When yet some places could no moisture get, [tains:
The windes grew gard'ners, and the clouds good foun-[tains.

Rain, do not hurt my flowers; but gently spend
Your hony drops: presse not to smell them here;
When they are ripe, their odour will ascend
And at your lodging with their thanks appeare.

How harsh are thorns to pears! and yet they make
A better hedge, and need less reparation.
How smooth are silks compared with a stake,
Or with a stone! yet make no good foundation.

Sometimes thou dost divide thy gifts to man,
Sometimes unite. The Indian nut alone
Is clothing, meat and trencher, drink and kan,
Boat, cable, sail and needle, all in one.

Most herbs that grow in brooks, are hot and dry.
Cold fruits warm kernells help against the winde.
The lemmon's juice and rinde cure mutually.
The whey of milk doth loose, the milk doth binde.

Thy creatures leap not, but expresse a feast,
Where all the guests sit close, and nothing wants.
Frogs marry fish and flesh; bats, bird and beast;
Sponges, non-sense and sense; mines, th' earth and [plants.

To show thou art not bound, as if thy lot
Were worse than ours, sometimes thou shiftest hands.
Most things move th' under-jaw; the Crocodile not.
Most things sleep lying, th' Elephant leans or stands.

But who hath praise enough? nay, who hath any?
None can expresse thy works, but he that knows them;
And none can know thy works, which are so many,
And so complete, but onely he that owes them.

All things that are, though they have sev'rall wayes,
Yet in their being joyn with one advice
To honour thee: and so I give thee praise
In all my other hymnes, but in this twice.

Each thing that is, although in use and name
It go for one, hath many wayes in store
To honour thee; and so each hymne thy fame
Extolleth many wayes, yet this one more.

93. HOPE.

I GAVE to Hope a watch of mine: but he
        An anchor gave to me.
Then an old prayer-book I did present:
        And he an optick sent.
With that I gave a viall full of tears:
        But he a few green eares.
Ah Loyterer! I'le no more, no more I'le bring:
        I did expect a ring.

94. SINNE'S ROUND.

SORRIE I am, my God, sorrie I am,
That my offences course it in a ring.
My thoughts are working like a busie flame,
Untill their cockatrice they hatch and bring:
And when they once have perfected their draughts,
My words take fire from my inflamed thoughts.

My words take fire from my inflamed thoughts,
Which spit it forth like the Sicilian hill.
They vent the wares, and passe them with their faults,
And by their breathing ventilate the ill.
But words suffice not, where are lewd intentions:
My hands do joyn to finish the inventions:

My hands do joyn to finish the inventions:
And so my sinnes ascend three stories high,
As Babel grew before there were dissentions.
Yet ill deeds loyter not: for they supplie
New thoughts of sinning; wherefore, to my shame,
Sorrie I am, my God, sorrie I am.

95. TIME.

MEETING with Time, slack thing, said I,
Thy sithe is dull; whet it for shame.
No marvell Sir, he did replie,
If it at length deserve some blame:
    But where one man would have me grinde it,
    Twentie for one too sharp do finde it.

Perhaps some such of old did passe,
Who above all things lov'd this life;
To whom thy sithe a hatchet was,
Which now is but a pruning-knife.
  Christ's coming hath made man thy debter,
  Since by thy cutting he grows better.

And in his blessing thou art blest:
For where thou onely wert before
An executioner at best,
Thou art a gard'ner now, and more.
An usher to convey our souls
Beyond the utmost starres and poles.

And this is that makes life so long,
While it detains us from our God.
Ev'n pleasures here increase the wrong:
And length of dayes lengthen the rod.
  Who wants the place, where God doth dwell,
  Partakes already half of hell.

Of what strange length must that needs be,
Which ev'n eternitie excludes!
Thus farre Time heard me patiently:
Then chafing said, This man deludes:
  What do I here before his doore?
  He doth not crave lesse time, but more.

96. GRATEFULNESSE.

THOU that hast giv'n so much to me,
Give one thing more, a grateful heart.
See how thy beggar works on thee
      By art.

He makes thy gifts occasion more,
And sayes, If he in this be crost,
All thou hast giv'n him heretofore
      Is lost.

But thou didst reckon, when at first
Thy word our hearts and hands did crave,
What it would come to at the worst
      To save.

Perpetuall knockings at thy doore,
Tears sullying thy transparent rooms,
Gift upon gift; much would have more,
                And comes.

This notwithstanding, thou wentst on,
And didst allow us all our noise:
Nay thou hast made a sigh and grone
                Thy joyes.

Not that thou hast not still above
Much better tunes, then grones can make;
But that these countrey-aires thy love
                Did take.

Wherefore I crie, and crie again;
And in no quiet canst thou be,
Till I a thankfull heart obtain
                Of thee:

Not thankfull, when it pleaseth me;
As if thy blessings had spare dayes:
But such a heart, whose pulse may be
                Thy praise.

97. PEACE.

SWEET PEACE, where dost thou dwell? I humbly crave,
            Let me once know.
    I sought thee in a secret cave,
        And ask'd, if Peace were there
A hollow winde did seem to answer, No:
            Go seek elsewhere.

I did; and going did a rainbow note:
              Surely, thought I,
    This is the lace of Peace's coat:
        I will search out the matter.
But while I lookt the clouds immediately
            Did break and scatter.

Then went I to a garden and did spy
            A gallant flower,
    The crown Imperiall: Sure, said I,
        Peace at the root must dwell.
But when I digg'd, I saw a worm devoure
            What show'd so well.

At length I met a rev'rend good old man:
                Whom when for Peace
    I did demand, he thus began:
                There was a Prince of old
At Salem dwelt, who liv'd with good increase
                Of flock and fold.

He sweetly liv'd; yet sweetnesse did not save
                His life from foes.
    But after death out of his grave
                There sprang twelve stalks of wheat:
Which many wondring at, got some of those
                To plant and set.

It prosper'd strangely, and did soon disperse
                Through all the earth:
    For they that taste it do rehearse,
                That vertue lies therein;
A secret vertue, bringing peace and mirth
                By flight of sinne.

Take of this grain, which in my garden grows,
                And grows for you;
    Make bread of it: and that repose
                And peace, which ev'ry where
With so much earnestnesse you do pursue
                Is onely there.

98. CONFESSION.

        O what a cunning guest
Is this same grief! within my heart I made
        Closets; and in them many a chest;
        And like a master in my trade,
In those chests, boxes; in each box, a till:
Yet grief knows all, and enters when he will.

        No scrue, no piercer can
Into a piece of timber work and winde,
        As God's afflictions into man,
        When he a torture hath design'd.
They are too subtill for the subt'llest hearts;
And fall, like rheumes, upon the tendrest parts.

          We are the earth; and they,
Like moles within us, heave and cast about:
          And till they foot and clutch their prey,
          They never cool, much lesse give out.
No smith can make such locks, but they have keyes;
Closets are halls to them; and hearts, high-wayes.

          Onely an open breast
Doth shut them out, so that they cannot enter;
          Or, if they enter, cannot rest,
          But quickly seek some new adventure.
Smooth open hearts no fastning have; but fiction
Doth give a hold and handle to affliction.

          Wherefore my faults and sinnes,
Lord, I acknowledge; take thy plagues away:
          For since confession pardon winnes,
          I challenge here the brightest day,
The clearest diamond: let them do their best,
They shall be thick and cloudie to my breast.

99. GEDDINESSE.

OH, what a thing is man! how farre from power,
          From setled peace and rest!
He is some twentie sev'rall men at least
          Each sev'rall houre.

One while he counts of heav'n, as of his treasure:
          But then a thought creeps in,
And calls him coward, who for fear of sinne
          Will lose a pleasure.

Now he will fight it out, and to the warres;
          Now eat his bread in peace,
And snudge in quiet: now he scorns increase;
          Now all day spares.

He builds a house, which quickly down must go,
          As if a whirlwinde blew
And crusht the building: and it's partly true,
          His minde is so.

O what a sight were Man, if his attires
          Did alter with his minde;
And like a Dolphin's skinne, his clothes combin'd
          With his desires!

Surely if each one saw another's heart,
                There would be no commerce,
No sale or bargain pass: all would disperse,
                And live apart.

Lord, mend or rather make us: one creation
                Will not suffice our turn:
Except thou make us dayly, we shall spurn
                Our own salvation.

100. THE BUNCH OF GRAPES.

JOY, I did lock thee up: but some bad man
                Hath let thee out again:
And now, methinks, I am where I began
                Sev'n years ago: one vogue and vein,
                One aire of thoughts usurps my brain,

I did toward Canaan draw; but now I am
Brought back to the Red sea, the sea of shame.

For as the Jews of old by God's command
                Travell'd, and saw no town;
So now each Christian hath his journeys spann'd:
                Their storie pennes and sets us down.
                A single deed is small renown.
God's works are wide, and let in future times;
His ancient justice overflows our crimes.

Then have we too our guardian fires and clouds:
                Our Scripture-dew drops fast:
We have our sands and serpents, tents and shrowds,
                Alas! our murmurings come not last.
                But where's the cluster? where's the taste
Of mine inheritance? Lord, if I must borrow,
Let me as well take up their joy, as sorrow.

But can he want the grape, who hath the wine?
                I have their fruit and more.
Blessed be God, who prosper'd *Noah's* vine,
                And made it bring forth grapes good store.
                But much more him I must adore,
Who of the law's sowre juice sweet wine did make,
Ev'n God himself, being pressed for my sake.

101. LOVE UNKNOWN.

DEARE friend, sit down, the tale is long and sad:
And in my faintings I presume your love
Will more complie, then help. A Lord I had,
And have, of whom some grounds, which may improve,
I hold for two lives, and both lives in me.
To him I brought a dish of fruit one day,
And in the middle plac'd my heart. But he
                        (I sigh to say)
Lookt on a servant, who did know his eye
Better than you know me, or (which is one)
Then I my self. The servant instantly
Quitting the fruit, seiz'd on my heart alone,
And threw it in a font, wherein did fall
A stream of bloud, which issu'd from the side
Of a great rock: I well remember all,
And have good cause: there it was dipt and died,
And washt, and wrung: the very wringing yet
Enforceth tears. *Your heart was foul, I fear.*
Indeed 'tis true. I did and do commit
Many a fault more than my lease will bear;
Yet still askt pardon, and was not denied.
But you shall heare. After my heart was well,
And clean and fair, as I one even-tide
                        (I sigh to tell)
Walkt by myself abroad, I saw a large
And spacious furnace flaming, and thereon
A boyling caldron, round about whose verge
Was in great letters set *AFFLICTION.*
The greatnesse shew'd the owner. So I went
To fetch a sacrifice out of my fold,
Thinking with that, which I did thus present,
To warm his love, which I did fear grew cold.
But as my heart did tender it, the man
Who was to take it from me, slipt his hand,
And threw my heart into the scalding pan;
My heart, that brought it (do you understand?)
The offerer's heart. *Your heart was hard, I fear.*
Indeed 'tis true. I found a callous matter
Began to spread and to expatiate there:
But with a richer drug, then scalding water,
I bath'd it often, ev'n with holy bloud,
Which at a board, while many drank bare wine,
A friend did steal into my cup for good,
Ev'n taken inwardly, and most divine
To supple hardnesses. But at the length

Out of the caldron getting, soon I fled
Unto my house, where to repair the strength
Which I had lost, I hasted to my bed:
But when I thought to sleep out all these faults,
                    (I sigh to speak)
I found that some had stuff'd the bed with thoughts,
I would say *thorns*. Deare, could my heart not break,
When with my pleasures ev'n my rest was gone?
Full well I understood, who had been there:
For I had giv'n the key to none, but one:
It must be he. *Your heart was dull, I fear.*
Indeed a slack and sleepie state of minde
Did oft possesse me, so that when I pray'd,
Though my lips went, my heart did stay behinde
But all my scores were by another paid,
Who took the debt upon him. Truly, Friend,
For ought I heare, your Master shows to you
More favour then you wot of. Mark the end.
The Font did onely, what was old, renew:
The Caldron suppled, what was grown too hard:
The Thorns did quicken, what was grown too dull:
All did but strive to mend, what you had marr'd.
Wherefore be cheer'd, and praise him to the full
Each day, each houre, each moment of the week,
Who fain would have you be, new, tender, quick.

102. MAN'S MEDLEY.

HEARK, how the birds do sing,
          And woods do ring.
All creatures have their joy, and man hath his.
          Yet if we rightly measure,
              Man's joy and pleasure
Rather hereafter, then in present, is.

          To this life things of sense
              Make their pretence:
In th' other Angels have a right by birth:
          Man ties them both alone,
              And makes them one,
With th' one hand touching heav'n, with th' other [earth.
          In soul he mounts and flies,
              In flesh he dies.
He wears a stuffe whose thread is course and round,
          But trimm'd with curious lace,
              And should take place
After the trimming, not the stuffe and ground.

    Not, that he may not here
      Taste of the cheer:
But as birds drink, and straight lift up their head;
     So must he sip and think
      Of better drink
He may attain to, after he is dead.

    But as his joyes are double,
      So is his trouble.
He hath two winters, other things but one:
     Both frosts and thoughts do nip:
      And bite his lip;
And he of all things fears two deaths alone.

    Yet ev'n the greatest griefs
      May be reliefs,
Could he but take them right, and in their wayes.
     Happie is he, whose heart
      Hath found the art
To turn his double pains to double praise.

     103. THE STORM.

IF as the windes and waters here below
      Do flie and flow,
My sighs and tears as busy were above;
      Sure they would move
And much affect thee, as tempestuous times
Amaze poore mortals, and object their crimes.

Starres have their storms, ev'n in a high degree,
      As well as we.
A throbbing conscience spurred by remorse
      Hath a strange force:

It quits the earth, and mounting more and more,
Dares to assault thee, and besiege thy doore.

There it stands knocking, to thy musick's wrong,
      And drowns the song.

Glorie and honour are set by till it
      An answer get.

Poets have wrong'd poore storms: such dayes are best;
They purge the aire without, within the breast.

104. PARADISE.

I BLESSE thee, Lord, because I GROW
Among thy trees, which in a ROW
To thee both fruit and order ow.

What open force, or hidden CHARM
Can blast my fruit, or bring me HARM,
While the inclosure is thine ARM?

Inclose me still for fear I START.
Be to me rather sharp and TART,
Than let me want thy hand and ART.

When thou dost greater judgements SPARE,
And with thy knife but prune and FARE,
Ev'n fruitfull trees more fruitfull ARE.

Such sharpnes shows the sweetest FREND:
Such cuttings rather heal than REND:
And such beginnings touch their END.

105. THE METHOD.

POORE heart, lament,
For since thy God refuseth still,
There is some rub, some discontent,
    Which cools his will.

Thy Father *could*
Quickly effect, what thou dost move;
For he is *Power:* and sure he *would;*
    For he is *Love.*

Go search this thing.
Tumble thy breast and turn thy book:
If thou hadst lost a glove or ring,
    Wouldst thou not look?

What do I see
Written above there? *Yesterday*
I did behave me carelessly,
    When I did pray.

       And should God's eare
To such indifferents chained be,
Who do not their own motions heare?
       Is God lesse free?

       But stay! what's there?
Late when I would have something done,
I had a motion to forbear,
       Yet I went on.

       And should God's care,
Which needs not man, be ty'd to those
Who heare not him, but quickly heare
       His utter foes?

       Then once more pray:
Down with thy knees, up with thy voice:
Seek pardon first, and God will say,
       Glad heart rejoyce.

106. DIVINITIE.

As men, for fear the starres should sleep and nod,
       And trip at night, have spheres supplied;
As if a starre were duller than a clod,
       Which knows his way without a guide:

Just so the other heav'n they also serve,
       Divinitie's transcendent skie:
Which with the edge of wit they cut and carve.
       Reason triumphs, and faith lies by.

Could not that wisdome, which first broacht the wine,
       Have thicken'd it with definitions?
And jagg'd his seamlesse coat, had that been fine,
       With curious questions and divisions?

But all the doctrine, which he taught and gave,
       Was cleare as heav'n, from whence it came.
At least those beams of truth, which onely save,
       Surpasse in brightnesse any flame.

Love God, and love your neighbour. Watch and pray.
       Do as you would be done unto.
O dark instructions, ev'n as dark as day!
       Who can these Gordian knots undo?

But he doth bid us take his bloud for wine.
        Bid what he please; yet I am sure,
To take and taste what he doth there designe,
        Is all that saves, and not obscure.

Then burn thy Epicycles, foolish man;
        Break all thy spheres, and save thy head;
Faith needs no staffe of flesh, but stoutly can
        To heav'n alone both go, and leade.

107. EPHES. IV. 30.

Grieve not the Holy Spirit, etc.

AND art thou grieved, sweet and sacred Dove,
        When I am sowre,
        And crosse thy love?
Grieved for me? the God of strength and power
        Griev'd for a worm, which when I tread,
        I passe away and leave it dead?

Then weep, mine eyes, the God of love doth grieve:
Weep foolish heart,
And weeping live;
For death is drie as dust. Yet if ye part,
        End as the night, whose sable hue
        Your sinnes expresse; melt into dew.

When sawcie mirth shall knock or call at doore,
Cry out, Get hence,
Or cry no more.
Almightie God doth grieve, he puts on sense:
        I sinne not to my grief alone,
        But to my God's too; he doth grone.

O take thy lute, and tune it to a strain,
Which may with thee
All day complain.

There can no discord but in ceasing be.
        Marbles can weep; and surely strings
        More bowels have, than such hard things.

Lord, I adjudge myself to tears and grief,
Ev'n endlesse tears
Without relief.

If a cleare spring for me no time forbears,
>   But runnes, although I be not drie;
>   I am no Crystall, what shall I?

Yet if I wail not still, since still to wail
Nature denies;
And flesh would fail,

If my deserts were masters of mine eyes:
>   Lord, pardon, for thy sonne makes good
>   My want of tears with store of bloud.

108. THE FAMILIE.

WHAT doth this noise of thoughts within my heart,
As if they had a part?
What do these loud complaints and pulling fears,
>   As if there were no rule or eares?

But, Lord, the house and familie are thine,
Though some of them repine.
Turn out these wranglers, which defile thy seat:
>   For where thou dwellest all is neat.

First Peace and Silence all disputes controll,
>   Then Order plaies the soul;
And giving all things their set forms and houres,
>   Makes of wilde woods sweet walks and bowres.

Humble Obedience neare the doore doth stand,
>   Expecting a command:
Then whom in waiting nothing seems more slow,
>   Nothing more quick when she doth go.

Joyes oft are there, and griefs as oft as joyes;
>   But griefs without a noise:
Tet speak they louder, then distemper'd fears:
>   What is so shrill as silent tears?

This is thy house, with these it doth abound:
>   And where these are not found,
Perhaps thou com'st sometimes, and for a day;
>   But not to make a constant stay.

109. THE SIZE.

      CONTENT thee, greedie heart.
Modest and moderate joyes to those, that have
Title to more hereafter when they part,
          Are passing brave.
      Let th' upper springs into the low
      Descend and fall, and thou dost flow.

      What though some have a fraught
Of cloves and nutmegs, and in cinamon sail?
If thou hast wherewithall to spice a draught,
          When griefs prevail,
      And for the future time art heir
      To th' Isle of spices, Is't not fair?

      To be in both worlds full
Is more then God was, who was hungrie here.
Wouldst thou his laws of fasting disanull?
          Enact good cheer?
      Lay out thy joy, yet hope to save it?
      Wouldst thou both eat thy cake, and have it?

      Great joyes are all at once;
But little do reserve themselves for more:
Those have their hopes; these what they have renounce,
          And live on score:
      Those are at home; these journey still,
      And meet the rest on Sion's hill.

      Thy Saviour sentenc'd joy,
And in the flesh condemn'd it as unfit,
At least in lump: for such doth oft destroy;
          Whereas a bit
      Doth tice us on to hopes of more,
      And for the present health restore.

      A Christian's state and case
Is not a corpulent, but a thinne and spare,
Yet active strength: whose long and bonie face
          Content and care
      Do seem to equally divide,
      Like a pretender, not a bride.

    Wherefore sit down, good heart;
Grasp not at much, for fear thou losest all.
If comforts fell according to desert,
     They would great frosts and snows destroy:
     For we should count, Since the last joy.

    Then close again the seam,
Which thou hast open'd; do not spread thy robe
In hope of great things. Call to mind thy dream,
     An earthly globe,
    On whose meridian was engraven,
   These seas are tears, and heav'n the haven.

110. ARTILLERIE.

As I one ev'ning sat before my cell,
Me thought a starre did shoot into my lap.
I rose, and shook my clothes, as knowing well,
That from small fires comes oft no small mishap:
  When suddenly I heard one say,
  Do as thou usest, disobey,
  Expell good motions from thy breast,
Which have the face of fire, but end in rest.

I, who had heard of musick in the spheres,
But not of speech in starres, began to muse:
But turning to my God, whose ministers
The starres and all things are; If I refuse,
  Dread Lord, said I, so oft my good;
  Then I refuse not ev'n with bloud
  To wash away my stubborn thought:
For I will do, or suffer what I ought.

But I have also starres and shooters too,
Born where thy servants both artilleries use,
My tears and prayers night and day do wooe,
And work up to thee; yet thou dost refuse.
  Not but I am (I must say still)
  Much more oblig'd to do thy will,
  Than thou to grant mine: but because
Thy promise now hath ev'n set thee thy laws.

Then we are shooters both, and thou dost deigne
To enter combate with us, and contest
With thine own clay. But I would parley fain:
Shunne not my arrows, and behold my breast.
     Yet if thou shunnest, I am thine:
     I must be so, if I am mine.
     There is no articling with thee:
I am but finite, yet thine infinitely.

111. CHURCH-RENTS AND SCHISMES.

BRAVE rose (alas!) where art thou? in the chair,
Where thou didst lately so triumph and shine,
A worm doth sit, whose many feet and hair
Are the more foul, the more thou wert divine.
This, this hath done it, this did bite the root
And bottome of the leaves: which when the winde
Did once perceive, it blew them under foot,
Where rude unhallow'd steps do crush and grinde
   Their beauteous glories; Onely shreds of thee,
   And those all bitten, in thy chair I see.

Why doth my Mother blush? is she the rose,
And shows it so? Indeed Christ's precious bloud
Gave you a colour once; which when your foes
Thought to let out, the bleeding did you good,
And made you look much fresher then before.
But when debates and fretting jealousies
Did worm and work within you more and more,
Your colour faded, and calamities
   Turned your ruddie into pale and bleak:
   Your health and beautie both began to break.

Then did your sev'rall parts unloose and start;
Which when your neighbours saw, like a north-winde
They rushed in, and cast them in the dirt
Where Pagans tread. O Mother deare and kinde,
Where shall I get me eyes enough to weep,
As many eyes as starres? since it is night,
And much of Asia and Europe fast asleep,
And ev'n all Africk; would at least I might
   With these two poore ones lick up all the dew,
   Which falls by night, and poure it out for you!

112. JUSTICE.

O DREADFULL justice, what a fright and terrour
               Wast thou of old,
               When sinne and errour
      Did show and shape thy looks to me,
       And through their glasse discolour thee!
He that did but look up, was proud and bold.

The dishes of thy ballance seem'd to gape,
               Like two great pits;
               The beam and scape
      Did like some tott'ring engine show:
      Thy hand above did burn and glow,
Danting the stoutest hearts, the proudest wits.

But now that Christ's pure vail presents the sight,
               I see no fears:
               Thy hand is white,
      Thy scales like buckets, which attend
      And interchangeably descend,
Lifting to heaven from this well of tears.

Forwhere before thou still didst call on me,
               Now I still touch
               And harp on thee,
      God's promises hath made thee mine:
      Why should I justice now decline?
Against me there isnone, but for me much.

113. THE PILGRIMAGE.

I TRAVELL'D on, seeing the hill, where lay
               My expectation.
      A long it was and weary way.
      The gloomy cave of Desperation
I left on th' one, and on the other side
               The rock of Pride.

And so I came to phansies medow strow'd
               With many a flower:
      Fain would I here have made abode,
      But I was quicken'd by my houre.
So to care's cops I came, and there got through
               With much ado.

That led me to the wilde of passion; which
                Some call the wold;
      A wasted place, but sometimes rich.
      Here I was robb'd of all my gold,
Save one good Angell, which a friend had tied
                Close to my side.

At length I got unto the gladsome hill,
                Where lay my hope,
      Where lay my heart; and climbing still,
      When I had gain'd the brow and top,
A lake of brackish waters on the ground
                Was all I found.

With that abash'd and struck with many a sting
                Of swarming fears,
      I fell, and cry'd, Alas my King;
      Can both the way and end be tears?
Yet taking heart I rose, and then perceiv'd
                I was deceived:

My hill was further: so I flung away,
                Yet heard a crie
      Just as I went, *None goes that way*
      And lives: If that be all, said I,
After so foul a journey death is fair,
                And but a chair.

114. THE HOLDFAST.

I THREATNED to observe the strict decree
      Of my deare God with all my power and might:
      But I was told by one, it could not be;
Yet I might trust in God to be my light.

Then will I trust, said I, in him alone.
      Nay, ev'n to trust in him, was also his:
      We must confesse, that nothing is our own.
Then I confesse that he my succour is:

But to have nought is ours, not to confesse
      That we have nought. I stood amaz'd at this,
      Much troubled, till I heard a friend expresse,
That all things were more ours by being his.
      What Adam had, and forfeited for all,
      Christ keepeth now, who cannot fail or fall.

115. COMPLAINING.

Do not beguile my heart,
Because thou art
My power and wisdome. Put me not to shame,
Because I am
Thy clay that weeps, thy dust that calls.

Thou art the Lord of glorie;
The deed and storie
Are both thy due: but I a silly flie,
That live or die,
According as the weather falls.

Art thou all justice, Lord?
Shows not thy word
More attributes? Am I all throat or eye
To weep or crie?
Have I no parts but those of grief?

Let not thy wrathfull power
Afflict my houre,
My inch of life: or let thy gracious power
Contract my houre,
That I may climbe and finde relief.

116. THE DISCHARGE.

BUSIE enquiring heart, what wouldst thou know?
Why dost thou prie,
And turn, and leer, and with a licorous eye
Look high and low;
And in thy lookings stretch and grow?
Hast thou not made thy counts, and summ'd up all?
Did not thy heart
Give up the whole, and with the whole depart?
Let what will fall:
That which is past who can recall?

Thy life is God's, thy time to come is gone,
And is his right.
He is thy night at noon: he is at night
Thy noon alone.
The crop is his, for he hath sown.

And well it was for thee, when this befell,
        That God did make
Thy businesse his, and in thy life partake:
        For thou canst tell,
          If it be his once, all is well.

Onely the present is thy part and fee.
        And happy thou,
If, though thou didst not beat thy future brow,
        Thou couldst well see
          What present things requir'd of thee.

They ask enough; why shouldst thou further go?
        Raise not the mudde
Of future depths, but drink the cleare and good.
        Dig not for wo
          In times to come; for it will grow.

Man and the present fit: if he provid,
        He breaks the square.
This houre is mine: if for the next I care,
        I grow too wide,
          And do encroach upon death's side:

For death each houre environs and surrounds
        He that would know
And care for future chances, cannot go
        Unto those grounds,
          But thro' a Church-yard which them bounds.

Things present shrink and die: but they that spend
        Their thoughts and sense
On future grief, do not remove it thence,
        But it extend,
          And draw the bottome out an end.

God chains the dog till night: wilt loose the chain,
        And wake thy sorrow?
Wilt thou forestall it, and now grieve to morrow,
        And then again
          Grieve over freshly all thy pain?

Either grief will not come: or if it must,
        Do not forecast:
And while it cometh, it is almost past.
        Away distrust:
          My God hath promis'd; he is just.

117. PRAISE.

KING of glorie, King of peace,
        I will love thee:
And that love may never cease,
        I will move thee.

Thou hast granted my request,
        Thou hast heard me:
Thou didst note my working breast,
        Thou hast spar'd me.

Wherefore with my utmost art
        I will sing thee,
And the cream of all my heart
        I will bring thee.

Though my sinnes against me cried,
        Thou didst cleare me;
And alone when they replied,
        Thou didst heare me.

Sev'n whole dayes, not one in seven,
        I will praise thee.
In my heart, though not in heaven,
        I can raise thee.

Thou grew'st soft and moist with tears,
        Thou relentedst.
And when Justice call'd for fears,
        Thou dissentedst.

Small it is, in this poore sort
        To enroll thee:
Ev'n eternitie is too short
        To extoll thee.

118. AN OFFERING.

COMB, bring thy gift. If blessings were as slow
As men's returns, what would become of fools?
What hast thou there? a heart? but is it pure?
Search well and see, for hearts have many holes.
Yet one pure heart is nothing to bestow:
In Christ two natures met to be thy cure.

O that within us hearts had propagation,
Since many gifts do challenge many hearts!
Yet one, if good, may title to a number;
And single things grow fruitfull by deserts.
In publick judgments one may be a nation.
And fence a plague, while others sleep and slumber.

But all I fear is lest thy heart displease,
As neither good, nor one: so oft divisions
Thy lusts have made, and not thy lusts alone;
Thy passions also have their set partitions.
These parcell out thy heart: recover these,
And thou mayst offer many gifts in one.

There is a balsome, or indeed a bloud, [close
Dropping from heav'n, which doth both cleanse and
All sorts of wounds; of such strange force it is.
Seek out this All-heal, and seek no repose,
Until thou finde, and use it to thy good:
Then bring thy gift; and let thy hymne be this;

SINCE my sadnesse
Into gladnesse,
    Lord thou dost convert,
O accept
What thou hast kept,
    As thy due desert.

    Had I many,
Had I any,
    (For this heart is none)
All were thine
And none of mine,
    Surely thine alone.
Yet thy favour
May give savour
    To this poore oblation;
And it raise
To be thy praise,
    And be my salvation.

119. LONGING.

WITH sick and famisht eyes,
With doubling knees and weary bones,
  To thee my cries,
  To thee my grones,
To thee my sighs, my tears ascend:
    No end?

My throat, my soul is hoarse;
My heart is wither'd like a ground
  Which thou dost curse.
  My thoughts turn round,
And make me giddie; Lord, I fall,
    Yet call.

From thee all pitie flows.
Mothers are kinde, because thou art,
  And dost dispose
  To them a part:
Their infants, them; and they suck thee
    More free.

Bowels of pitie, heare!
Lord of my soul, love of my minde,
  Bow down thine eare!
  Let not the winde
Scatter my words, and in the same
    Thy name!

Look on my sorrows round!
Mark well my furnace! O what flames,
  What heats abound!
  What griefs, what shames!
Consider, Lord; Lord, bow thine eare,
    And heare!

Lord Jesu, thou didst bow
Thy dying head upon the tree:
  O be not now
  More dead to me!
Lord, heare! *Shall he that made the eare*
    Not heare?

Behold, thy dust doth stirre;
It moves, it creeps, it aims at thee:
   Wilt thou deferre
   To succour me,
Thy pile of dust, wherein each crumme
      Sayes, Come?

To thee help appertains.
Hast thou left all things to their course,
   And laid the reins
   Upon the horse?
Is all lockt? hath a sinner's plea
      No key?

Indeed the world's thy book,
Where all things have their leafe assign'd:
   Yet a meek look
   Hath interlin'd.
Thy board is full, yet humble guests
      Finde nests.

Thou tamest, while I die,
And fall to nothing: thou dost reigne,
   And rule on high,
   While I remain
In bitter grief: yet am I stil'd
      Thy childe.

Lord, didst thou leave thy throne,
Not to relieve? how can it be,
   That thou art grown
   Thus hard to me?
Were sinne alive, good cause there were
      To bear.

But now both sinne is dead,
And all thy promises live and bide.
   That wants his head;
   These speak and chide,
And in thy bosome poure my tears,
      As theirs.

   Lord JESU, heare my heart,
Which hath been broken now so long,
    That ev'ry part
    Hath got a tongue!
Thy beggars grow; rid them away
     To-day.

   My love, my sweetnesse, heare!
By these thy feet, at which my heart
    Lies all the yeare,
    Pluck out thy dart,
And heal my troubled breast which cryes,
     Which dyes.

120. THE BAG.

AWAY despair; my gracious Lord doth heare,
  Though windes and waves assault my keel,
  He doth preserve it: he doth steer,
  Ev'n when the boat seems most to reel.
  Storms are the triumph of his art:
Well may he close his eyes, but not his heart.

Hast thou not heard, that my Lord JESUS died?
  Then let me tell thee a strange storie.
  The God of power, as he did ride
  In his majestick robes of glorie,
  Resolv'd to light; and so one day
He did descend, undressing all the way.

The starres his tire of light and rings obtain'd,
  The cloud his bow, the fire his spear,
  The sky his azure mantle gain'd.
  And when they ask'd, what he would wear;
  He smil'd, and said as he did go,
He had new clothes a making here below.

When he was come, as travellers are wont,
  He did repair unto an inne.
  Both then, and after, many a brunt
  He did endure to cancell sinne:
  And having giv'n the rest before,
Here he gave up his life to pay our score.

But as he was returning, there came one
    That ran upon him with a spear.
    He, who came hither all alone,
    Bringing nor man, nor arms, nor fear,
    Receiv'd the blow upon his side,
And straight he turn'd, and to his brethren cry'd,

If ye have any thing to send or write,
    (I have no bag, but here is room)
    Unto my father's hands and sight
    (Beleeve me) it shall safely come.
    That I shall minde, what you impart;
Look, you may put it very neare my heart.

Or if hereafter any of my friends
    Will use me in this kinde, the doore
    Shall still be open; what he sends
    I will present, and somewhat more,
    Not to his hurt. Sighs will convey
Anything to me. Heark despair, away.

121. THE JEWS.

    POORE nation, whose sweet sap and juice
Our cyens have purloin'd, and left you drie:
Whose streams we got by the Apostles' sluce,
And use in baptisme, while ye pine and die:
Who by not keeping once, became a debter;
    And now by keeping lose the letter;

    Oh that my prayers! mine, alas!
Oh that some Angel might a trumpet sound;
At which the Church falling upon her face
Should crie so loud, untill the trump were drown'd,
And by that crie of her deare Lord obtain,
    That your sweet sap might come again!

122. THE COLLAR.

I STRUCK the board, and cry'd, No more;
    I will abroad.
    What? shall I ever sigh and pine?
My lines and life are free; free as the rode,
    Loose as the winde, as large as store.
        Shall I be still in suit?
    Have I no harvest but a thorn
    To let me bloud, and not restore
What I have lost with cordiall fruit?
        Sure there was wine,
    Before my sighs did drie it: there was corn,
        Before my tears did drown it.
    Is the yeare onely lost to me?
        Have I no bayes to crown it?
No flowers, no garlands gay? all blasted?
        All wasted?
    Not so, my heart: but there is fruit,
        And thou hast hands.
    Recover all thy sigh-blown age
On double pleasures: leave thy cold dispute
Of what is fit, and not forsake thy cage,
        Thy rope of sands,
Which pettie thoughts have made, and made to thee
    Good cable, to enforce and draw,
        And be thy law,
    While thou didst wink and wouldst not see.
        Away; take heed:
        I will abroad.
Call in thy death's head there: tie up thy fears.
        He that forbears]
        To suit and serve his need,
        Deserves his load.
But as I rav'd and grew more fierce and wilde,
        At every word,
    Methought I heard one calling, *Childe:*
        And I reply'd, *My Lord.*

123. THE GLIMPSE.

        WHITHER away delight?
Thou cam'st but now; wilt thou so soon depart,
        And give me up to night?
For many weeks of lingring pain and smart
But one half hour of comfort for my heart?

   Methinks delight should have
More skill in musick, and keep better time.
   Wert thou a winde or wave,
They quickly go and come with lesser crime:
Flowers look about, and die not in their prime.

   Thy short abode and stay
Feeds not, but addes to the desire of meat.
   Lime begg'd of old (they say)
A neighbour spring to cool his inward heat;
Which by the spring's accesse grew much more great.

   In hope of thee my heart
Pickt here and there a crumme, and would not die;
   But constant to his part,
When as my fears foretold this, did replie,
A slender thread a gentle guest will tie.

   Yet if the heart that wept
Must let thee go, return when it doth knock.
   Although thy heap be kept
For future times, the droppings of the stock
May oft break forth, and never break the lock.

   If I have more to spinne,
The wheel shall go, so that thy stay be short.
   Thou knowst how grief and sinne
Disturb the work. O make me not their sport,
Who by thy coming may be made a court!

124. ASSURANCE.

   O SPITEFULL bitter thought!
Bitterly spitefull thought! Couldst thou invent
So high a torture? Is such poyson bought?
Doubtlesse, but in the way of punishment,
   When wit contrives to meet with thee,
   No such rank poyson can there be.

   Thou said'st but even now,
That all was not so fair, as I conceiv'd,
Betwixt my God and me; that I allow
And coin large hopes; but, that I was deceiv'd:
   Either the league was broke, or neare it;
   And, that I had great cause to fear it.

    And what to this? what more
Could poyson, if it had a tongue, expresse?
What is thy aim? wouldst thou unlock the doore
To cold despairs, and gnawing pensivenesse?
    Wouldst thou raise devils? I see, I know,
    I writ thy purpose long ago.

    But I will to my Father,
Who heard thee say it. O most gracious Lord,
If all the hope and comfort that I gather,
Were from myself, I had not half a word,
    Not half a letter to oppose
    What is objected by my foes.

    But thou art my desert:
And in this league, which now my foes invade,
Thou art not onely to perform thy part,
But also mine; as when the league was made.
    Thou didst at once thyself indite,
    And hold my hand, while I did write.

    Wherefore if thou canst fail,
Then can thy truth and I: but while rocks stand,
And rivers stirre, thou canst not shrink or quail:
Yea, when both rocks and all things shall disband,
    Then shalt thou be my rock and tower,
    And make their ruine praise thy power.

    Now foolish thought go on,
Spin out thy thread, and make thereof a coat
To hide thy shame: for thou hast cast a bone,
Which bounds on thee, and will not down thy throat.
    What for it self love once began,
    Now love and truth will end in man.

125. THE CALL.

COME, my Way, my Truth, my Life:
Such a Way, as gives us breath:
Such a Truth, as ends all strife:
Such a Life, as killeth death.

Come, my Light, my Feast, my Strength:
Such a Light as shows a feast:
Such a Feast, as mends in length:
Such a Strength, as makes his guest.

Come, my Joy, my Love, my Heart:
Such a Joy, as none can move:
Such a Love, as none can part:
Such a Heart, as joyes in love.

126. CLASPING OF HANDS.

LORD, thou art mine, and I am thine,
If mine I am: and thine much more,
Than I or ought, or can be mine.
Yet to be thine, doth me restore;
So that again I now am mine,
And with advantage mine the more.
Since this being mine, brings with it thine,
And thou with me dost thee restore.
    If I without thee would be mine,
    I neither should be mine nor thine.

Lord, I am thine, and thou art mine:
So mine thou art, that something more
I may presume thee mine, then thine.
For thou didst suffer to restore
Not thee, but me, and to be mine:
And with advantage mine the more,
Since thou in death wast none of thine,
Yet then as mine didst me restore.
    O be mine still! still make me thine;
    Or rather make no Thine and Mine!

127. PRAISE.

LORD, I will mean and speak thy praise,
    Thy praise alone.
My busie heart shall spin it all my dayes:
    And when it stops for want of store,
Then will I wring it with a sigh or grone,
    That thou mayst yet have more.

When thou dost favour any action,
    It runnes, it flies:
All things concurre to give it a perfection.
    That which had but two legs before,
When thou dost blesse, hath twelve: one wheel doth
    To twentie then, or more. [rise

  But when thou dost on businesse blow,
     It hangs, it clogs:
Not all the teams of Albion in a row
  Can hale or draw it out of doore.
Legs are but stumps, and Pharaoh's wheels but logs.
    And struggling hinders more.

  Thousands of things do thee employ
     In ruling all
This spacious globe: Angels must have their joy,
  Devils their rod, the sea his shore,
The windes their stint: and yet when I did call,
    Thou heardst my call, and more.

  I have not lost one single tear:
     But when mine eyes
Did weep to heav'n, they found a bottle there
  (As we have boxes for the poore)
Readie to take them in; yet of a size
    That would contain much more.

  But after thou hadst slipt a drop
     From thy right eye
(Which there did hang like streamers neare the top
  Of some fair church to show the sore
And bloudie battell which thou once didst trie)
    The glasse was full and more.

  Wherefore I sing. Yet since my heart,
     Though press'd, runnes thin;
O that I might some other hearts convert,
  And so take up at use good store:
That to thy chests there might be coming in
    Both all my praise, and more!

128. JOSEPH'S COAT.

WOUNDED I sing, tormented I indite,
Thrown down I fall into a bed, and rest:
Sorrow hath chang'd its note: such is his will
Who changeth all things, as him pleaseth best.
  For well he knows, if but one grief and smart
Among my many had his full career,
Sure it would carrie with it ev'n my heart,
And both would runne until they found a biere
  To fetch the bodie; both being due to grief.
But he hath spoil'd the race; and giv'n to anguish

One of Joyes coats, ticing it with relief
To linger in me, and together languish.
    I live to shew his power, who once did bring
    My *joyes* to *weep,* and now my *griefs* to *sing.*

129. THE PULLEY.

    WHEN God at first made man,
Having a glasse of blessings standing by;
Let us (said he) poure on him all we can:
Let the world's riches, which dispersed lie,
    Contract into a span.

    So strength first made a way;
Then beautie flow'd, then wisdome, honour, pleasure:
When almost all was out, God made a stay,
Perceiving that alone, of all his treasure,
    Rest in the bottome lay.

    For if I should (said he)
Bestow this jewell also on my creature,
He would adore my gifts in stead of me,
And rest in Nature, not the God of Nature:
    So both should losers be.

    Yet let him keep the rest,
But keep them with repining restlesnesse:
Let him be rich and wearie, that at least,
If goodnesse leade him not, yet wearinesse
    May tosse him to my breast.

130. THE PRIESTHOOD.

BLEST Order, which in power dost so excell,
That with th' one hand thou liftest to the sky,
And with the other throwest down to hell
In thy just censures; fain would I draw nigh;
Fain put thee on, exchanging my lay-sword
    For that of th' holy word.

But thou art fire, sacred and hallow'd fire;
And I but earth and clay: should I presume
To wear thy habit, the severe attire
My slender compositions might consume.
I am both foul and brittle, much unfit
    To deal in holy writ.

Yet have I often seen, by cunning hand
And force of fire, what curious things are made
Of wretched earth. Where once I scorn'd to stand,
That earth is fitted by the fire and trade
Of skilfull artists, for the boards of those
              Who make the bravest shows.

But since those great ones, be they ne'er so great,
Come from the earth, from whence those vessels come;
So that at once both feeder, dish, and meat,
Have one beginning and one finall summe:
I do not greatly wonder at the sight,
              If earth in earth delight.

But th' holy men of God such vessels are,
As serve him up, who all the world commands.
When God vouchsafeth to become our fare,
Their hands convey him, who conveys their hands:
O what pure things, most pure must those things be,
              Who bring my God to me!

Wherefore I dare not, I, put forth my hand
To hold the Ark, although it seem to shake
Through th' old sinnes and new doctrines of our land.
Onely, since God doth often vessels make
Of lowly matter for high uses meet,
              I throw me at his feet.

There will I lie, untill my Maker seek
For some mean stuffe whereon to show his skill:
Then is my time. The distance of the meek
Doth flatter power. Lest good come short of ill
In praising might, the poore do by submission
              What pride by opposition.

131. THE SEARCH.

WHITHER, O, whither art thou fled,
              My Lord, my Love?
My searches are my daily bread;
              Yet never prove.

My knees pierce th' earth, mine eies the skie:
              And yet the sphere
And centre both to me denie
              That thou art there.

Yet can I mark how herbs below
                    Grow green and gay;
As if to meet thee they did know,
                    While I decay.

Yet can I mark how starres above
                    Simper and shine,
As having keyes unto thy love,
                    While poore I pine.

I sent a sigh to seek thee out,
                    Deep drawn in pain,
Wing'd like an arrow: but my scout
                    Returns in vain.

I tun'd another (having store)
                    Into a grone,
Because the search was dumbe before:
                    But all was one.

Lord, dost thou some new fabrick mold
                    Which favour winnes,
And keeps thee present, leaving th' old
                    Unto their sinnes?

Where is my God? what hidden place
                    Conceals thee still?
What covert dare eclipse thy face?
                    Is it thy will?

O let not that of any thing:
                    Let rather brasse,
Or steel, or mountains be thy ring,
                    And I will passe.

Thy will such an intrenching is,
                    As passeth thought:
To it all strength, all subtilties
                    Are things of nought.

Thy will such a strange distance is,
                    As that to it
East and West touch, the poles do kisse,
                    And parallels meet.

Since then my grief must be as large
                As is thy space,
Thy distance from me; see my charge,
                Lord, see my case.

O take these barres, these lengths away;
                Turn, and restore me:
Be not Almightie, let me say,
                Against, but for me.

When thou dost turn, and wilt be neare;
                What edge so keen,
What point so piercing can appeare
                To come between?

For as thy absence doth excell
                All distance known:
So doth thy nearnesse bear the bell,
                Making two one.

132. GRIEF.

O WHO will give me tears? Come all ye springs,
Dwell in my head and eyes: come, clouds, and rain:
My grief hath need of all the watry things,
That nature hath produc'd. Let ev'ry vein
Suck up a river to supply mine eyes,
My weary weeping eyes too drie for me,
Unlesse they get new conduits, new supplies,
To bear them out, and with my state agree.
What are two shallow foords, two little spouts
Of a lesse world? the greater is but small,
A narrow cupboard for my griefs and doubts,
Which want provision in the midst of all.
Verses, ye are too fine a thing, too wise
For my rough sorrows: cease, be dumbe and mute,
Give up your feet and running to mine eyes,
And keep your measures for some lover's lute,
Whose grief allows him musick and a ryme:
For mine excludes both measure, tune, and time.
                      Alas, my God!

133. THE CROSSE.

      WHAT is this strange and uncouth thing
To make me sigh, and seek, and faint, and die,
Untill I had some place, where I might sing,
          And serve thee; and not onely I,
But all my wealth, and familie might combine
To set thy honour up, as our designe.

      And then when after much delay,
Much wrastling, many a combate, this deare end,
So much desir'd, is giv'n, to take away
          My power to serve thee: to unbend.
All my abilities, my designes confound,
And lay my threatnings bleeding on the ground.

      One ague dwelleth in my bones,
Another in my soul (the memorie
What I would do for thee, if once my grones
          Could be allow'd for harmonie)
I am in all a weak disabled thing,
Save in the sight thereof, where strength doth sting.

      Besides, things sort not to my will,
Ev'n when my will doth studie thy renown:
Thou turnest th' edge of all things on me still,
          Taking me up to throw me down:
So that, ev'n when my hopes seem to be sped,
I am to grief alive, to them as dead.

      To have my aim, and yet to be
Farther from it than when I bent my bow;
To make my hopes my torture, and the fee
          Of all my woes another wo,
Is in the midst of delicates to need,
And ev'n in Paradise to be a weed.

      Ah my deare Father, ease my smart!
These contrarieties crush me: these crosse actions
Doe winde a rope about, and cut my heart:
          And yet since these thy contradictions
Are properly a crosse felt by thy sonne
With but foure words, my words, *Thy will be done.*

134. THE FLOWER.

How fresh, O Lord, how sweet and clean
Are thy returns! ev'n as the flowers in spring;
    To which, besides their own demean,
The late-past frosts tributes of pleasure bring.
        Grief melts away
        Like snow in May,
    As if there were no such cold thing.

    Who would have thought my shrivel'd heart
Could have recover'd greennesse? It was gone
    Quite under ground; as flowers depart
To see their mother-root, when they have blown;
        Where they together
        All the hard weather,
Dead to the world, keep house unknown.

    These are thy wonders, Lord of power,
Killing and quickning, bringing down to hell
    And up to heaven in an houre;
Making a chiming of a passing-bell.
        We say amisse,
        This or that is:
    Thy word is all, if we could spell.

O that I once past changing were,
Fast in thy Paradise, where no flower can wither!
    Many a spring I shoot up fair,
Offring at heav'n, growing and groning thither:
        Nor doth my flower
        Want a spring-showre,
My sinnes and I joining together.

    But while I grow in a straight line,
Still upwards bent, as if heav'n were mine own,
    Thy anger comes, and I decline:
What frost to that? what pole is not the zone
        Where all things burn,
        When thou dost turn,
    And the least frown of thine is shown?

  And now in age I bud again,
After so many deaths I live and write;
  I once more smell the dew and rain,
And relish versing: O my onely light,
    It cannot be
    That I am he,
  On whom thy tempests fell all night.

  These are thy wonders, Lord of love,
To make us see we are but flowers that glide:
  Which when we once can finde and prove,
Thou hast a garden for us, where to bide
    Who would be more,
    Swelling through store,
  Forfeit their Paradise by their pride.

135. DOTAGE.

FALSE glozing pleasures, casks of happinesse,
Foolish night-fires, womens' and childrens' wishes,
Chases in arras, guilded emptinesse,
Shadows well mounted, dreams in a career,
Embroider'd lyes, nothing between two dishes;
    These are the pleasures here.

True earnest sorrows, rooted miseries,
Anguish in grain, vexations ripe and blown,
Sure-footed griefs, solid calamities,
Plain demonstrations, evident and cleare,
Fetching their proofs ev'n from the very bone;
    These are the sorrows here.

But oh the folly of distracted men,
Who griefs in earnest, joyes in jest pursue;
Preferring, like brute beasts, a loathsome den
Before a court, ev'n that above so cleare,
Where are no sorrows, but delights more true
    Then miseries are here!

136. THE SONNE.

LET forrain nations of their language boast,
What fine varietie each tongue affords:
I like our language, as our men and coast;
Who cannot dresse it well, want wit, not words.
How neatly do we give one onely name
To parents' issue and the sunne's bright starre!
A senne is light and fruit; a fruitfull flame
Chasing the father's dimnesse, carried far
From the first man in th' East, to fresh and new
Western discov'ries of posteritie.
So in one word our Lord's humilitie
We turn upon him in a sense most true:
    For what Christ once in humblenesse began,
    We him in glorie call, *The Sonne of Man.*

137. A TRUE HYMNE.

    MY joy, my life, my crown!
    My heart was meaning all the day,
        Somewhat it fain would say:
And still it runneth mutt'ring up and down
With only this, *My joy, my life, my crown.*

    Yet slight not these few words;
    If truly said, they may take part
        Among the best in art.
The finenesse which a hymne or psalme affords,
Is, when the soul unto the line accords.

    He who craves all the minde,
    And all the soul, and strength, and time,
        If the words onely ryme,
Justly complains, that somewhat is behinde
To make his verse, or write a hymne in kinde.

    Whereas if th' heart be moved,
    Although the verse be somewhat scant,
        God doth supplie the want.
As when th' heart sayes (sighing to be approved)
O, could I love! and stops; God writeth, *Loved.*

138. THE ANSWER.

MY comforts drop and melt away like snow:
I shake my head, and all the thoughts and ends,
Which my fierce youth did bandie, fall and flow
Like leaves about me, or like summer friends,
Flyes of estates and sunne-shine. But to all,
Who think me eager, hot, and undertaking,
But in my prosecutions slack and small;
As a young exhalation, newly waking,
Scorns his first bed of dirt, and means the sky;
But cooling by the way, grows pursie and slow,
And settling to a cloud, doth live and die
In that dark state of tears: to all, that so
    Show me, and set me, I have one reply,
Which they that know the rest, know more then I.

139. A DIALOGUE-ANTHEM.

Christian, Death.

Chr. ALAS, poore death! where is thy glorie?
    Where is thy famous force, thy ancient sting?
Dea. Alas, poore mortall, void of storie,
    Go spell and reade how I have kill'd thy King.
Chr. Poore death! and who was hurt thereby?
    Thy curse being laid on him makes thee accurst.
Dea. Let losers talk, yet thou shall die;
    These arms shall crush thee. *Chr,* Spare not, do thy worst.
    I shall be one day better then before:
    Thou so much worse, that thou shalt be no more.

140. THE WATER-COURSE.

THOU who dost dwell and linger here below,
Since the condition of this world is frail,
Where of all plants afflictions soonest grow;
If troubles overtake thee, do not wail:
    For who can look for lesse, that loveth   { Life
                                                  { Strife

But rather turn the pipe, and waters course
To serve thy sinnes, and furnish thee with store
Of sov'raigne tears, springing from true remorse:
That so in purenesse thou mayst him adore
    Who gives to man, as he sees fit,   { Salvation.
                                               { Damnation.

141. SELF-CONDEMNATION.

THOU who condemnest Jewish hate,
For choosing Barabbas a murderer
      Before the Lord of glorie;
   Look back upon thine own estate,
Call home thine eye (that busie wanderer)
      That choice may be thy storie.

   He that doth love, and love amisse
This world's delights before true Christian joy,
      Hath made a Jewish choice:
   The world an ancient murderer is;
Thousands of souls it hath and doth destroy
      With her enchanting voice.

   He that hath made a sorrie wedding
Between his soul and gold, and hath preferr'd
      False gain before the true,
   Hath done what he condemnes in reading:
For he hath sold for money his deare Lord,
      And is a Judas-Jew.

   Thus we prevent the last great day,
And judge our selves. That light which sin and
      Did before dimme and choke, [passion
   When once those snuffes are ta'en away,
Shines bright and cleare, ev'n unto condemnation,
      Without excuse or cloak.

142. BITTER-SWEET.

AH, my deare angrie Lord,
Since thou dost love, yet strike;
Cast down, yet help afford;
Sure I will do the like.

I will complain, yet praise;
I will bewail, approve:
And all my sowre-sweet dayes
I will lament, and love.

143. THE GLANCE.

WHEN first thy sweet and gracious eye
Vouchsaf'd ev'n in the midst of youth and night
To look upon me, who before did lie
    Weltring in sinne;

I felt a sugred strange delight,
Passing all cordials made by any art,
Bedew, embalme, and overrunne my heart,
    And take it in.

Since that time many a bitter storm
My soul hath felt, ev'n able to destroy,
Had the malicious and ill-meaning harm
    His swing and sway:

But still thy sweet originall joy,
Sprung from thine eye, did work within my soul,
And surging griefs, when they grew bold, controll,
    And got the day.

If thy first glance so powerfull be,
A mirth but open'd, and seal'd up again;
What wonders shall we feel, when we shall see
    Thy full-ey'd love!

When thou shalt look us out of pain,
And one aspect of thine spend in delight
More then a thousand sunnes disburse in light,
    In heav'n above.

144. THE TWENTY-THIRD PSALME.

THE God of love my shepherd is,
    And he that doth me feed:
While he is mine, and I am his,
    What can I want or need?

He leads me to the tender grasse,
    Where I both feed and rest;
Then to the streams that gently passe:
    In both I have the best.

Or if I stray, he doth convert,
  And bring my minde in frame:
And all this not for my desert,
  But for his holy name.

Yea, in death's shadie black abode
  Well may I walk, not fear:
For thou art with me, and thy rod
  To guide, thy staffe to bear.

Nay, thou dost make me sit and dine,
  Ev'n in my enemies' sight;
My head with oyl, my cup with wine
  Runnes over day and night.

Surely thy sweet and wondrous love
  Shall measure all my dayes;
And as it never shall remove,
  So neither shall my praise.

145. MARIE MAGDALENE.

WHEN blessed Marie wip'd her Saviour's feet,
(Whose precepts she had trampled on before)
And wore them for a jewell on her head,
  Shewing his steps should be the street,
  Wherein she thenceforth evermore
With pensive humblenesse would live and tread:

She being stain'd herself, why did she strive
To make him clean, who could not be defil'd?
Why kept she not her tears for her own faults,
  And not his feet? Though we could dive
  In tears like seas, our sinnes are pil'd
Deeper then they, in words, and works, and thoughts.

Deare soul, she knew who did vouchsafe and deigne
To bear her filth; and that her sinnes did dash
Ev'n God himself: wherefore she was not loth,
  As she had brought wherewith to stain,
  So to bring in wherewith to wash:
And yet in washing one, she washed both.

146. AARON.

HOLINESSE on the head,
Light and perfections on the breast,
Harmonious bells below, raising the dead
    To lead them unto life and rest:
        Thus are true Aarons drest.

Profanenesse in my head,
Defects and darknesse in my breast
A noise of passions ringing me for dead
    Unto a place where is no rest:
        Poore priest thus am I drest.

Onely another head
I have, another heart and breast,
Another musick, making live not dead,
    Without whom I could have no rest:
        In him I am well drest.

Christ is my onely head,
My alone onely heart and breast,
My only musick, striking me ev'n dead;
    That to the old man I may rest,
        And be in him new drest.

So holy in my head,
Perfect and light in my deare breast,
My doctrine tun'd by Christ, (who is not dead,
    But lives in me while I do rest).
        Come, people; Aaron's drest.

147. THE ODOUR.

2 Cor. II.

How sweetly doth *My Master* sound! *My Master!*
    As amber-greese leaves a rich scent
        Unto the taster:
    So do these words a sweet content,
In orientali fragrancie, *My Master.*

With these all day I do perfume my minde,
    My mind ev'n thrust into them both;
        That I might finde
    What cordials make this curious broth,
This broth of smells, that feeds and fats my minde.

My Master, shall I speak? O that to thee
    My Servant were a little so,
        As flesh may be;
    That these two words might creep and grow
To some degree of spicinesse to thee!

Then should the Pomander, which was before
    A speaking sweet, mend by reflection,
        And tell me more:
    For pardon of my imperfection
Would warm and work it sweeter than before.

For when *My Master,* which alone is sweet,
    And ev'n in my unworthinesse pleasing,
        Shall call and meet,
    My servant, as thee not displeasing,
That call is but the breathing of the sweet.

This breathing would with gains by sweetning me
    (As sweet things traffick: when they meet)
        Return to thee.
    And so this new commerce and sweet
Should all my life employ, and busie me.

148. THE FOIL.

    IF we could see below
The sphere of vertue, and each shining grace,
    As plainly as that above doth show;
This were the better skie, the brighter place.

    God hath made starres the foil
To set off vertues; griefs to set off sinning:
    Yet in this wretched world we toil,
As if grief were not foul, nor vertue winning.

149. THE FORERUNNERS.

The harbingers are come. See, see their mark;
White is their colour, and behold my head.
But must they have my brain? must they dispark
Those sparkling notions, which therein was bred?
    Must dulnesse turn me to a clod?
Yet have they left me, *Thou art still my God.*

Good men ye be, to leave me my best room,
Ev'n ail my heart, and what is lodged there:
I passe not, I, what of the rest become,
So, *Thou art still my God,* be out of fear.
    He will be pleased with that dittie;
And if I please him, I write fine and wittie.

Farewell sweet phrases, lovely metaphors:
But will ye leave me thus? when ye before
Of stews and brothels onely knew the doores,
Then did I wash you with my tears, and more,
    Brought you to Church well drest and clad:
My God must have my best, ev'n all I had.

Lovely enchanting language, sugar-cane,
Hony of roses, whither wilt thou flie?
Hath some fond lover tic'd thee to thy bane?
And wilt thou leave the Church, and love a stie?
    Fie, thou wilt soil thy broider'd coat,
And hurt thyself, and him that sings the note.

Let foolish lovers, if they will love dung,
With canvas, not with arras clothe their shame:
Let follie speak in her own native tongue.
True beautie dwells on high: ours is a flame
    But borrow'd thence to light us thither.
Beautie and beauteous words should go together.

Yet if you go, I passe not; take your way:
For, *Thou art still my God,* is all that ye
Perhaps with more embellishment can say.
Go birds of spring: let winter have his fee;
    Let a bleak palenesse chalk the doore,
So all within be livelier then before.

150. THE ROSE.

PRESSE me not to take more pleasure
    In this world of sugred lies,
And to use a larger measure
    Than my strict, yet welcome size.

First, there is no pleasure here:
    Colour'd griefs indeed there are,
Blushing woes, that look as cleare,
    As if they could beautie spare.

Or if such deceits there be,
    Such delights I meant to say;
There are no such things to me,
    Who have pass'd my right away.

But I will not much oppose
    Unto what you now advise:
Onely take this gentle rose,
    And therein my answer lies.

What is fairer then a rose?
    What is sweeter? yet it purgeth.
Purgings enmitie disclose,
    Enmitie forbearance urgeth.

If then all that worldlings prize
    Be contracted to a rose;
Sweetly there indeed it lies,
    But it biteth in the close.

So this flower doth judge and sentence
    Worldly joyes to be a scourge:
For they all produce repentance,
    And repentance is a purge.

But I health, not physick choose:
    Onely though I you oppose,
Say that fairly I refuse,
    For my answer is a rose.

151. DISCIPLINE.

THROW away thy rod,
Throw away thy wrath:
    O my God,
Take the gentle path.

For my heart's desire
Unto thine is bent:
    I aspire
To a full consent.

Not a word or look
I affect to own,
    But by book,
And thy book alone.

Though I fail, I weep:
Though I halt in pace,
          Yet I creep
To the throne of grace.

Then let wrath remove;
Love will do the deed:
          For with love
Stonie hearts will bleed.

Love is swift of foot;
Love's a man of warre,
          And can shoot,
And can hit from forre.

Who can scape his bow?
That which wrought on thee,
          Brought thee low,
Needs must work on me.

Throw away thy rod;
Though man frailties hath,
          Thou art God:
Throw away thy wrath.

152. THE INVITATION.

COME ye hither all, whose taste
          Is your waste;
Save your cost, and mend your fare.
God is here prepar'd and drest,
          And the feast,
God, in whom all dainties are.

Come ye hither all, whom wine
          Doth define,
Naming you not to your good:
Weep what ye have drunk amisse,
          And drink this,
Which before ye drink is bloud.

Come ye hither all, whom pain
          Doth arraigne,
Bringing all your sinnes to sight:
Taste and fear not: God is here
          In this cheer,
And on sinne doth cast the fright.

Come ye hither all, whom joy
                    Doth destroy,
While ye graze without your bounds:
Here is joy that drowneth quite
                    Your delight,
As a floud the lower grounds.

Come ye hither all, whose love
                    Is your dove,
And exalts you to the skie:
Here is love, which, having breath
                    Ev'n in death,
After death can never die.

Lord I have invited all,
                    And I shall
Still invite, still call to thee:
For it seems but just and right
                    In my sight,
Where is all, there all should be.

153. THE BANQUET.

WELCOME sweet and sacred cheer,
                    Welcome deare;
With me, in me, live and dwell:
For thy neatnesse passeth sight,
                    Thy delight
Passeth tongue or taste or tell.

O what sweetnesse from the bowl
                    Fills my soul,
Such as is, and makes divine!
Is some starre (fled from the sphere)
                    Melted there,
As we sugar melt in wine?

Or hath sweetnesse in the bread
                    Made a head
To subdue the smell of sinne,
Flowers, and gummes, and powders giving
                    All their living,
Lest the enemie should winne?

Doubtlesse, neither starre nor flower
                    Hath the power
Such a sweetnesse to impart:
Onely God, who gives perfumes,
                    Flesh assumes,
And with it perfumes my heart.

But as Pomanders and wood
                    Still are good,
Yet being bruis'd are better sented;
God, to show how farre his love
                    Could improve,
Here, as broken, is presented.

When I had forgot my birth,
                    And on earth
In delights of earth was drown'd;
God took bloud, and needs would be
                    Spilt with me,
And so found me on the ground.

Having rais'd me to look up,
                    In a cup
Sweetly he doth meet my taste.
But I still being low and short,
                    Farre from court,
Wine becomes a wing at last.

For with it alone I flie
                    To the skie:
Where I wipe mine eyes, and see
What I seek, for what I sue;
                    Him I view
Who hath done so much for me.

Let the wonder of this pitie
                    Be my dittie,
And take up my lines and life:
Hearken under pain of death,
                    Hands and breath,
Strive in this, and love the strife.

154. THE POSIE.

    LET wits contest,
And with their words and posies windows fill:
    Lesse than the least
Of all thy mercies, is my posie still.

    This on my ring,
This by my picture, in my book I write;
    Whether I sing,
Or say, or dictate, this is my delight.

    Invention rest;
Comparisons go play; wit use thy will:
    Lesst than the least
Of all God's mercies, is my posie still.

155. A PARODIE.

SOUL'S joy, when thou art gone,
        And I alone,
        Which cannot be,
Because thou dost abide with me,
    And I depend on thee;

Yet when thou dost suppresse
        The cheerfulnesse
        Of thy abode,
And in my powers not stirre abroad,
    But leave me to my load:

O what a damp and shade
        Doth me invade!
        No stormie night
Can so afflict or so affright
    As thy eclipsed light.

Ah Lord! do not withdraw,
        Lest want of aw
        Make sinne appeare;
And when thou dost but shine lesse cleare,
    Say, that thou art not here.

  And then what life I have,
    While Sinne doth rave,
    And falsly boast,
That I may seek, but thou art lost;
    Thou and alone thou know'st.

O what a deadly cold
    Doth me infold!
    I half beleeve,
That Sinne says true: but while I grieve.
    Thou com'st and dost relieve.

156. THE ELIXER.

  TEACH me, my God and King,
    In all things thee to see,
And what I do in any thing,
    To do it as for thee:

    Not rudely, as a beast,
    To runne into an action;
But still to make thee prepossest,
    And give it his perfection.

    A man that looks on glasse,
    On it may stay his eye;
Or if he pleaseth, through it passe,
    And then the heav'n espie.

    All may of thee partake:
    Nothing can be so mean,
Which with his tincture (for thy sake)
    Will not grow bright and clean.

    A servant with this clause
    Makes drudgerie divine:
Who sweeps a room, as for thy laws,
    Makes that and th' action fine.

    This is the famous stone
    That turneth all to gold:
For that which God doth touch and own
    Cannot for lesse be told.

157. A WREATH.

A WREATHED garland of deserved praise,
Of praise deserved, unto thee I give,
I give to thee, who knowest all my wayes,
My crooked winding wayes, wherein I live,
Wherein I die, not live; for life is straight,
Straight as a line, and ever tends to thee,
To thee, who art more farre above deceit,
Than deceit seems above simplicitie.
Give me simplicitie, that I may live,
So live and like, that I may know thy wayes,
Know them and practise them: then shall I give
For this poore wreath, give thee a crown of praise.

158. DEATH.

DEATH, thou wast once an uncouth hideous thing,
        Nothing but bones,
     The sad effect of sadder grones:
Thy mouth was open, but thou couldst not sing.

For we consider'd thee as at some six
        Or ten yeares hence,
     After the losse of life and sense,
Flesh being tnrn'd to dust, and bones to sticks.

We lookt on this side of thee, shooting short;
        Where we did finde
     The shells of fledge souls left behinde,
Dry dust, which sheds no tears, but may extort.

But since our Saviour's death did put some bloud
        Into thy face;
     Thou art grown fair and full of grace,
Much in request, much sought for, as a good.

For we do now behold thee gay and glad,
        As at dooms-day;
     When souls shall wear their new aray,
And all thy bones with beautie shall be clad.

Therefore we can go die as sleep, and trust
        Half that we have
     Unto an honest faithfull grave;
Making our pillows either down, or dust.

159. DOOMS-DAY.

COME away,
Make no delay.
Summon all the dust to rise,
Till it stirre, and rubbe the eyes;
While this member jogs the other,
Each one whispering, *Live you, brother?*

Come away,
Make this the day.
Dust, alas, no musick feels,
But thy trumpet: then it kneels,
As peculiar notes and strains
Cure Tarantulaes raging pains.

Come away,
O make no stay!
Let the graves make their confession,
Lest at length they plead possession:
Fleshes stubbornnesse may have
Read that lesson to the grave.

Come away,
Thy flock doth stray.
Some to the windes their bodie lend,
And in them may drown a friend:
Some in noisome vapours grow
To a plague and publick wo.

Come away,
Help our decay.
Man is out of order hurl'd,
Parcel'd out to all the world.
Lord, thy broken consort raise,
And the musick shall be praise.

160. JUDGEMENT.

ALMIGHTIE Judge, how shall poore wretches brook
       Thy dreadfull look,
Able a heart of iron to appall,
       When thou shalt call
For ev'ry man's peculiar book?

What others mean to do, I know not well;
              Yet I heare tell,
That some will turn thee to some leaves therein
              So void of sinne,
      That they in merit shall excell.

But I resolve, when thou shalt call for mine,
              That to decline,
And thrust a Testament into thy hand:
              Let that be scann'd.
      There thou shalt finde my faults are thine.

161. HEAVEN.

O WHO will show me those delights on high?
            Echo.   *I.*
Thou Echo, thou art mortall, all men know.
            Echo.   *No.*
Wert thou not born among the trees and leaves?
            Echo.   *Leaves.*
And are there any leaves, that still abide?
            Echo.   *Bide.*
What leaves are they? impart the matter wholly.
            Echo.   *Holy.*
Are holy leaves the Echo then of blisse?
            Echo.   *Yes.*
Then tell me what is that supreme delight?
            Echo.   *Light.*
Light to the minde: what shall the will enjoy?
            Echo.   *Joy.*
But are there cares and businesse with the pleasure?
            Echo.   *Leisure.*
Light, joy, and leisure; but shall they persever?
            Echo   *Ever.*

162. LOVE.

LOVE bade me welcome: yet my soul drew back,
            Guiltie of dust and sinne.
But quick-ey'd Love, observing me grow slack
            From my first entrance in,
Drew nearer to me, sweetly questioning,
            If I lacked any thing.

A guest, I answer'd, worthy to be here:
        Love said, you shall be he.
I the unkinde, ungratefull? Ah my deare,
        I cannot look on thee.
Love took my hand, and smiling did reply,
        Who made the eyes but I?

Truth Lord, but I have marr'd them: let my shame
        Go where it doth deserve.
And know you not, sayes Love, who bore the blame?
        My deare, then I will serve.
You must sit down, sayes Love, and taste my meat:
        So I did sit and eat.

        Glorie be to God on high, and on earth peace,
            good mill towards men.

II. THE CHURCH MILITANT.

ALMIGHTIE LORD, who from thy glorious throne
Seest and rulest all things ev'n as one:
The smallest ant or atome knows thy power,
Known also to each minute of an hour:
Much more do Common-weals acknowledge thee,
And wrap their policies in thy decree,
Complying with thy counsels, doing nought
Which doth not meet with an eternall thought.
But above all, thy Church and Spouse doth prove
Not the decrees of power, but bands of love.
Early didst thou arise to plant this vine,
Which might the more indeare it to be thine.
Spices come from the East; so did thy Spouse
Trimme as the light, sweet as the laden boughs
Of *Noah's* shadie vine, chaste as the dove,
Prepar'd and fitted to receive thy love.
The course was westward, that the sunne might light
As well our understanding as our sight.
Where th' Ark did rest, there *Abraham* began
To bring the other Ark from *Canaan.*
Moses pursu'd this: but King *Solomon*
Finish'd and fixt the old religion.
When it grew loose, the Jews did hope in vain
By nailing Christ to fasten it again.
But to the Gentiles he bore crosse and all,
Rending with earthquakes the partition-wall.
Onely whereas the Ark in glorie shone,
Now with the crosse, as with a staffe, alone,
Religion, like a pilgrime, westward bent,
Knocking at all doores, ever as she went.
Yet as the sunne, though forward be his flight,
Listens behinde him, and allows some light,
Till all depart: so went the Church her way,
Letting, while one foot stept, the other stay
Among the eastern nations for a time,
Till both removed to the western clime.
To *Egypt* first she came, where they did prove
Wonders of anger once, but now of love.
The ten Commandments there did flourish more
Than the ten bitter plagues had done before.
Holy *Macarius* and great *Anthonie*
Made *Pharaoh Moses,* changing th' historie.
Goshen was darknesse, *Egypt* full of lights,
Nilus for monsters brought forth Israelites.
Such power hath mightie Baptisme to produce,

For things misshapen, things of highest use.
How deare to me, O God, thy counsels are!
    Who may with thee compare?
Religion thence fled into *Greece,* where arts
Gave her the highest place in all men's hearts.
Learning was pos'd, Philosophic was set,
Sophisters taken in a fisher's net.
Plato and *Aristotle* were at a losse,
And wheel'd about again to spell *Christ-Crosse.*
Prayers chas'd syllogismes into their den,
And *Ergo* was transform'd into *Amen.*
Though *Greece* took horse as soon as *Egypt* did,
And *Rome* as both; yet *Egypt* faster rid,
And spent her period and prefixed time
Before the other. *Greece* being past her prime,
Religion went to *Rome,* subduing those,
Who, that they might subdue, made all their foes.
The Warrier his deere skarres no more resounds,
But seems to yeeld Christ hath the greater wounds;
Wounds willingly endur'd to work his blisse,
Who by an ambush lost his Paradise.
The great heart stoops, and taketh from the dust
A sad repentance, not the spoils of lust:
Quitting his spear, lest it should pierce again
Him in his members, who for him was slain.
The shepherd's hook grew to a scepter here,
Giving new names and numbers to the yeare.
But th' Empire dwelt in *Greece,* to comfort them,
Who were cut short in *Alexander's* stemme.
In both of these Prowesse and Arts did tame
And tune men's hearts against the Gospel came:
Which using, and not fearing skill in th' one,
Or strength in th' other, did erect her throne,
Many a rent and stlruggling th' Empire knew
(As dying things are wont,) untill it flew
At length to *Germanie,* still westward bending,
And there the Churches festivall attending:
That as before Empire and Arts made way,
(For no lesse Harbingers would serve then they)
So they might still, and point us out the place,
Where first the Church shou!d raise her down-cast face.
Strength levels grounds, Art makes a garden there;
Then showres Religion, and makes all to bear.
Spain in the Empire shar'd with *Germanie,*
But *England* in the higher victorie;
Giving the Church a crown to keep her state,
And not go lesse than she had done of late.
Constantine's British line meant this of old,

And did this mysterie wrap up and fold
Within a sheet of paper, which was rent
From time's great Chronicle, and hither sent.
Thus both the Church and Sunne together ran
Unto the farthest old meridian.
How deare to me, O God, thy counsels are!
        Who may with thee compare?
Much about one and the same time and place,
Both where and when the Church began her race,
Sinne did set out of Eastern *Babylon,*
And travell'd westward also: journeying on
He chid the Church away, where e're he came,
Breaking her peace, and tainting her good name.
At first he got to *Egypt,* and did sow
Gardens of gods, which ev'ry yeare did grow,
Fresh and fine deities. They were at great cost,
Who for a god clearely a sallet lost.
Ah, what a thing is man devoid of grace,
Adoring garlick with an humble face,
Begging his food of that which he may eat,
Starving the while he worshippeth his meat!
Who makes a root his god, how low is he,
If God and man be sever'd infinitely!
What wretchednesse can give him any room,
Whose house is foul, while he adores his broom?
None will beleeve this now, though money be
In us the same transplanted foolerie.
Thus Sinne in *Egypt* sneaked for a while;
His highest was an ox or crocodile,
And such poore game. Thence he to *Greece* doth
And being craftier much then Goodnesse was, [passe,
He left behinde him garrisons of sinnes,
To make good that which ev'ry day he winnes.
Here Sinne took heart, and for a garden-bed
Rich shrines and oracles he purchased:
He grew a gallant, and would needs foretell
As well what should befall, as what befell.
Nay, he became a poet, and would serve
His pills of sublimate in that conserve.
The world came both with hands and purses full
To this great lotterie, and all would pull.
But all was glorious cheating, brave deceit,
Where some poore truths were shuffled for a bait
To credit him, and to discredit those,
Who after him should braver truths disclose.
From *Greece* he went to *Rome:* and as before
He was a God, now he's an Emperour.
Nero and others lodg'd him bravely there,

Put him in trust to rule the Romane sphere.
Glorie was his chief instrument of old:
Pleasure succeeded straight, when that grew cold:
Which soon was blown to such a mightie flame,
That though our Saviour did destroy the game,
Disparking oracles, aed all their treasure,
Setting affliction to encounter pleasure;
Yet did a rogue with hope of carnall joy,
Cheat the most subtill nations. Who so coy,
So trimme, as *Greece* and *Egypt?* yet their hearts
Are given over, for their curious arts,
To such Mahometan stupidities,
As the old heathen would deem prodigies.
How deare to me, O God, thy counsels are!
        Who may with thee compare?
Onely the West and *Rome* doth keep them free
From this contagious infidelitie.
And this is all the Rock, whereof they boast,
As *Rome* will one day finde unto her cost.
Sinne not being able to extirpate quite
The Churches here, bravely resolv'd one night
To be a Church man too, and wear a Mitre:
The old debauched ruffian would turn writer.
I saw him in his studie, where he sate
Busie in controversies sprung of late.
A gown and pen became him wondrous well:
His grave aspect had more of heav'n then hell:
Onely there was a handsome picture by,
To which he lent a corner of his eye.
As Sinne in *Greece* a Prophet was before,
And in old *Rome* a mightie Emperour;
So now being Priest he plainly did professe
To make a jest of Christ's three offices:
The rather since his scatter'd jugglings were
United now in one both time and sphere.
From *Egypt* he took pettie deities,
From *Greece* oracular infallibilities,
And from old *Rome* the libertie of pleasure,
By free dispensings of the Churches treasure.
Then in memoriall of his ancient throne,
He did surname his palace, *Babylon.*
Yet that he might the better gain all nations,
And make that name good by their transmigrations;
From all these places, but at divers times,
He took fine vizards to conceal his crimes:
From *Egypt* Anchorisme and retirednesse,
Learning from *Greece,* from old Rome stateliness;
And blending these, he carri'd all men's eyes,

While Truth sat by, counting his victories:
Whereby he grew apace, and scorn'd to use
Such force as once did captivate the Jews;
But did bewitch, and finelly work each nation
Into a voluntarie transmigration.
All poste to *Rome:* Princes submit their necks
Either t' his publick foot or private tricks.
It did not fit his gravitie to stirre,
Nor his long journey, nor his gout and furre:
Therefore he sent out able ministers,
Statesmen within, without doores cloisterers;
Who without spear, or sword, or other drumme,
Than what was in their tongue, did overcome;
And having conquer'd, did so strangely rule,
That the whole world did seem but the Pope's mule.
As new and old *Rome* did one Empire twist;
So both together are one Antichrist;
Yet with two faces, as their *Janus* was,
Being in this their old crackt looking-glasse.
How deare to me, O God, thy counsels are!
      Who may with thee compare?
Thus Sinne triumphs in Western *Babylon;*
Yet not as Sinne, but as Religion.
Of his two thrones he made the latter best,
And to defray his journey from the east.
Old and new *Babylon* are to hell and night,
As is the moon and sunne to heav'n and light.
When th' one did set, the other did take place,
Confronting equally the law and grace.
They are hell's land-marks, Satan's double crest:
They are Sinne's nipples, feeding th' east and west.
But as in vice the copie still exceeds
The pattern, but not so in vertuous deeds;
So though Sinne made his latter seat the better,
The latter Church is to the first a debter.
The second Temple could not reach the first:
And the late reformation never durst
Compare with ancient times and purer yeares;
But in the Jews and us deserveth tears.
Nay, it shall ev'ry yeare decrease and fade;
Till such a darknesse do the world invade
At Christ's last coming, as his first did finde:
Yet must there such proportions be assign'd
To these diminishings, as is between
The spacious world and *Jurie* to be seen.
Religion stands on tip-toe in our land,
Readie to passe to the *American* strand.
When height of malice, and prodigious lusts,

Impudent sinning, witchcrafts, and distrusts,
(The marks of future bane,) shall fill our cup
Unto the brimme, and make our measure up;
When *Sein* shall swallow *Tiber,* and the *Thames*
By letting in them both, pollutes her streams:
When *Italie* of us shall have her will,
And all her calendar of sinnes fulfill;
Whereby one may foretell, what sinnes next yeare
Shall both in *France* and *England* domineer:
Then shall Religion to *America* flee:
They have their times of Gospel, ev'n as we.
My God, thou dost prepare for them a way,
By carrying first their gold from them away:
For gold and grace did never yet agree:
Religion alwaies sides with povertie.
We think we rob them, but we think amisse:
We are more poore, and they more rich by this.
Thou wilt revenge their quarrell, making grace
To pay our debts, and leave our ancient place
To go to them, while that, which now their nation
But lends to us, shall be our desolation.
Yet as the Church shall thither westward flie,
So Sinne shall trace and dog her instantly:
They have their period also and set times
Both for their vertuous actions and their crimes.
And where of old the Empire and the Arts
Usher'd the Gospel ever in men's hearts,
Spain hath done one; when Arts perform the other,
The Church shall come, and Sinne the Church shall smother:
That when they have accomplished the round,
And met in th' east their first and ancient sound,
Judgement may meet them both, and search them round.
Thus do both lights, as well in Church as Sunne,
Light one another, and together runne.
Thus also Sinne and Darknesse follow still
The Church and Sunne with all their power and skill.
But as the Sunne still goes both west and east:
So also did the Church by going west
Still eastward go; because it drew more neare
To time and place, where judgement shall appeare.
How deare to me, O God, thy counsels are!
      Who may with thee compare?

L'ENVOY.

KING *of glorie, King of peace,*
With the one make warre to cease;
With the other blesse thy sheep,
Thee to love, in thee to sleep.
Let not Sinne devoure thy fold,
Bragging that thy bloud is cold;
That thy death is also dead,
While his conquests dayly spread;
That thy flesh hath lost his food,
And thy Crosse is common wood.
Choke him, let him say no more,
But reserve his breath in store,
Till thy conquest and his fall
Make his sighs to use it all;
And then bargain with the winde
To discharge what is behinde.

>*Blessed be God alone,*
>*Thrice blessed Three in One.*

JACULA PRUDENTUM;

OR, OUTLANDISH PROVERBS, SENTENCES, &C.

SELECTED BY MR. GEORGE HERBERT,

LATE ORATOR OF THE UNIVERSITY OP CAMBRIDGE.

[FIRST PRINTED IN 1640.]

OLD men go to death, death comes to young men.
Man proposeth, God disposeth.
He begins to die that quits his desires.
A handful of good life is better than a bushel of learning.
He that studies his content, wants it.
Every day brings its bread with it.
Humble hearts have humble desires.
He that stumbles and falls not, mends his pace.
The house shows the owner.
He that gets out of debt, grows rich.
All is well with him who is beloved of his neighbours.
Building and marrying of children are great wasters.
A good bargain is a pick-purse.
The scalded dog fears cold water.
Pleasing ware is half sold.
Light burdens, long borne, grow heavy.
The wolf knows what the ill beast thinks.
Who hath none to still him may weep out his eyes.
When all sins grow old, covetousness is young.
If ye would know a knave, give him a staff.
You cannot know wine by the barrel.
A cool mouth, and warm feet, live long.
A horse made, and a man to make.
Look not for musk in a dog's kennel.
Not a long day, but a good heart, rids work.
He pulls with a long rope, that waits for another's death.
Great strokes make not sweet music.
A cask and an ill custom must be broken.
A fat housekeeper makes lean executors.
Empty chambers make foolish maids.
The gentle hawk half mans herself.
The devil is not always at one door.
When a friend asks, there is no to-morrow.
God sends cold according to clothes.
One sound blow will serve to undo us all.
He loseth nothing, that looseth not God.
The German's wit is in his fingers.

At dinner my man appears.
Who gives to all, denies all.
Quick believers need broad shoulders.
Who remove stones, bruise their fingers.
Benefits please like flowers while they are fresh.
Between the business of life and the day of death, a space ought to be interposed.
All came from and will go to others.
He that will take the bird, must not scare it.
He lives unsafely that looks too near on things.
A gentle housewife mars the household.
A crooked log makes a straight fire.
He hath great need of a fool that plays the fool himself.
A merchant that gains not, loseth.
Let not him that fears feathers come among wild-fowl.
Love, and a cough, cannot be hid.
A dwarf on a giant's shoulder, sees further of the two.
He that sends a fool, means to follow him.
Babbling curs never want fore ears.
Better the feet slip than the tongue.
For washing his hands, none sells his lands.
A lion's skin is never cheap.
The goat must browse where she is tied.
Nothing id to be presumed on, or despaired of.
Who hath a wolf for his mate, needs a dog for his man.
In a good house all is quickly ready.
A bad dog never sees the wolf.
God oft hath a great share in a little house.
Ill ware is never cheap.
A cheerful look makes a dish a feast.
If all fools had baubles, we should want fuel.
Virtue never grows old.
Evening words are not like to morning.
Were there no fools, bad ware would not pass.
Never had ill workman good tools.
He stands not surely that never slips.
Were there no hearers, there would be no backbiters.
Everything is of use to a housekeeper.
When prayers are done, my lady is ready.
Cities seldom change religion only.
At length the fox turns monk.
Flies are busiest about lean horses.
Hearken to reason, or she will be heard.
The bird loves her nest.
Everything new is fine.
When a dog is a drowning, every one offers him drink.
Better a bare foot that none.
Who is so deaf as he that will not hear?

He that is warm thinks all so.
At length the fox is brought to the furrier.
He that goes barefoot must not plant thorns.
They that are booted are not always ready.
He that will learn to pray, let him go to sea.
In spending lies the advantage.
He that lives well, is learned enough.
Ill vessels seldom miscarry.
A full belly neither fights nor flies well.
All truths are not to be told.
An old wise man's shadow is better than a young buzzard's sword.
Noble housekeepers need no doors.
Every ill man hath his ill day.
Sleep without supping, and wake without owing.
I gave the mouse a hole, and she is become my heir.
Assail who will, the valiant attends.
Whither goest, grief? where I am wont.
Praise day at night, and life at the end.
Whither shall the ox go where he shall not labour?
Where you think there is bacon, there is no chimney.
Mend your clothes, and you may hold out this year.
Press a stick, and it seems a youth.
The tongue walks where the teeth speed not.
A fair wife and a frontier castle breed quarrels.
Leave jesting whiles it pleaseth, lest it turns to earnest.
Deceive not thy physician, confessor, nor lawyer.
Ill natures, the more you ask them, the more they stick.
Virtue and a trade are the best portion for children.
The chicken is the country's, but the city eats it.
He that gives thee a capon, give him the leg and the wing.
He that lives ill, fear follows him.
Give a clown your finger, and he will take your hand.
Good is to be sought out, and evil attended.
A good paymaster starts not at assurances.
No alchymy to saving.
To a grateful man give money when he asks.
Who would do ill ne'er wants occasion.
To fine folks a little ill finely wrapt.
A child correct behind, and not before.
To a fair day, open the window, but make you ready as to a foul.
Keep good men company, and you shall be of the number.
No love to a father's.
The mill gets by going.
To a boiling pot flies come not.
Make haste to an ill way, that you may get out of it.
A snow year, a rich year.
Better to be blind than to see ill.
Learn weeping, and thou shalt laugh gaining.

Who hath no more bread than need, must not keep a dog.
A garden must be looked unto and dressed as the body.
The fox, when he cannot reach the grapes, says they are not ripe.
Water trotted is as good as oats.
Though the mastiff be gentle, yet bite him not by the lip.
Though a he be well dressed, it is ever overcome.
Though old and wise, yet still advise.
Three helping one another, bear the burthen of six.
Slander is a shipwreck by a dry tempest.
Old wine and an old friend are good provisions.
Happy is he that chastens himself.
Well may he smell fire whose gown burns.
The wrongs of a husband or master are not reproached.
Welcome evil if thou comest alone.
Love your neighbour, yet pull not down your hedge.
The bit that one eats, no friend makes.
A drunkard's purse is a bottle.
She spins well that breeds her children.
Good is the *mora* that makes all sure.
Play with a fool at home, and he will play with you in the market.
Every one stretcheth his legs according to his coverlet.
Autumnal agues are long or mortal.
Marry your son when you will; your daughter when you can.
Dally not with money or women.
Men speak of the fair as things went with them there.
The best remedy against an ill man, is much ground between both.
The mill cannot grind with water that's past.
Corn is cleaned with wind, and the soul with chastenings.
Good words are worth much, and cost little.
To buy dear is not bounty.
Jest not with the eye, or with religion.
The eye and religion can bear no jesting.
Without favour none will know you, and with it you will not know yourself.
Buy at a fair, but sell at home.
Cover yourself with your shield, and care not for cries.
A wicked man's gift hath a touch of his master.
None is a fool always, every one sometimes.
From a choleric man withdraw a little; from him that says nothing, for ever.
Debtors are liars.
Of all smells, bread; of all tastes, salt.
In a great river great fish are found: but take heed lest you be drowned.
Ever since we wear clothes, we know not one another.
God heals, and the physician hath the thanks.
Hell is full of good meanings and wishings.
Take heed of still waters, the quick pass away.
After the house is finished, leave it.
Our own actions are our security, not others' judgments.
Think of ease, but work on.

He that lies long a bed, his estate feels it.
Whether you boil snow or pound it, you can have but water of it.
One stroke fells not an oak.
God complains not, but doth what is fitting.
A diligent scholar, and the master's paid.
Milk says to wine, Welcome, friend.
They that know one another, salute afar off.
Where there is no honour, there is no grief.
Where the drink goes in, there the wit goes out.
He that stays does the business.
Alms never make poor. Or thus,
Great alms-giving lessens no man's living.
Giving much to the poor doth enrich a man's store.
It takes much from the account, to which his sin doth amount.
It adds to the glory both of soul and body.
Ill comes in by ells, and goes out by inches.
The smith and his penny both are black.
Whose house is of glass, must not throw stones at another.
If the old dog bark, he gives counsel.
The tree that grows slowly, keeps itself for another.
I wept when I was born, and every day shews why.
He that looks not before, finds himself behind.
He that plays his money, ought not to value it.
He that riseth first, is first drest.
Diseases of the eye are to be cured with the elbow.
The hole calls the thief.
A gentleman's greyhound and a salt box, seek them at the fire.
A child's service is little, yet he is no little fool that despiseth it.
The river past, and God forgotten.
Evils have their comfort; good none can support (to wit) with a moderate and contented heart.
Who must account for himself and others, must know both.
He that eats the hard, shall eat the ripe.
The miserable man maketh a penny of a farthing, and the liberal of a farthing sixpence.
The honey is sweet, but the bee stings.
Weight and measure take away strife.
The son full and tattered, the daughter empty and fine.
Every path hath a puddle.
In good years corn is hay, in ill years straw is corn.
Send a wise man on an errand, and say nothing unto him.
In life you loved me not, in death you bewail me.
Into a mouth shut flies fly not.
The heart's letter is read in the eyes.
The ill that comes out of our mouth falls into our bosom.
In great pedigrees there are governors and chandlers.
In the house of a fiddler, all fiddle.
Sometimes the best gain is to lose.

Working and making a fire doth discretion require.
One grain fills not a sack, but helps his fellows.
It is a great victory that comes without blood.
In war, hunting, and love, men for one pleasure a thousand griefs prove.
Reckon right, and February hath one and thirty days.
Honour without profit is a ring on the finger.
Estate in two parishes is bread in two wallets.
Honour and profit lie not in one sack.
A naughty child is better sick than whole.
Truth and oil are ever above.
He that riseth betimes, hath something in his head.
Advise none to marry or go to war.
To steal the hog, and give the feet for alms.
The thorn comes forth with the point forwards.
One hand washeth another, and both the face.
The fault of the horse is put on the saddle.
The corn hides itself in the snow as an old man in furs.
The Jews spend at Easter, the Moors at marriages, the Christians in suits.
Fine dressing is a foul house swept before the doors.
A woman and a glass are ever in danger.
An ill wound is cured, not an ill name.
The wise hand doth not all that the foolish mouth speaks.
On painting and fighting look aloof.
Knowledge is folly except grace guide it.
Punishment is lame, but it comes.
The more women look in their glass, the less they look to their house.
A long tongue is a sign of a short hand.
Marry a widow before she leave mourning.
The worst of law is, that one suit breeds twenty.
Providence is better than a rent.
What your glass tells you, will not be told by counsel.
There are more men threatened than stricken.
A fool knows more in his house, than a wise man in another's.
I had rather ride on an ass that carries me, than a horse that throws me.
The hard gives more than he that hath nothing.
The beast that goes always, never wants blows.
Good cheap is dear.
It costs more to do ill than to do well.
Good words quench more than a bucket of water.
An ill agreement is better than a good judgment.
There is more talk than trouble.
Better spare to have of thine own, than ask of other men.
Better good afar off, than evil at hand.
Fear keeps the garden better than the gardener.
I had rather ask of my sire brown bread, than borrow of my neighbour white.
Your pot broken seems better than my whole one.
Let an ill man lie in thy straw, and he looks to be thy heir.
By suppers more have been killed than Galen ever cured.

While the discreet advise, the fool doth his business.
A mountain and a river are good neighbours.
Gossips are frogs, they drink and talk.
Much spends the traveller more than the abider.
Prayers and provender hinder no journey.
A well-bred youth neither speaks of himself, nor, being spoken to, is silent.
A journeying woman speaks much of all, and all of her.
The fox knows much, but more he that catcheth him.
Many friends in general, one in special.
The fool asks much, but he is more fool that grants it.
Many kiss the hand they wish cut off.
Neither bribe, nor lose thy right.
In the world who knows not to swim, goes to the bottom.
Choose not a house near an inn (viz. for noise): or in a corner (for filth).
He is a fool that thinks not that another thinks.
Neither eyes on letters, nor hands in coffers.
The lion is not so fierce as they paint him.
Go not for every grief to the physician, nor for every quarrel to the lawyer, nor for every thirst to the pot.
Good service is a great enchantment.
There would be no great ones, if there were no little ones.
It is no sure rule to fish with a cross-bow.
There were no ill language, if it were not ill taken.
The groundsel speaks not, save what it heard at the hinges.
The best mirror is an old friend.
Say no ill of the year till it be past.
A man's discontent is his worst evil.
Fear nothing but sin.
The child says nothing, but what it heard by the fire.
Call me not an olive, till thou see me gathered.
That is not good language which all understand not.
He that burns his house, warms himself for once.
He will burn his house to warm his hands.
He will spend a whole year's rent at one meal's meat.
All is not gold that glisters.
A blustering night, a fair day.
Be not idle, and you shall not be longing.
He is not poor that hath little, but he that desireth much.
Let none say, I will not drink water.
He wrongs not an old man that steals his supper from him.
The tongue talks at the head's cost.
He that strikes with his tongue, must ward with his head.
Keep not ill men company, lest you increase the number.
God strikes not with both hands, for to the sea he made heavens, and to rivers fords.
A rugged stone grows smooth from hand to hand.
No lock will hold against the power of gold.
The absent party is still faulty.

Peace and patience, and death with repentance.
If you lose your time, you cannot get money nor gain.
Be not a baker, if your head be of butter.
Ask much to have a little.
Little sticks kindle the fire; great ones put it out.
Another's bread costs dear.
Although it rain, throw not away thy watering pot.
Although the sun shine, leave not thy cloak at home.
A little with quiet is the only diet.
In vain is the mill-clack, if the miller his hearing lack.
By the needle you shall draw the thread, and by that which is past, see how that which is to come will be drawn on.
Stay a little, and news will find you.
Stay till the lame messenger come, if you will know the truth of the thing.
When God will, no wind but brings rain.
Though you rise early, yet the day comes at his time, and not till then.
Pull down your hat on the wind's side.
As the year is, your pot must seeth.
Since you know all, and I nothing, tell me what I dreamed last night.
When the fox preacheth, beware geese.
When you are an anvil, hold you still; when you are a hammer, strike your fill.
Poor and liberal, rich and covetous.
He that makes his bed ill, lies there.
He that labours and thrives, spends gold.
He that sows, trusts in God.
He that lies with the dogs, riseth with fleas.
He that repairs not a part, builds all.
A discontented man knows not where to sit easy.
Who spits against heaven, it falls in his face.
He that dines and leaves, lays the cloth twice.
Who eats his cock alone, must saddle his horse alone.
He that is not handsome at twenty, nor strong at thirty, nor rich at forty, nor wise at fifty, will never be handsome, strong, rich, or wise.
He that doth what he will, doth not what he ought.
He that will deceive the fox must rise betimes.
He that lives well, sees afar off.
He that hath a mouth of his own, must not say to another, Blow.
He that will be served, must be patient.
He that gives thee a bone, would not have thee die.
He that chastens one, chastens twenty.
He that hath lost his credit, is dead to the world.
He that hath no ill fortune, is troubled with good.
He that demands, misseth not, unless his demands be foolish.
He that hath no honey in his pot, let him have it in his mouth.
He that takes not up a pin, slights his wife.
He that owes nothing, if he makes not mouths at us, is courteous.
He that loseth his due, gets not thanks.
He that believes all, misseth; he that believeth nothing, hits not.

Pardons and pleasantness are great revengers of slanders.
A married man turns his staff into a stake.
If you would know secrets, look them in grief or pleasure.
Serve a noble disposition, though poor, the time comes that he will repay thee.
The fault is as great as he that is faulty.
If folly were grief, every house would weep.
He that would be well old, must be old betimes.
Sit in your place, and none can make you rise.
If you could run as you drink, you might catch a hare.
Would you know what money is, go borrow some.
The morning sun never lasts a day.
Thou hast death in thy house, and dost bewail another's.
All griefs with bread are less.
All things require skill, but an appetite.
All things have their place, knew we how to place them.
Little pitchers have wide ears.
We are fools one to another.
This world is nothing except it tend to another.
There are three ways, the universities, the sea, the court.
God comes to see without a bell.
Life without a friend, is death without a witness.
Clothe thee in war, arm thee in peace.
The horse thinks one thing, and he that saddles him another.
Mills and wives ever want.
The dog that licks ashes, trust not with meal.
The buyer needs a hundred eyes, the seller not one.
He carries well, to whom it weighs not.
The comforter's head never aches.
Step after step the ladder is ascended.
Who likes not the drink, God deprives him of bread.
To a crazy ship all winds are contrary.
Justice pleaseth few in their own house.
In time comes he, whom God sends.
Water afar off quencheth not fire.
In sports and journeys men are known.
An old friend is a new house.
Love is not found in the market.
Dry feet, warm head, bring safe to bed.
He is rich enough that wants nothing.
One father is enough to govern one hundred sons, but not a hundred sons one father.
Far shooting never killed bird.
An upbraided morsel never choked any.
Dearths foreseen come not.
An ill labourer quarrels with his tools.
He that falls into the dirt, the longer he stays there the fouler he is.
He that blames would buy.
He that sings on Friday will weep on Sunday.

The charges of building, and making of gardens, are unknown.
My house, my house, though thou art small, thou art to me the Escurial.
A hundred load of thought will not pay one of debts.
He that comes of a hen must scrape.
He that seeks trouble never misses.
He that once deceives, is ever suspected.
Being on sea, sail; being on land, settle.
Who doth his own business, fouls not his hands.
He that makes a good war, makes a good peace.
He that works after his own manner, his head aches not at the matter.
Who hath bitter in his mouth, spits not all sweet.
He that hath children, all his morsels are not his own.
He that hath the spice, may season as he list.
He that hath a head of wax, must not walk in the sun.
He that hath love in his breast, hath spurs in his sides.
He that respects not is not respected.
He that hath a fox for his mate, hath need of a net at his girdle.
He that hath right, fears; he that hath wrong, hopes.
He that hath patience, hath fat thrushes for a farthing.
Never was strumpet fair.
He that measures not himself is measured.
He that hath one hog, makes him fat; and he that hath one son, makes him a fool.
Who lets his wife go to every feast, and his horse drink at every water, shall neither have good wife nor good horse.
He that speaks sows, and he that holds his peace gathers.
He that hath little is the less dirty.
He that lives most dies most.
He that hath one foot in the straw hath another in the spittle.
He that is fed at another's hand, may stay long ere he be full.
He that makes a thing too fine, breaks it.
He that bewails himself hath the cure in his hands.
He that would be well, needs not go from his own house.
Counsel breaks not the head.
Fly the pleasure that bites to-morrow.
He that knows what may be gained in a day, never steals.
Money refused loseth its brightness.
Health and money go far.
Where your will is ready, your feet are light.
A great ship asks deep waters.
Woe to the house where there is no chiding.
Take heed of the vinegar of sweet wine.
Fools bite one another, but wise men agree together.
Trust not one night's ice.
Good is good, but better carries it.
To gain teacheth how to spend.
Good finds good.
The dog gnaws the bone because he cannot swallow it.
The crow bewails the sheep, and then eats it.

Building is a sweet impoverishing.
The first degree of folly is to hold one's self wise, the second to possess it, the third to despise counsel.
The greatest step is that out of doors.
To weep for joy is a kind of manna.
The first service a child doeth his father is to make him foolish.
The resolved mind hath no cares.
In the kingdom of a cheater, the wallet is carried before.
The eye will have his part.
The good mother says not, Will you? but gives.
A house and a woman suit excellently.
In the kingdom of blind men, the one-eyed is king.
A little kitchen makes a large house.
War makes thieves, and peace hangs them.
Poverty is the mother of health.
In the morning mountains, in the evening fountains.
The back door robs the house.
Wealth is like rheum, it falls on the weakest parts.
The gown is his that wears it, and the world his that enjoys it.
Hope is the poor man's bread.
Virtue now is in herbs, and stones, and words only.
Fine words dress ill deeds.
Labour as long lived, pray as even dying.
A poor beauty finds more lovers than husbands.
Discreet women have neither eyes nor ears.
Things well fitted abide.
Prettiness dies first.
Talking pays no toll.
The master's eye fattens the horse, and his foot the ground.
Disgraces are like cherries, one draws another.
Praise a hill, but keep below.
Praise the sea, but keep on land.
In choosing a wife, and buying a sword, we ought not to trust another.
The wearer knows where the shoe wrings.
Fair is not fair, but that which pleaseth.
There is no jolity but hath a smack of folly.
He that's long a giving knows not how to give.
The filth under the white snow the sun discovers.
Every one fastens where there is gain.
All feet tread not in one shoe.
Patience, time, and money accommodate all things.
For want of a nail the shoe is lost, for want of a shoe the horse is lost, for want of a horse the rider is lost.
Weight justly, and sell dearly.
Little wealth little care.
Little journeys and good cost bring safe home.
Gluttony kills more than the sword.
When children stand quiet, they have done some ill.

A little and good fills the trencher.
A penny spared is twice got.
When a knave is in a plum-tree, he hath neither friend nor kin.
Short boughs, long vintage.
Health without money is half an ague.
If the wife erred not, it would go hard with fools.
Bear with evil, and expect good.
He that tells a secret is another's servant.
If all fools wore white caps, we should seem a flock of geese.
Water, fire, and soldiers, quickly make room.
Pension never enriched a young man.
Under water, famine; under snow, bread.
The lame goes as far as your staggerer.
He that loseth is merchant, as well as he that gains.
A jade eat as much as a good horse.
All things in their being are good for something.
One flower makes no garland.
A fair death honours the whole life.
One enemy is too much.
Living well is the best revenge.
One fool makes a hundred.
One pair of ears draws dry a hundred tongues.
A fool may throw a stone into a well, which a hundred wise men cannot pull out.
One slumber finds another.
On a good bargain think twice.
To a good spender God is the treasurer.
A curst cow hath short horns.
Music helps not the tooth-ache.
We cannot come to honour under coverlet.
Great pains quickly find ease.
To the counsel of fools a wooden bell.
The choleric man never wants woe.
Help thyself, and God will help thee.
At the game's end we shall see who gains.
There are many ways to fame.
Love is the true price of love.
Love rules his kingdom without a sword.
Love makes all hearts gentle.
Love makes a good eye squint.
Love asks faith, and faith firmness.
A sceptre is one thing, and a ladle another.
Great trees are good for nothing but shade.
He commands enough that obeys a wise man.
Fair words make me look to my purse.
Though the fox run the chicken hath wings.
He plays well that wins.
Tou must strike in measure, when there are many to strike on one anvil.
The shortest answer is doing.

It is a poor stake that cannot stand one year in the ground.
He that commits a fault thinks every one speaks of it.
He that is foolish in the fault, let him be wise in the punishment.
The blind eats many a fly.
He that can make a fire well can end a quarrel.
The tooth-ache is more ease than to deal with ill people.
He that would have what he hath not, should do what he doth not.
He that hath no good trade it is to his loss.
The offender never pardons.
He that lives not well one year, sorrows seven after.
He that hopes not for good, fears not evil.
He that is angry at a feast, is rude.
He that mocks a cripple ought to be whole.
When the tree is fallen, all go with their hatchet.
He that hath horns in his bosom let him not put them on his head.
He that burns most, shines most.
He that trusts in a lie, shall perish in truth.
He that blows in the dust, fills his eyes with it.
Bells call others, but themselves enter not into the church.
Of fair things, the Autumn is fair.
Giving is dead, restoring very sick.
A gift much expected is paid, not given.
Two ill meals make the third a glutton.
The royal crown cures not the head-ache.
'Tis hard to be wretched, but worse to be known so.
A feather in hand is better than a bird in the air.
It is better to be the head of a lizard than the tail of a lion.
Good and quickly seldom meet.
Folly grows without watering.
Happier are the hands compassed with iron, than a heart without thoughts.
If the staff be crooked, the shadow cannot be straight.
To take the nuts from the fire with the dog's foot.
He is a fool that makes a wedge with his fist.
Valour that parleys, is near yielding.
Thursday come, and the week is gone.
A flatterer's throat is an open sepulchre.
There is great force hidden in a sweet command.
The command of custom is great.
To have money is a fear, not to have it a grief.
The cat sees not the mouse ever.
Little dogs start the hare, the great get her.
Willows are weak, yet they bind other wood.
A good payer is master of another's purse.
The thread breaks where it is weakest.
Old men, when they scorn young, make much of death.
God is at the end, when we think he is furthest off it.
A good judge conceives quickly, judges slowly.
Rivers need a spring.

He that contemplates hath a day without night.
Give losers leave to talk.
Loss embraceth shame.
Gaming, women, and wine, while they laugh, they make men pine.
The fat man knoweth not what the lean thinketh.
Wood half burnt is easily kindled.
The fish adores the bait.
He that goeth far hath many encounters.
Every bee's honey is sweet.
The slothful is the servant of the counters.
Wisdom hath one foot on land, and another on sea.
The thought hath good legs, and the quill a good tongue.
A wise man needs not blush for changing his purpose.
The March sun raises, but dissolves not.
Time is the rider that breaks youth.
The wine in the bottle doth not quench thirst.
The sight of a man hath the force of a lion.
An examined enterprise goes on boldly.
In every art it is good to have a master.
In every country dogs bite.
In every country the sun rises in the morning.
A noble plant suits not with a stubborn ground.
You may bring a horse to the river, but he will drink when and what he pleaseth.
Before you make a friend, eat a bushel of salt with him.
Speak fitly, or be silent wisely.
Skill and confidence are an unconquered army.
I was taken by a morsel, says the fish.
A disarmed peace is weak.
The balance distinguisheth not between gold and lead.
The persuasion of the fortunate sways the doubtful.
To be beloved is above all bargains.
To deceive oneself is very easy.
The reasons of the poor weigh not.
Perverseness makes one squint-eyed.
The evening praises the day, and the morning a frost.
The table robs more than the thief.
When ago is jocund, it makes sport for death.
True praise roots and spreads.
Fears are divided in the midst.
The soul needs few things, the body many.
Astrology is true, but the astrologers cannot find it.
Tie it well, and let it go.
Empty vessels sound most.
Send not a cat for lard.
Foolish tongues talk by the dozen.
Love makes one fit for any work.
A pitiful mother makes a scald head.
An old physician, and a young lawyer.

Talk much, and err much, says the Spaniard.
Some make a conscience of spitting in the church, yet rob the altar.
An idle head is a box for the wind.
Show me a liar, and I will show thee a thief.
A bean in liberty is better than a comfort in prison.
None is born master.
Show a good man his error, and he turns it to a virtue; but an ill, it doubles his fault.
None is offended but by himself.
None says his garner is full.
In the husband wisdom, in the wife gentleness.
Nothing dries sooner than a tear.
In a leopard the spots are not observed.
Nothing lasts but the church.
A wise man cares not for what he cannot have.
It is not good fishing before the net.
He cannot be virtuous that is not rigorous.
That which will not be spun, let it not come between the spindle and the distaff.
When my house bums, it is not good playing at chess.
No barber shaves so close but another finds work.
There is no great banquet, but some fares ill.
A holy habit cleanseth not a foul soul.
Forbear not sowing because of birds.
Mention not a halter in the house of him that was hanged.
Speak not of a dead man at the table.
A hat is not made for one shower.
No sooner is a temple built to God, but the devil builds a chapel hard by.
Every one puts his fault on the times.
You cannot make a windmill go with a pair of bellows.
Pardon all but thyself.
Every one is weary, the poor in seeking, the rich in keeping, the good in learning.
The escaped mouse ever feels the taste of the bait.
A little wind kindles, much puts out the fire.
Dry bread at home is better than roast meat abroad.
More have repented speech than silence.
The covetous spends more than the liberal.
Divine ashes are better than earthly meal.
Beauty draws more than oxen.
One father is more than a hundred schoolmasters.
One eye of the master's sees more than ten of the servants'.
When God will punish, he will first take away the under standing.
A little labour, much health.
When it thunders the thief becomes honest.
The tree that God plants, no winds hurt it.
Knowledge is no burthen.
It is a bold mouse that nestles in the cat's ear.
Long jesting was never good.

If a good man thrive, all thrive with him.
If the mother had not been in the oven, she had never sought her daughter there.
If great men would have care of little ones, both would last long.
Though you see a church-man ill, yet continue in the church still.
Old praise dies unless you feed it.
If things were to be done twice, all would be wise.
Had you the world on your chess-board, you could not fill all to your mind.
Suffer and expect.
If fools should not fool it, they shall lose their season.
Love and business teach eloquence.
That which two will, takes effect.
He complains wrongfully on the sea, that twice suffers shipwreck.
He is only bright that shines by himself.
A valiant man's look is more than a coward's sword.
The effect speaks, the tongue needs not.
Divine grace was never slow.
Reason lies between the spur and the bridle.
It is a proud horse that will not carry his own provender.
Three women make a market.
Three can hold their peace if two be away.
It is an ill counsel that hath no escape.
All our pomp the earth covers.
To whirl the eyes too much, shows a kite's brain.
Comparisons are odious.
All keys hang not on one girdle.
Great businesses turn on a little pin.
The wind in one's face makes one wise.
All the arms of England will not arm fear.
One sword keeps another in the sheath.
Be what thou wouldst seem to be.
Let all live as they would die.
A gentle heart is tied with an easy thread.
Sweet discourse makes short days and nights.
God provides for him that trusteth.
He that will not have peace, God gives him war.
To him that will, ways are not wanting.
To a great night, a great lanthorn.
To a child all weather is cold.
Where there is peace, God is.
None is so wise, but the fool overtakes him.
Fools give to please all but their own.
Prosperity lets go the bridle.
The friar preached against stealing, and had a goose in his sleeve.
To be too busy gets contempt.
February makes a bridge, and March breaks it.
A horse stumbles that hath four legs.
The best smell is bread, the best savour salt, the best love that of children.
That is the best gown that goes up and down the house.

The market is the best garden.
The first dish pleaseth all.
The higher the ape goes, the more he shows his tail.
Night is the mother of councils.
God's mill grinds slow, but sure.
Every one thinks his sack heaviest.
Drought never brought dearth.
All complain.
Gamesters and race-horses never last long.
It is a poor sport that is not worth the candle.
He that is fallen cannot help him that is down.
Every one is witty for his own purpose.
A little let lets an ill workman.
Good workmen are seldom rich.
By doing nothing we learn to do ill.
A great dowry is a bed full of brambles.
No profit to honour, no honour to religion.
Every sin brings its punishment with it.
Of him that speaks ill, consider the life more than the word.
You cannot bide an eel in a sack.
Give not Saint Peter so much, to leave Saint Paul nothing.
You cannot slay a stone.
The chief disease that reigns this year is folly.
A sleepy master makes his servant a lout.
Better speak truth rudely, than lie covertly.
He that fears leaves, let him not go into the wood.
One foot is better than two crutches.
Better suffer ill, than do ill.
Neither praise nor dispraise thyself, thy actions serve the turn.
Soft and fair goes far.
The constancy of the benefit of the year in their seasons argues a Deity.
Praise none too much, for all are fickle.
It is absurd to warm one in his armour.
Lawsuits consume time, and money, and rest, and friends.
Nature draws more than ten teams.
He that hath a wife and children, wants not business.
A ship and a woman aro ever repairing.
He that fears death, lives not.
He that pities another, remembers himself.
He that doth what he should not, shall feel what he would not.
He that marries for wealth, sells his liberty.
He that once hits, is ever bending.
He that serves, must serve.
He that lends, gives.
He that preacheth, giveth alms.
He that cockers his child, provides for his enemy.
A pitiful look asks enough.
Who will sell the cow, must say the word.

Service is no inheritance.
The faulty stands on his guard.
A kinsman, a friend, or whom you entreat, take not to serve you, if you will be served neatly.
At court, every one for himself.
To a crafty man, a crafty and a half.
He that is thrown, would ever wrestle.
He that serves well, need not ask his wages.
Fair language grates not the tongue.
A good heart cannot lie.
Good swimmers at length are drowned.
Good land, evil way.
In doing we learn.
It is good walking with a horse in one's hand.
God, and parents, and our master, can never be required.
An ill deed cannot bring honour.
A small heart hath small desires.
All are not merry that dance lightly.
Courtesy on one side only lasts not long.
Wine-counsels seldom prosper.
Weening is not measure.
The best of the sport is to do the deed, and say nothing.
If thou thyself canst do it, attend no other's help or hand.
Of a little thing, a little displeaseth.
He warms too near that burns.
God keep me from four houses, a usurer's, a tavern, a spital, and a prison.
In an hundred ells of contention there is not an inch of love.
Do what thou oughtest, and come what come can.
Hunger makes dinners, pastime suppers.
In a long journey straw weighs.
Women laugh when they can, and weep when they will.
War is death's feast.
Set good against evil.
He that brings good news knocks hard.
Beat the dog before the lion.
Haste comes not alone.
You must lose a fly to catch a trout.
Better a snotty child than his nose wiped off.
He is not free that draws his chain.
He goes not out of his way that goes to a good inn.
There comes nought out of the sack, but what was there.
A little given seasonably, excuses a great gift.
He looks not well to himself that looks not ever.
He thinks not well, that thinks not again.
Religion, credit, and the eye are not to be touched.
The tongue is not steel, yet it cuts.
A white wall is the paper of a fool.
They talk of Christmas so long, that it comes.

That is gold which is worth gold.
It is good tying the sack before it be full.
Words are women, deeds are men.
Poverty is no sin.
A stone in a well is not lost.
He can give little to his servant that licks his knife.
Promising is the eve of giving.
He that keeps his own, makes war.
The wolf must die in his own skin.
Goods are theirs that enjoy them.
He that sends a fool, expects one.
He that can stay, obtains.
He that gains well and spends well, needs no account book.
He that endures is not overcome.
He that gives all before he dies, provides to suffer.
He that talks much of his happiness, summons grief.
He that loves the tree, loves the branch.
Who hastens a glutton, chokes him.
Who praiseth St Peter, doth not blame St Paul.
He that hath not the craft, let him shut up shop.
He that knows nothing, doubts nothing.
Green wood makes a hot fire.
He that marries late, marries ill.
He that passeth a winter's day, escapes an enemy.
The rich knows not who is his friend.
A morning sun, and a wine-bred child, and a Latin-bred woman, seldom end well.
To a close shorn sheep, God gives wind by measure.
A pleasure long expected, is dear enough sold.
A poor man's cow dies a rich man's child.
The cow knows not what her tail is worth till she has lost it.
Choose a horse made, and a wife to make.
It is an ill air where we gain nothing.
He hath not lived, that lives not after death.
So many men in court, and so many strangers.
He quits his place well, that leaves his friend here.
That which sufficeth is not little.
Good news may he told at any time, but ill in the morning.
He that would be a gentleman, let him go to an assault.
Who pays the physician does the cure.
None knows the weight of another's burthen.
Every one hath a fool in his sleeve.
One hour's sleep before midnight is worth three after.
In a retreat the lame are foremost.
It is more pain to do nothing than something.
Amongst good men two men suffice.
There needs a long time to know the world's puke.
The offspring of those that are very young, or very old, lasts not.

A tyrant is most tyrant to himself.
Too much taking heed is loss.
Craft against craft, makes no living.
The reverend are ever before.
France is a meadow that cuts thrice a year.
It is easier to build two chimneys, than to maintain one.
The court hath no almanack.
He that will enter into Paradise, must have a good key.
When you enter into a house, leave the anger ever at the door.
He hath no leisure who useth it not.
It is a wicked thing to make a dearth one's garner.
He that deals in the world needs four sieves.
Take heed of an ox before, of a horse behind, of a monk on all sides.
The year does nothing else but open and shut.
The ignorant hath an eagle's wings and an owl's eyes.
There are more physicians in health than drunkards.
The wife is the key of the house.
The law is not the same at morning and at night.
War and physic are governed by the eye.
Half the world knows not how the other half lives.
Death keeps no calendar.
Ships fear fire more than water.
The least foolish is wise.
The chief box of health is time.
Silks and satins put out the fire in the chimney.
The first blow is as much as two.
The life of man is a winter way.
The way is an ill neighbour.
An old man's staff is the rapper of death's door.
Life is half spent, before we know what it is.
The singing man keeps his shop in his throat.
The body is more dressed than the soul.
The body is sooner dressed than the soul.
The physician owes all to the patient, but the patient owes nothing to him but a little money.
The little cannot be great, unless he devour many.
Time undermines us.
The choleric drinks, the melancholic eats, the phlegmatic sleeps.
The apothecary's mortar spoils the luter s music.
Conversation makes one what he is.
The deaf gains the injury.
Years know more than books.
Wine is a turn-coat (first a friend, then an enemy.)
Wine ever pays for his lodging.
Wine makes all sorts of creatures at table.
Wine that cost nothing is digested before it be drunk.
Trees eat but once.
Armour is light at table.

Good horses make short miles.
Castles are forests of stones.
The dainties of the great are the tears of the poor.
Parsons are souls' waggoners.
Children when they are little make parents fools, when they are great they make them mad.
The master absent, and the house dead.
Dogs are fine in the field.
Sins are not known till they be acted.
Thorns whiten, yet do nothing.
All are presumed good till they are found in a fault.
The great put the little on the hook.
The great would have none great, and the little all little.
The Italians are wise before the deed, the Germans in the deed, the French after the deed.
Every mile is two in winter.
Spectacles are death's arquebuse.
Lawyers' houses are built on the heads of fools.
The house is a fine house when good folks are within.
The best bred have the best portion.
The first and last frosts are the worst.
Gifts enter every where without a wimble.
Princes have no way.
Knowledge makes one laugh, but wealth makes one dance
The citizen is at his business before he rise.
The eyes have one language every where.
It is better to have wings than horns.
Better be a fool than a knave.
Count not four, except you have them in a wallet.
To live peaceably with all, breeds good blood.
You may be on land, yet not in a garden.
You cannot make the fire so low, but it will get out.
We know not who lives or dies.
An ox is taken by the horns, and a man by the tongue.
Many things are lost for want of asking.
No church-yard is so handsome, that a man would desire straight to be buried there.
Cities are taken by the ears.
Once a year a man may say, On his conscience.
We leave more to do when we die, than we have done.
With customs we live well, but laws undo us.
To speak of a usurer at the table, mars the wine.
Pains to get, care to keep, fear to lose.
For a morning rain, leave not your journey.
One fair day in winter makes not birds merry.
He that learns a trade, hath a purchase made.
When all men have what belongs to them, it cannot be much.
Though God take the sun out of the heaven, yet we must have patience.

When a man sleeps, his head is in his stomach.
When one is on horseback, he knows all things.
When God is made the master of a family, he orders the disorderly.
When a lackey comes to hell's door, the devils lock the gates.
He that is at ease, seeks dainties.
He that bath charge of souls, transports them not in bundles.
He that tells his wife news, is but newly married.
He that is in a town in May, loseth his spring.
He that is in a tavern, thinks he is in a vine-garden.
He that praiseth himself, spattereth himself.
He that is a master, must serve (another).
He that is surprised at the first frost, feels it all the winter after.
He a beast doth die, that hath done no good to his country.
He that follows the Lord, hopes to go before.
He that dies without the company of good men, puts not himself into a good way.
Who hath no head, needs no heart.
Who hath no haste in his business, mountains to him seem valleys.
Speak not of my debts, unless you mean to pay them.
He that is not in the wars, is not out of danger.
He that gives me small gifts, would have me live.
He that is his own counsellor, knows nothing sure but what he hath laid out.
He that hath lands, hath quarrels.
He that goes to bed thirsty, riseth healthy.
Who will make a door of gold, must knock a nail every day.
A trade is better than service.
He that lives in hope, danceth without music.
To review one's store is to mow twice.
Saint Luke was a saint and physician, yet is dead.
Without business, debauchery.
Without danger we cannot get beyond danger.
Health and sickness surely are men's double enemies.
If gold knew what gold is, gold would get gold, I wis.
Little losses amaze, great tame.
Choose none for thy servant who have served thy betters.
Service without reward is punishment.
If the husband be not at home, there is nobody.
An oath that is not to be made, is not to be kept.
The eye is bigger than the belly.
If you would be at ease, all the world is not.
Were it not for the bone in the leg, all the world would turn carpenters.
If you must fly, fly well.
All that shakes falls not.
All beasts of prey are strong, or treacherous.
If the brain sows not corn, it plants thistles.
A man well mounted is ever choleric.
Every one is a master and servant.
A piece of a church-yard fits every body.

One mouth doth nothing without another.
A master of straw eats a servant of steel.
An old cat sports not with her prey.
A woman conceals what she knows not.
He that wipes the child's nose, kisseth the mother's cheek.[6]
Gentility is nothing but ancient riches.
To go where the king goes afoot.
To go upon the Franciscan's hackney.
Amiens was taken by the Fox, and retaken by the Lion.
After death the doctor.
Ready money is a ready medicine.
It is the philosophy of the distaff.
It is a sheep of Beery, it is marked on the nose: applied to those that have a blow.
To build castles in Spain.
An idle youth, a needy age.
Silk doth quench the fire in the kitchen.
The words ending in *ique,* do mock the physician; as
Hectique, Paralitique, Apoplectique, Lethargique.
He that trusts much obliges much, says the Spaniard.
He that thinks amiss, concludes worse.
A man would live in Italy (a place of pleasure) but he would choose to die in Spain, where they say the Catholic religion is professed with greatest strictness.
Whatsoever was the father of a disease, an ill diet was the mother.
Frenzy, heresy, and jealousy, seldom cured.
There is no heat of affection but is joined with some idleness of brain, says the Spaniard.
The war is not done so long as my enemy lives.
Some evils are cured by contempt.
Power seldom grows old at Court.
Danger itself the best remedy for danger.
Favour will as surely perish as life.
Fear the beadle of the law.
Heresy is the school of pride.
For the same man to be a heretic and a good subject, is impossible.
Heresy may be easier kept out than shook off.
Infants' manners are moulded more by the example of parents, than by stars at their nativities.
They favour learning whose actions are worthy of a learned pen.
Modesty sets off one newly come to honour.
No naked man is sought after to be rifled.
There is no such conquering weapon as the necessity of conquering.
Nothing secure unless suspected.
No tie can oblige the perfidious.
Spies are the ears and eyes of princes.

---

[6] The proverbs which follow were added to the second edition.

The life of spies is to know, not to be known.
Religion a stalking horse to shoot other fowl.
It is a dangerous fire begins in the bed straw.
Covetousness breaks the bag.
Fear keeps and looks to the vineyard, and not the owner.
The noise is greater than the nuts.
Two sparrows on one ear of corn make an ill agreement.
The world is now a-days, God save the conqueror.
Unsound minds, like unsound bodies, if you feed, you poison.
Not only ought fortune to be pictured on a wheel, but every thing else in this world.
All covet, all lose.
Better is one *Accipe,* than twice to say, *Dabo tibi.*
An ass endures his burden, but not more than his burden.
Threatened men eat bread, says the Spaniard.
The beads in the hand, and the devil in capuch; or, cape of the cloak.
He that will do thee a good turn, either he will be gone or die.
I escaped the thunder, and fell into the lightning.
A man of a great memory without learning, hath a rock and a spindle, and no staff to spin.
The death of wolves is the safety of the sheep.
He that is once born, once must die.
He that hath but one eye, must be afraid to lose it.
He that makes himself a sheep, shall be eat by the wolf.
He that steals an egg, will steal an ox.
He that will be surety, shall pay.
He that is afraid of leaves, goes not to the wood.
In the mouth of a bad dog falls often a good bone.
Those that God loves, do not live long.
Still fisheth he that catcheth one.
All flesh is not venison.
A city that parleys is half gotten.
A dead bee maketh no honey.
An old dog barks not in vain.
They that hold the greatest farms, pay the least rent: (applied to rich men that are unthankful to God.)
Old camels carry young camels' skins to the market.
He that hath time and looks for better time, time comes that he repents himself of time.
Words and feathers the wind carries away.
Of a pig's tail you can never make a good shaft.
The bath of the blackmoor hath sworn not to whiten.
To a greedy eating horse a short halter.
The devil divides the world between atheism and superstition.
Such a saint, such an offering.
We do it soon enough, if that we do be well.
Cruelty is more cruel, if we defer the pain.
What one day gives us, another takes away from us.

To seek in a sheep five feet when there are but four.
A scabbed horse cannot abide the comb.
God strikes with his finger, and not with all his arm.
God gives his wrath by weight, and without weight his mercy.
Of a new prince, new bondage.
New things are fair.
Fortune to one is mother, to another is stepmother.
There is no man, though never so little, but sometimes he can hurt.
The horse that draws after him his halter, is not altogether escaped.
We must recoil a little, to the end we may leap the better.
No love is foul nor prison fair.
No day so clear, but hath dark clouds.
No hair so small, but hath his shadow.
A wolf will never make war against another wolf.
We must love, as looking one day to hate.
It is good to have some friends both in heaven and hell.
It is very hard to shave an egg.
It is good to hold the ass by the bridle.
The healthful man can give counsel to the sick.
The death of a young wolf doth never come too soon.
The rage of a wild boar is able to spoil more than one wood.
Virtue flies from the heart of a mercenary man.
The wolf eats oft of the sheep that have been warned.
The mouse that hath but one hole is quickly taken.
To play at chess when the house is on fire.
The itch of disputing is the scab of the church.
Follow not truth too near the heels, lest it dash out thy teeth.
Either wealth is much increased, or moderation is much decayed.
Say to pleasure, Gentle Eve, I will none of your apple.
When war begins, then hell openeth.
There is a remedy for everything, could men find it.
There is an hour wherein a man might be happy all his life could he find it.
Great fortune brings with it great misfortune.
A fair day in winter is the mother of a storm.
Woe be to him that reads but one book.
Tithe, and be rich.

Take heed of { The wrath of a mighty man, and the tumult of the people.
{ Mad folks in a narrow place.
{ Credit decayed, and people that have nothing.
{ A young wench, a prophetess, and a Latin bred woman.
{ A person marked, and a widow thrice married.
{ Foul dirty ways, and long sickness.
{ Wind that comes in at a hole, and a reconciled enemy.
{ A step-mother; the very name of her sufficeth.

Princes are venison in heaven.
Critics are like brushers of noblemen's clothes.
He is a great necromancer, for he asks counsel of the dead: *i.e.* books.
A man is known to be mortal by two things, sleep and lust.

Love without end, hath no end, says the Spaniard: meaning, if it were not begun on particular ends, it would last.

Stay awhile, that we may make an end the sooner.

Presents of love fear not to be ill taken of strangers.

To seek these things is lost labour: Geese in an oil pot, fat hogs among Jews, and wine in a fishing net.

Some men plant an opinion they seem to eradicate.

The philosophy of princes is to dive into the secrets of men, leaving the secrets of nature to those that have spare time.

States have their conversions and periods as well as natural bodies.

Great deservers grow intolerable presumera.

The love of money and the love of learning rarely meet.

Trust no friend with that you need, fear him as if he were your enemy.

Some had rather lose their friend than their jest.

Marry your daughters betimes, lest they marry themselves.

Soldiers in peace are like chimneys in summer.

Here is a talk of the Turk and the Pope, but my next neighbour doth me more harm than either of them both.

Civil wars of France made a million of atheists, and thirty thousand witches.

We bachelors laugh and show our teeth, but you married men laugh till your hearts ache.

The devil never assails a man except he find him either void of knowledge, or of the fear of God.

There is nobody will go to hell for company.

Much money makes a country poor, for it sets a dearer price on everything.

The virtue of a coward is suspicion.

A man's destiny is always dark.

Every man's censure is first moulded in his own nature.

Money wants no followers.

Your thoughts close, and your countenance loose.

Whatever is made by the hand of man, by the hand of man may be overturned.

THE PROSE OF GEORGE HERBERT

A PRIEST TO THE TEMPLE;

OR, THE COUNTRY PARSON,

HIS CHARACTER, AND RULE OF HOLY LIFE.

[FIRST PRINTED IN 1652.]

THE AUTHOR TO THE READER.

Being desirous (through the mercy of God) to please him, for whom I am, and live, and who giveth me my desires and performances; and considering with myself, that the way to please him is to feed my flock diligently and faithfully, since our Saviour hath made that the argument of a Pastor's love, I have resolved to set down the form and character of a true Pastor, that I may have a mark to aim at: which also I will set as high as I can, since he shoots higher that threatens the moon, than he that aims at a tree. Not that I think, if a man do not all which is here expressed, he presently sins, and displeases God, but that it is a good strife to go as far as we can in pleasing him, who hath done so much for us. The Lord prosper the intention to myself and others, who may not despise my poor labours, but add to those points which I have observed, until the book grow to a complete pastoral.

GEO. HERBERT.

1632.

A PRIEST TO THE TEMPLE.

CHAPTER I. OF A PASTOR.

A Pastor is the deputy of Christ for the reducing of man to the obedience of God. This definition is evident, and contains the direct steps of pastoral duty and authority. For first, man fell from God by disobedience. Secondly, Christ is the glorious instrument of God for the revoking of man. Thirdly, Christ being not to continue on earth, but after he had fulfilled the work of reconciliation, to be received up into heaven, he constituted deputies in his place, and these are Priests. And therefore St Paul in the beginning of his Epistles, professeth this: and in the first to the Colossians[1] plainly avoucheth that he fills up that which is behind of the afflictions of Christ in his flesh, for his body's sake, which is the Church, wherein is contained the complete definition of a minister. Out of this charter of the priesthood may be plainly gathered both the dignity thereof and the duty: The dignity, in that a priest may do that which Christ did, and by his authority, and as his vicegerent. The duty, in that a priest is to do that which Christ did, and after his manner, both for doctrine and life.

CHAPTER II. THEIR DIVERSITIES.

Of Pastors (intending mine own nation only, and also therein setting aside the reverend prelates of the church, to whom this discourse ariseth not) some live in the universities, some in noble houses, some in parishes residing on their cures. Of those that live in the universities, some live there in office, whose rule is that of the apostle, Romans, xii. 6. "Having gifts, differing according to the grace that is given to us, whether prophecy, let us prophesy according to the proportion of faith; or ministry, let us wait on our ministering; or he that teacheth, on teaching, &c.; he that ruleth let him do it with diligence," &c. Some in a preparatory way, whose aim and labour must be not only to get knowledge, but to subdue and mortify all lusts and affections: and not to think, that when they have read the Fathers or Schoolmen, a minister is made, and the thing done. The greatest and hardest preparation is within: for unto the godly saith God, "Why dost thou preach my laws, and takest my covenant in thy mouth?" Psalm i. 16. Those that live in noble houses are called Chaplains, whose duty and obligation being the same to the houses they live in, as a Parson's to his parish, in describing the one (which is indeed the bent of my discourse) the other will be manifest. Let not chaplains think themselves so free, as many of them do, and because they have different names, think their office different. Doubtless they are Parsons of the families they live, in, and are entertained to that end, either by an open or implicit covenant. Before they are in orders, they may be received for companions or discoursers; but after a man is once minister, he cannot agree to come into any house, where he shall not exercise what he is, unless he forsake his plough, and look back. Wherefore they are not to be over-submissive and base, but to keep up with the lord and lady of the house, and to preserve a boldness with them and all, even so far as reproof to their very face, when occasion calls, but seasonably and discreetly. They who do not thus, while they remember their earthly lord, do much forget their heavenly; they wrong the priesthood, neglect their duty, and shall be so far from that

---

[1] Chap. i. 24.

which they seek with their over-submissiveness and cringing, that they shall ever be despised. They who for the hope of promotion neglect any necessary admonition or reproof, sell (with Judas) their Lord and Master.

CHAPTER III. THE PARSON'S LIFE.

The country Parson is exceeding exact in his life, being holy, just, prudent, temperate, bold, grave, in all his ways. And because the two highest points of life, wherein a Christian is most seen, are patience and mortification; patience in regard of afflictions, mortification in regard of lusts and affections, and the stupifying and deading of all the clamorous powers of the soul, therefore he hath thoroughly studied these, that he may be an absolute master and commander of himself, for all the purposes which God hath ordained him. Yet in these points he labours most in those things which are most apt to scandalize his parish. And first, because country people live hardly, and therefore as feeling their own sweat, and consequently knowing the price of money, are offended much with any who, by hard usage, increase their travail, the country Parson is very circumspect in avoiding all covetousness, neither being greedy to get nor niggardly to keep, nor troubled to lose any worldly wealth; but in all his words and actions slighting and disesteeming it, even to a wondering that the world should so much value wealth, which in the day of wrath hath not one dram of comfort for us. Secondly, because luxury is a very visible sin, the Parson is very careful to avoid all kinds thereof, but especially that of drinking, because it is the most popular vice; into which if he come, he prostitutes himself both to shame and sin, and by having fellowship with the unfruitful works of darkness, he disableth himself of authority to reprove them; for sins make all equal whom they find together; and then they are worst who ought to be best. Neither is it for the servant of Christ to haunt inns, or taverns, or alehouses, to the dishonour of his person and office. The Parson doth not so, but orders his life in such a fashion, that when death takes him, as the Jews and Judas did Christ, he may say as He did, "I sat daily with you teaching in the Temple." Thirdly, because country people (as indeed all honest men) do much esteem their word, it being the life of buying and selling and dealing in the world; therefore the Parson is very strict in keeping his word, though it be to his own hindrance, as' knowing that if he be not so, he will quickly be discovered and disregarded: neither will they believe him in the pulpit, whom they cannot trust in his conversation. As for oaths, and apparel, the disorders thereof are also very manifest. The Parson's yea is yea, and nay, nay; and his apparel plain, but reverend and clean, without spots, or dust, or smell; the purity of his mind breaking out, and dilating itself even to his body, clothes, and habitation.

CHAPTER IV. THE PARSON'S KNOWLEDGE.

The country Parson is full of all knowledge. They say it is an ill mason that refuseth any stone: and there is no knowledge but, in a skilful hand, serves either positively as it is, or else to illustrate some other knowledge. He condescends even to the knowledge of tillage and pasturage, and makes great use of them in teaching, because people by what they understand are best led to what they understand not. But the chief and top of his knowledge consists in the book of books, the storehouse and magazine of life and comfort, the Holy Scriptures. There he sucks, and lives. In the Scriptures he finds four things; precepts for life, doctrines for knowledge, examples for illustration, and promises for comfort: these he hath digested severally. But for the understanding of these; the means he useth are, first, a holy life, remembering what his Master saith, that "if any do God's will, he shall know of the doctrine," John vii; and assuring himself that wicked men, however learned, do not know the Scriptures, because they feel them not, and because they are not understood but with the same Spirit that writ them. The second means is prayer, which if it be necessary even in temporal things, how much more in things of another world, where the well is deep, and we have nothing of ourselves to draw with? Wherefore he ever begins the reading of the Scripture with some short inward ejaculation, as, "Lord open mine eyes, that I may see the wondrous things of thy law, &C."[1] The third means is a diligent collation of Scripture with Scripture. For all truth being consonant to itself, and all being penned by one and the self-same Spirit, it cannot be but that an industrious and judicious comparing of place with place, must be a singular help for the right understanding of the Scriptures. To this may be added the consideration of any text with the coherence thereof, touching what goes before, and what follows after, as also the scope of the Holy Ghost. When the apostles would have called down fire from heaven, they were reproved, as ignorant of what spirit they were. For the Law required one thing, and the Gospel another: yet as diverse, not as repugnant: therefore the spirit of both is to be considered, and weighed.

The fourth means are commenters and fathers, who have handled the places controverted, which the Parson by no means refuseth. As he doth not so study others, as to neglect the grace of God in himself, and what the Holy Spirit teacheth him; so doth he assure himself, that God in all ages hath had his servants, to whom he hath revealed his truth, as well as to him; and that as one country doth not bear all things, that there may be a commerce, so neither hath God opened or will open all to one, that there may be a traffic in knowledge between the servants of God, for the planting both of love and humility. Wherefore he hath one comment at least upon every book of Scripture, and ploughing with this, and his own meditations, he enters into the secrets of God treasured in the holy Scripture.

CHAPTER V. THE PARSON'S ACCESSORY KNOWLEDGES.

The country Parson hath read the Fathers also, and the Schoolmen, and the later writers, or a good proportion of all, out of all which he hath compiled a book and body of divinity, which is the storehouse of his sermons, and which he preacheth all his life; but diversely clothed, illustrated, and enlarged. For though the world is full of such composures, yet every man's own is fittest, readiest, and most savoury to him. Besides, this being to be done in his younger and preparatory times, it is an honest joy ever after to look upon his well-spent hours. This body he made by way of expounding the Church Catechism, to which all divinity may easily be reduced. For it being indifferent in itself to choose any method, that is best to be chosen of which there is likeliest to be most use. Now catechizing being a work of singular and admirable benefit to the Church of God, and a thing required under canonical obedience, the expounding of our catechism must needs be the most useful form. Yet hath the Parson, besides this laborious work, a slighter form of catechizing, fitter for country people; according as his audience is, so he useth one or other, or sometimes both, if his audience be intermixed. He greatly esteems also of cases of conscience, wherein he is much vexed. And indeed, herein is the greatest ability

---

[1] Psalm cxix. 18.

of a Parson, to lead his people exactly in the ways of truth, so that they neither decline to the right hand nor to the left. Neither let any think this a slight thing. For every one hath not digested, when it is a sin to take something for money lent, or when not; when it is a fault to discover another's fault, or when not; when the affections of the soul in desiring and procuring increase of means or honour be a sin of covetousness or ambition, and when not; when the appetites of the body in eating, drinking, sleep, and the pleasure that comes with sleep, be sins of gluttony, drunkenness, sloth, lust, and when not; and so in many circumstances of actions. Now if a shepherd know not what grass will bane, or which not, how is he fit to be a shepherd? Wherefore the Parson hath thoroughly canvassed all the particulars of human actions, at least all those which he observeth are most incident to his parish.

CHAPTER VI. THE PARSON PRAYING.

The country Parson, when he is to read divine services, composeth himself to all possible reverence; lifting up his heart and hands and eyes, and using all other gestures which may express a hearty and unfeigned devotion. This he doth, first, as being truly touched and amazed with the majesty of God, before whom he then presents himself; yet not as himself alone, but as presenting with himself the whole congregation; whose sins he then bears, and brings with his own to the heavenly altar to be bathed and washed in the sacred laver of Christ's blood. Secondly, as this is the true reason of his inward fear, so he is content to express this outwardly to the utmost of his power; that being at first affected himself, he may affect also his people, knowing that no sermon moves them so much to reverence, which they forget again when they come to pray, as a devout behaviour in the very act of praying. Accordingly his voice is humble, his words treatable and slow; yet not so slow neither as to let the fervency of the supplicant hang and die between speaking, but with a grave liveliness, between fear and zeal, pausing yet pressing, he performs his duty. Besides his example, he having often instructed his people how to carry themselves in divine service, exacts of them all possible reverence, by no means enduring either talking, or sleeping, or gazing, or leaning, or half-kneeling, or any undutiful behaviour in them, but causing them, when they sit, to stand, or kneel, to do all in a straight and steady posture, as attending to what is done in the Church, and every one, man and child, answering aloud both Amen, and all other answers, which are on the clerk's and people's part to answer; which answers also are to be done not in a huddling or slubbering fashion gaping or scratching the head, or spitting even in the midst of their answer, but gently and pausably, thinking what they say; so that while they answer, "As it was in the beginning," &c. they meditate as they speak, that God hath ever had his people, that have glorified him as well as now, and that he shall have so for ever. And the like in other answers. This is that which the apostle calls a reasonable service (Romans xii.), when we speak not as parrots, without reason, or offer up such sacrifices as they did of old, which was of beasts devoid of reason; but when we use our reason, and apply our powers to the service of Him that gives them. If there be any of the gentry or nobility of the parish who sometimes make it a piece of state not to come at the beginning of service with their poor neighbours, but at mid-prayers, both to their own loss and of theirs also who gaze upon them when they come in, and neglect the present service of God, he by no means suffers it, but after divers gentle admonitions, if they persevere, he causes them to be presented: or if the poor churchwardens be affrighted with their greatness, notwithstanding his instruction that they ought not to be so, but even to let the world sink, so they do their duty, he presents them himself; only protesting to them, that not any ill-will draws him to it, but the debt and obligation of his calling, being to obey God rather than men.

CHAPTER VII. THE PARSON PREACHING.

The country Parson preacheth constantly; the pulpit is his joy and his throne. If he at any time intermit, it is either for want of health, or against some great festival, that he may the better celebrate it, or for the variety of the hearers, that he may be heard at his return more attentively. When he intermits, he is ever well supplied by some able man, who treads in his steps, and will not throw down what he hath built; whom also he entreats to press some point, that he himself hath often urged with no great success, that so, in the mouth of two or three witnesses, the truth may be more established. When he preacheth, he procures attention by all possible art, both by earnestness of speech, it being natural to men to think that where is much earnestness there is somewhat worth hearing, and by a diligent and busy cast of his eye on his auditors, with letting them know that he observes who marks and who not; and with particularizing of his speech now to the younger sort, then to the elder; now to the poor, and now to the rich: This is for you; and, This is for you; for particulars ever touch, and awake more than generals. Herein also he serves himself of the judgments of God, as of those of ancient times, so especially of the late ones; and those most which are nearest to his parish; for people are very attentive at such discourses, and think it behoves them to be so, when God is so near them, and even over their heads. Sometimes he tells them stories and sayings of others, according as his text invites him; for them also men heed and remember better than exhortations, which, though earnest, yet often die with the sermon, especially with country people, which are thick and heavy, and hard to raise to a point of zeal and fervency, and need a mountain of fire to kindle them; but stories and sayings they will well remember. He often tells them that sermons are dangerous things; that none goes out of church as he came in, but either better or worse; that none is careless before his Judge, and that the Word of God shall judge us. By these and other means the Parson procures attention. The character of his sermon is holiness; he is not witty, or learned, or eloquent, but holy: a character that Hermogenes never dreamed of, and therefore he could give no precept thereof. But it is gained, first, by choosing texts of devotion, not controversy; moving and ravishing texts, whereof the Scriptures are full. Secondly, by dipping and seasoning all our words and sentences in our hearts, before they come into our mouths, truly affecting and cordially expressing all that we say; so that the auditors may plainly perceive that every word is heart-deep. Thirdly, by turning often, and making many apostrophes to God; as, O Lord, bless my people and teach them this point; or, O my Master, on whose errand I come, let me hold my peace, and do thou speak thyself; for thou art love, and when thou teachest, all are scholars. Some such irradiations scatteringly in the sermon carry great holiness in them. The prophets are admirable in this. So Isaiah lxiv. "O that thou wouldst rend the heavens, that thou wouldst come down," &c. And Jeremiah x., after he had complained of the desolation of Israel, turns to God suddenly, "O Lord, I know that the way of man is not in himself," &c. Fourthly, by frequent wishes of the people's good, and joying therein, though he himself were with St Paul even sacrificed upon the service of their faith. For there is no greater sign of holiness than the procuring and rejoicing in another's good. And herein St Paul excelled in all his Epistles. How did he put the Romans in all his prayers, Rom. i. 9; and ceased not to give thanks for the Ephesians, Eph. i. 16; and for the Corinthians, chap. i. 4; and for the Philippians made request with joy, chap. i. 4; and is in contention for them, whether to live or die; be with them, or Christ, verse 23, which, setting aside his care of his flock, were a madness to doubt of? What an admirable epistle is the Second to the Corinthians! how full of affections! he joys, and he is sorry, he grieves, and he glories; never was there such care of a flock expressed, save in the great Shepherd of the fold, who first shed tears over Jerusalem, and afterwards blood. Therefore this care may be learned there, and then woven into sermons, which will make them appear exceeding reverend and holy. Lastly, by an often urging of the presence and majesty of God, by these or such like speeches: Oh let us all take heed what we do! God sees us; he sees whether I speak as I ought or you hear as you ought: he sees hearts as we see faces; he is among us, for if we be here he must be here, since we are here by him, and without him could not be here. Then turning the discourse to his majesty: And he is a great God and terrible, as great in mercy, so great in judgment. There are but two devouring elements, fire and water; he hath both in him: "His voice is as the sound of many waters," Revelation i., and "He himself is a consuming fire," Hebrews, xii. Such discourses show very holy. The Parson's method in handling of a text consists of two parts: First, a plain and evident declaration of the meaning of the text; and, secondly, some choice observations drawn out of the whole text, as it lies entire, and unbroken in the Scripture itself. This he thinks natural, and sweet, and grave. Whereas the other way of crumbling a text into small parts, as the person speaking or spoken to the subject and object, and the like, hath neither in it sweetness, nor gravity, nor variety, since the words apart are not Scripture, but a dictionary, and may be considered alike in all the Scripture. The Parson exceeds not an hour in preaching, because all ages have thought that a competency; and he that profits not in that time will less afterwards, the same affection which made him not profit before making him then weary, and so he grows from not relishing to loathing.

CHAPTER VIII. THE PARSON ON SUNDAYS.

The country Parson, as soon as he awakes on Sunday morning, presently falls to work, and seems to himself so as a market-man is when the market-day comes, or a shopkeeper when customers come in. His thoughts are full of making the best of the day, and contriving it to his best gains. To this end, besides his ordinary prayers, he makes a peculiar one for a blessing on the exercises of the day. That nothing befall him unworthy of that Majesty before which he is to present himself, but that all may be done with reverence to His glory, and with edification to his flock, humbly beseeching his Master, that how or whenever he punish him, it be not in his ministry. Then he turns to request for his people that the Lord would be pleased to sanctify them all, that they may come with holy hearts and awful minds into the congregation, and that the good God would pardon all those who come with less prepared hearts than they ought. This done, he sets himself to the consideration of the duties of the day; and if there be any extraordinary addition to the customary exercises, either from the time of the year, or from the State, or from God; by a child born, or dead, or any other accident, he contrives how and in what manner to induce it to the best advantage. Afterwards when the hour calls, with his family attending him, he goes to church, at his first entrance humbly adoring and worshipping the invisible majesty and presence of Almighty God, and blessing the people either openly or to himself. Then having read divine service twice fully, and preached in the morning, and catechized in the afternoon, he thinks he hath in some measure, according to poor and frail man, discharged the public duties of the congregation. The rest of the day he spends either in reconciling neighbours that are at variance, or in visiting the sick, or in exhortations to some of his flock by themselves, whom his sermons cannot or do not reach. And every one is more awaked, when we come and say, Thou art the man. This way he finds exceeding useful and winning; and these exhortations he calls his privy purse, even as princes have theirs, besides their public disbursements. At night he thinks it a very fit time, both suitable to the joy of the day and without hinderance to public duties, either to entertain some of his neighbours or to be entertained of them, where he takes occasion to discourse of such things as are both profitable and pleasant, and to raise up their minds to apprehend God's good blessing to our church and state; that order is kept in the one, and peace in the other, without disturbance or interruption of public divine offices. As he opened the day with prayer, so he closeth it, humbly beseeching the Almighty to pardon and accept our poor services, and to improve them, that we may grow therein, and that our feet may be like hinds' feet, ever climbing up higher and higher unto Him.

CHAPTER IX. THE PARSON'S STATE OF LIFE.

The country Parson considering that virginity is a higher state than matrimony, and that the ministry requires the best and highest things, is rather unmarried than married. But yet as the temper of his body may be, or as the temper of his parish may be, where he may have occasion to converse with women, and that among suspicious men, and other like circumstances considered, he is rather married than unmarried. Let him communicate the thing often by prayer unto God, and as his grace shall direct him, so let him proceed. If he be unmarried and keep house, he hath not a woman in his house, but finds opportunities of having his meat dressed and other services done by men-servants at home, and his linen washed abroad. If he be unmarried and sojourn, he never talks with any woman alone, but in the audience of others, and that seldom, and then also in a serious manner, never jestingly or sportfully. He is very circumspect in all companies, both of his behaviour, speech, and very looks, knowing himself to be both suspected and envied. If he stands steadfast in his heart, having no necessity, but hath power over his own will, and hath so decreed in his heart that he will keep himself a virgin, he spends his days in fasting and prayer, and blesseth God for the gift of continency, knowing that it can no way be preserved but only by those means by which at first it was obtained. He therefore thinks it not enough for him to observe the fasting days of the Church, and the daily prayers enjoined him by authority, which he observeth out of humble conformity and obedience; but adds to them, out of choice and devotion, some other days for fasting, and hours for prayers; and by these he keeps his body tame, serviceable, and healthful, and his soul fervent, active, young, and lusty as an eagle. He often readeth the lives of the primitive monks, hermits, and virgins, and wondereth not so much at their patient suffering and cheerful dying under persecuting emperors (though that indeed be very admirable), as at their daily temperance, abstinence, watchings, and constant prayers and mortifications in the times of peace and prosperity. To put on the profound humility and the exact temperance of our Lord Jesus, with other exemplary virtues of that sort, and to keep them on in the sunshine and noon of prosperity, he findeth to be as necessary, and as difficult at least, as to be clothed with perfect patience and Christian fortitude in the cold midnight storms of persecution and adversity. He keepeth his watch and ward, night and day, against the proper and peculiar temptations of his state of life, which are principally these two, spiritual pride and impurity of heart; against these ghostly enemies he girdeth up his loins, keeps the imagination from roving, puts on the whole armour of God, and by the virtue of the shield of faith he is not afraid of the pestilence that walketh in darkness [carnal impurity], nor of the sickness that destroyeth at noon-day [ghostly pride and self-conceit]. Other temptations he hath, which like mortal enemies may sometimes disquiet him likewise; for the human soul being bounded and kept in her sensitive faculty, will run out more or less in her intellectual. Original concupiscence is such an active thing, by reason of continual inward or outward temptations, that it is ever attempting or doing one mischief or other. Ambition or untimely desire of promotion to a higher state or place, under colour of accommodation or necessary provision, is a common temptation to men of any eminence, especially being single men. Curiosity in prying into high speculative and unprofitable questions, is another great stumbling-block to the holiness of scholars. These and many other spiritual wickednesses in high places doth the Parson fear, or experiment, or both; and that much more being single than if he were married; for then commonly the stream of temptations is turned another way, into covetousness, love of pleasure, or ease, or the like. If the Parson be unmarried, and means to continue so, he doth at least as much as hath been said. If he be married, the choice of his wife was made rather by his ear than by his eye; his judgment, not his affection, found out a fit wife for him, whose humble and liberal disposition he preferred before beauty, riches, or honour. He knew that (the good instrument of God to bring woman to heaven) a wise and loving husband could, out of humility, produce any special grace of faith, patience, meekness, love, obedience, &c., and out of liberality make her fruitful in all good works. As he is just in all things, so is he to his wife also, counting nothing so much his own as that he may be unjust unto it. Therefore he gives her respect both afore her servants and others, and half at least of the government of the house, reserving so much of the affairs as serve for a diversion for him; yet never so giving over the reins, but that be sometimes looks how things go, demanding an account, but not by the way of an account. And this must be done the oftener, or the seldomer, according as he is satisfied of his wife's discretion.

CHAPTER X. THE PARSON IN HIS HOUSE.

The Parson is very exact in the governing of his house, making it a copy and model for his parish. He knows the temper and pulse of every person in his house, and accordingly either meets with their vices or advanceth their virtues. His wife[7] is either religious, or night and day he is winning her to it. Instead of the qualities of the world, he requires only three of her; first, a training up of her children and maids in the fear of God, with prayers, and catechizing, and all religious duties. Secondly, a curing and healing of all wounds and sores with her own hands; which skill either she brought with her, or he takes care she shall learn it of some religious neighbour. Thirdly, a providing for her family in such sort, as that neither they want a competent sustentation, nor her husband be brought in debt. His children he first makes Christians, and then Commonwealth's men; the one he owes to his heavenly country, the other to his earthly, having no title to either, except he do good to both. Therefore having seasoned them with all piety, not only of words in praying and reading, but in actions, in visiting other sick children, and tending their wounds, and sending his charity by them to the poor, and sometimes giving

---

[7] "A priest's wife can challenge to precedence or place but that which she purchases by her obliging humility."—Herbert to his Wife.

them a little money to do it of themselves, that they get a delight in it, and enter favour with God, who weighs even children's actions; 1 Kings xiv. 12, 13. He afterwards turns his care to fit all their dispositions with some calling, not sparing the eldest, but giving him the prerogative of his father's profession, which happily for his other children he is not able to do. Yet in binding them apprentices (in case he think fit to do so) he takes care not to put them into vain trades, and unbefitting the reverence of their father's calling, such as are taverns for men, and lace-making for women; because those trades, for the most part, serve but the vices and vanities of the world, which he is to deny and not augment. However, he resolves with himself never to omit any present good deed of charity, in consideration of providing a stock for his children; but assures himself, that money, thus lent to God, is placed surer for his children's advantage, than if it were given to the chamber of London.[8] Good deeds, and good breeding, are his two great stocks for his children; if God give any thing above those, and not spent in them, he blesseth God, and lays it out as he sees cause. His servants are all religious, and were it not his duty to have them so, it were his profit, for none are so well served as by religious servants, both because they do best, and because what they do is blessed and prospers. After religion, he teacheth them that three things make a complete servant, truth, and diligence, and neatness or cleanliness. Those that can read are allowed times for it, and those that cannot are taught; for all in his house are either teachers or learners, or both, so that his family is a school of religion, and they all account that to teach the ignorant is the greatest alms. Even the walls are not idle, but something is written or painted there, which may excite the reader to a thought of piety: especially the 101st Psalm, which is expressed in a fair table, as being the rule of a family. And when they go abroad, his wife among her neighbours is the beginner of good discourses, his children among children, his servants among other servants; so that as in the house of those that are skilled in music all are musicians, so in the house of a preacher all are preachers. He suffers not a lie or equivocation by any means in his house, but counts it the art and secret of governing, to preserve a directness and open plainness in all things; so that all his house knows that there is no help for a fault done but confession. He himself, or his wife, takes account of sermons, and how every one profits, comparing this year with the last: and besides the common prayers of the family, he straightly requires of all to pray by themselves before they sleep at night, and stir out in the morning, and knows what prayers they say, and till they have learned them, makes them kneel by him; esteeming that this private praying is a more voluntary act in them, than when they are called to others' prayers, and that which when they leave the family they carry with them. He keeps his servants between love and fear, according as he finds them; but generally he distributes it thus: to his children he shews more love than terror, to his servants more terror than love; but an old good servant boards a child. The furniture of his house is very plain, but clean, whole, and sweet, as sweet as his garden can make; for he hath no money for such things, charity being his only perfume, which deserves cost when he can spare it. His fare is plain and common, but wholesome; what he hath is little, but very good; it consisteth most of mutton, beef, and veal: if he adds any thing for a great day, or a stranger, his garden or orchard supplies it, or his barn and yard: he goes no further for any entertainment, lest he go into the world, esteeming it absurd that he should exceed who teacheth others temperance. But those which his home produceth, he refuseth not, as coming cheap and

---

[8] "To a good spender God is the treasurer." "He that's long a-giving knows not how to give."—Jacula Prudentum.

easy, and arising from the improvement of things which otherwise would be lost. Wherein he admires and imitates the wonderful providence and thrift of the great Householder of the world: for there being two things which as they are are unuseful to man, the one for smallness, as crumbs and scattered corn, and the like; the other for the foulness, as wash and dirt, and things thereinto fallen, God hath provided creatures for both; for the first, poultry, for the second, swine. These save man the labour and doing that which either he could not do, or was not fit for him to do, by taking both sorts of food into them, do as it were and dress and prepare both for man in themselves, by growing themselves fit for his table. The Parson in his house observes fasting days; and particularly, as Sunday is his day of joy, so Friday his day of humiliation, which he celebrates not only with abstinence of diet, but also of company, recreation, and all outward contentments; and besides, with confession of sins and all acts of mortification. Now fasting days contain a treble obligation: First, of eating less that day than on other days; secondly, of eating no pleasing or over-nourishing things, as the Israelites did eat sour herbs; thirdly, of eating no flesh, which is but the determination of the second rule by authority to this particular. The two former obligations are much more essential to a true fast than the third and last; and fasting days were fully performed by keeping the two former, had not authority interposed; so that to eat little, and that unpleasant, is the natural rule of fasting, although it be flesh. For since fasting in Scripture language is an afflicting of our souls, if a piece of dry flesh at my table be more unpleasant to me than some fish there certainly to eat the flesh and not the fish, is to keep the fasting day naturally. And it is observable, that the prohibiting of flesh came from hot countries, where both flesh alone, and much more with wine, is apt to nourish more than in cold regions, and where flesh may be much better spared, and with more safety than elsewhere, where both the people and the drink being cold and phlegmatic, the eating of flesh is an antidote to both. For it is certain, that a weak stomach, being prepossessed with flesh, shall much better brook and bear a draught of beer, than if it had taken before either fish or roots, or such things; which will discover itself by spitting, and rheum, or phlegm. To conclude, the Parson, if he be in full health, keeps the three obligations, eating fish, or roots, and that for quantity little, for quality unpleasant. If hb body be weak and obstructed, as most students are, he cannot keep the last obligation, nor suffer others in his house that are so, to keep it; but only the two former, which also in diseases of exinanition (as consumptions) must be broken; for meat was made for man, not man for meat. To all this may be added, not for emboldening the unruly, but for the comfort of the weak, that not only sickness breaks these obligations of fasting, but sickliness also. For it is as unnatural to do anything that leads me to a sickness, to which I am inclined, as not to get out of that sickness, when I am in it, by any diet. One thing is evident, that an English body, and a student's body, are two great obstructed vessels, and there is nothing that is food, and not physic, which doth less obstruct than flesh moderately taken; as being immoderately taken, it is exceedingly obstructive. And obstructions are the cause of most diseases.

CHAPTER XI. THE PARSON'S COURTESY.

The country Parson owing a debt of charity to the poor, and of courtesy to his other parishioners, he so distinguisheth that he keeps his money for the poor and his table for those that are above alms. Not but that the poor are welcome also to his table, whom he sometimes purposely takes home with him, setting them close by him, and carving for them, both for his own humility and their comfort, who are much cheered with such friendlinesse. But since both is to be done, the better sort invited, and meaner relieved, he chooseth rather to give the poor money, which they can better employ to their own advantage, and suitably to their needs, than so much given in meat at dinner. Having then invited some of his parish, he taketh his times to do the like to the rest; so that in the compass of the year, he hath them all with him, because country people are very observant of such things, and will not be persuaded but being not invited they are hated; which persuasion the Parson by all means avoids, knowing that where there are such conceits, there is no room for his doctrine to enter. Yet doth he oftenest invite those whom he sees take best courses, that so both they may be encouraged to persevere, and others spurred to do well, that they may enjoy the like courtesy. For though he desire that all should live well and virtuously, not for any reward of his but for virtue's sake, yet that will not be so; and therefore as God, although we should love him only for his own sake, yet out of his infinite pity hath set forth heaven for a reward to draw men to piety, and is content, if at least so, they will become good; so the country Parson, who is a diligent observer and tracker of God's ways, sets up as many encouragements to goodness as he can, both in honour, and profit, and fame; that he may, if not the best way, yet any way, make his parish good.

CHAPTER XII. THE PARSON'S CHARITY.

The country Parson is full of charity; it is his predominant element: for many and wonderful things are spoken of thee, thou great virtue! To charity is given the covering of sins, 1 Pet. iv. 8; and the forgiveness of sins, Matthew vi. 14, Luke vii. 47; the fulfilling of the law, Romans xiii. 10; the life of faith, James ii. 26; the blessings of this life, Proverbs xxii. 9, Psalm xli. 2; and the reward of the next, Matthew xxv. 35. In brief, it is the body of religion, John xiii. 35; and the top of Christian virtues, 1 Corinthians xiii. Wherefore all his works relish of charity. When he riseth in the morning, he bethinketh himself what good deeds he can do that day, and presently doth them; counting that day lost wherein he hath not exercised his charity. He first considers his own parish, and takes care that there be not a beggar or idle person in his parish, but that all be in a competent way of getting their living. This he effects either by bounty, or persuasion, or by authority, making use of that excellent statute which binds all parishes to maintain their own. If his parish be rich, he exacts this of them; if poor, and he able, he easeth them therein. But he gives no set pension to any; for this in time will lose the name and effect of charity with the poor people, though not with God; for then they will reckon upon it as on a debt; and if it be taken away, though justly, they will murmur, and repine as much as he that is disseized of his own inheritance. But the Parson having a double aim, and making a hook of his charity, causeth them still to depend on him; and so by continual and fresh bounties, unexpected to them, but resolved to himself, he wins them to praise God more, to live more religiously, and to take more pains in their vocation, as not knowing when they shall be relieved; which otherwise they would reckon upon and turn to idleness. Besides this general provision, he hath other times of opening his hand; as at great festivals and communions; not suffering any that day that he receives to want a good meal suiting to the joy of the occasion. But specially, at hard times, and dearths, he even parts his living and life among them, giving some corn outright, and selling other at under rates; and when his own stock serves not, working those that are able to the same charity, still pressing it in the pulpit and out of the pulpit, and never leaving them till he obtain his desire. Yet in all his charity, he distinguisheth, giving them most who live best, and take most pains, and are most charged: so is his charity in effect a sermon. After the consideration of his own parish, he enlargeth himself, if he be able, to the neighbourhood; for that also is some kind of obligation; so doth he also to those at his door, whom God puts in his way, and makes his neighbours. But these he helps not without some testimony, except the evidence of the misery bring testimony with it. For though these testimonies also may be falsified, yet considering that the law allows these in case they be true, but allows by no means to give without testimony, as he obeys authority in the one, so that being once satisfied, he allows his charity some blindness in the other; especially, since of the two commands, we are more enjoined to be charitable than wise. But evident miseries have a natural privilege and exemption from all law. Whenever he gives anything, and sees them labour in thanking of him, he exacts of them to let him alone, and say rather, God be praised! God be glorified! that so the thanks may go the right way, and thither only where they are only due. So doth he also before giving make them say their prayers first, or the Creed and Ten Commandments, and as he finds them perfect, rewards them the more. For other givings are lay and secular; but this is to give like a priest.

CHAPTER XIII. THE PARSON'S CHURCH.

The country Parson hath a special care of his church, that all things there be decent, and befitting His name, by which it is called. Therefore, first, he takes order that all things be in good repair; as walls plastered, windows glazed, floor paved, seats whole, firm, and uniform, especially that the pulpit and desk, and communion table and font, be as they ought for those great duties that are performed in them. Secondly, that the church be swept and kept clean without dust or cobwebs, and at great festivals strewed and stuck with boughs, and perfumed with incense. Thirdly, that there be fit and proper texts of Scripture everywhere painted, and that all the painting be grave and reverend, not with light colours or foolish antics. Fourthly, that all the books appointed by authority be there, and those not torn or fouled, but whole and clean, and well bound; and that there be a fitting and sightly communion cloth of fine linen, with a handsome and seemly carpet of good and costly stuff or cloth, and all kept sweet and clean, in a strong and decent chest, with a chalice and cover, and a stoop or flagon, and a basin for alms and offerings; besides which, he hath a poor-man's box conveniently seated to receive the charity of well-minded people, and to lay up treasure for the sick and needy. And all this he doth, not as out of necessity, or as putting a holiness in the things, but as desiring to keep the middle way between superstition and slovenliness, and as following the Apostle's two great and admirable rules in things of this nature, the first whereof is, Let all things be done decently and in order: The second, Let all things be done to edification, 1 Cor. xiv. For these two rules comprise and include the double object of our duty, God and our neighbour; the first being for the honour of God, the second for the benefit of our neighbour. So that they excellently score out the way, and fully and exactly contain, even in external and indifferent things, what course is to be taken, and put them to great shame who deny the Scripture to be perfect.

CHAPTER XIV. THE PARSON IN CIRCUIT.

The country Parson, upon the afternoons in the weekdays, takes occasion sometimes to visit in person now one quarter of his parish now another. For there he shall find his flock most naturally as they are, wallowing in the midst of their affairs: whereas on Sunday it is easy for them to compose themselves to order, which they put on as their holiday clothes, and come to church in frame, but commonly the next day put off both. When he comes to any house, first he blesseth it, and then as he finds the persons of the house employed, so he forms his discourse. Those that he finds religiously employed, he both commends them much, and furthers them when he is gone, in their employment; as if he finds them reading, he furnisheth them with good books; if curing poor people, he supplies them with receipts, and instructs them further in that skill, shewing them how acceptable such works are to God, and wishing them ever to do the cures with their own hands, and not to put them over to servants. Those that he finds busy in the works of their calling, he commendeth them also: for it is a good and just thing for every one to do their own business. But then he admonisheth them of two things; first that they dive not too deep into worldly affairs, plunging themselves over head and ears into carking and caring; but that they so labour, as neither to labour anxiously, nor distrustfully, nor profanely. Then they labour anxiously, when they overdo it, to the loss of their quiet and health: then distrustfully, when they doubt God's providence, thinking that their own labour is the cause of their thriving, as if it were in their own hands to thrive or not to thrive. Then they labour profanely, when they set themselves to work like brute beasts, never raising their thoughts to God, nor sanctifying their labour with daily prayer; when on the Lord's day they do unnecessary servile work, or in time of divine service on other holy days, except in the cases of extreme poverty, and in the seasons of seed-time and harvest. Secondly, he adviseth them so to labour for wealth and maintenance, as that they make not that the end of their labour, but that they may have wherewithal to serve God the better, and to do good deeds. After these discourses, if they be poor and needy whom he thus finds labouring, he gives them somewhat; and opens not only his mouth, but his purse to their relief, that so they go on more cheerfully in their vocation, and himself be ever the more welcome to them. Those that the Parson finds idle or ill-employed, he chides not at first, for that were neither civil nor profitable, but always in the close, before he departs from them; yet in this he distinguisheth, for if he be a plain countryman, he reproves him plainly; for they are not sensible of fineness; if they be of higher quality, they commonly are quick, and sensible, and very tender of reproof; and therefore he lays his discourse so, that he comes to the point very leisurely, and oftentimes, as Nathan did, in the person of another, making them to reprove themselves. However, one way or other, he ever reproves them, that he may keep himself pure, and not be entangled in others' sins. Neither in this doth he forbear, though there be company by: for as when, the offence is particular, and against me, I am to follow our Saviour's rule, and to take my brother aside, and reprove him; so when the offence is public, and against God,. I am then to follow the apostle's rule, 1 Timothy v. 20, and to rebuke openly that which is done openly. Besides these occasional discourses, the Parson questions what order is kept in the house, as about prayers, morning and evening on their knees, reading of Scripture, catechizing, singing of psalms at their work on holy days: who can read, who not; and sometimes he hears the children read himself, and blesseth, encouraging also the servants to learn to read, and offering to have them taught on holy days by his servants. If the Parson were ashamed of particularizing in these things, he were not fit to be a Parson; but he holds the rule, that nothing is little in God's service; if it once have the honour of that name, it grows great instantly. Wherefore neither disdaineth he to enter into the poorest cottage, though he even creep into it, and though it smell never so loathsomely. For both God is there also, and those for whom God died: and so much the rather doth he so, as his access to the poor is more comfortable than to the rich; and in regard of himself, it is more humiliation. These are the Parson's general aims in his circuit; but with these he mingles other discourses for conversation sake, and to make his higher purposes slip the more easily.

CHAPTER XV. THE PARSON COMFORTING.

The country Parson, when any of his cure is sick, or afflicted with loss of friend, or estate, or any ways distressed, fails not to afford his best comforts, and rather goes to them than sends for the afflicted, though they can and otherwise ought to come to him. To this end he hath thoroughly digested all the points of consolation, as having continual use of them, such as are from God's general providence extended even to lilies; from his particular, to his Church; from his promises; from the example of all saints that ever were: from Christ himself, perfecting our redemption no other way than by sorrow; from the benefit of affliction, which softens and works the stubborn heart of man; from the certainty both of deliverance and reward, if we faint not; from the miserable comparison of the moments of griefs here with the weight of joys hereafter. Besides this, in his visiting the sick, or otherwise afflicted, he followeth the Church's counsel, namely, in persuading them to particular confession; labouring to make them understand the great good use of this ancient and pious ordinance, and how necessary it is in some cases: he also urgeth them to do some pious charitable works, as a necessary evidence and fruit of their faith, at that time especially: the participation of the holy sacrament, how comfortable and sovereign a medicine it is to all sin-sick souls; what strength, and joy, and peace it administers against all temptations, even to death itself, he plainly and generally intimateth to the disaffected or sick person, that so the hunger and thirst after it may come rather from themselves than from his persuasion.

CHAPTER XVI. THE PARSON A FATHER.[9]

The country Parson is not only a father to his flock, but also professeth himself thoroughly of the opinion, carrying; it about with him as fully as if he had begot his whole parish. And of this he makes great use. For by this means, when any sins, he hateth him not as an officer, but pities him as a father: and even in those wrongs which either in tithing or otherwise are done to his own person, he considers the offender as a child, and forgives, so he may have any sign of amendment; so also, when, after many admonitions, any continue to be refractory, yet he gives him not over, but is long before he proceed to disinheriting, or perhaps never goes so far; knowing that some are called at the eleventh

---

[9] "Sir, the life of a parson, of a conscientious clergyman, is not easy. I have always considered a clergyman as the father of a larger family than he is able to maintain."—Johnson by Croker, vii. 152.

hour, and therefore he still expects, and waits, lest he should determine God's hour of coming; which as he cannot, touching the last day, so neither touching the intermediate days of conversion.

CHAPTER XVII. THE PARSON IN JOURNEY.

The country Parson, when a just occasion calleth him out of his parish (which he diligently and strictly weigheth, his parish being all his joy and thought), leaveth not his ministry behind him; but is himself wherever he is. Therefore those he meets on the way he blesseth audibly, and with those he overtakes, or that overtake him, he begins good discourses, such as may edify, interposing some short and honest refreshments, which may make his other discourses more welcome and less tedious. And when he comes to his inn, he refuseth not to join, that he may enlarge the glory of God to the company he is in, by a due blessing of God for their safe arrival, and saying grace at meat, and at going to bed by giving the host notice, that he will have prayers in the hall, wishing him to inform his guests thereof, that if any be willing to partake, they may resort thither. The like he doth in the morning, using pleasantly the outlandish proverb, that prayers and provender never hinder journey. When he comes to any other house, where his kindred or other relations give him any authority over the family, if he be to stay for a time, he considers diligently the state thereof to God-ward, and that in two points: First, what disorders there are either in apparel, or diet, or too open a buttery, or reading vain books, or swearing, or breeding up children to no calling, but in idleness, or the like. Secondly, what means of piety, whether daily prayers be used, grace, reading of Scriptures, and other good books; how Sundays, holydays, and fasting days are kept. And accordingly, as he finds any defect in these, he first considers with himself, what kind of remedy fits the temper of the house best, and then he faithfully and boldly applieth it, yet seasonably and discreetly, by taking aside the lord or lady, or master or mistress of the house, and shewing them clearly, that they respect them most who wish them best, and that not a desire to meddle with others' affairs, but the earnestness to do all the good he can, mores him to say thus and thus.

CHAPTER XVIII. THE PARSON IN SENTINEL.

The country Parson, wherever he is, keeps God's watch; that is, there is nothing spoken or done in the company where he is, but comes under his test and censure: if it be well spoken or done, he takes occasion to commend and enlarge it; if ill, he presently lays hold of it, lest the poison steal into some young and unwary spirits, and possess them even before they themselves heed it. But this he doth discreetly, with mollifying and suppling words: This was not so well said, as it might have been forborne; we cannot allow this, or else the thing will admit interpretation; your meaning is not thus, but thus; or, so far indeed what you say is true, and well said; but this will not stand: this is called keeping God's watch, when the baits which the enemy lays in company are discovered and avoided: this is to be on God's side, and be true to his party. Besides, if he perceive in company any discourse tending to ill, either by the wickedness or quarrelsomeness thereof, he either prevents it judiciously, or breaks it off seasonably by some diversion. Wherein a pleasantness of disposition is of great use, men being willing to sell the interest and engagement of their discourses for no price sooner than that of mirth;[10] whether the nature of man, loving refreshment, gladly betakes itself, even to the loss of honour.

CHAPTER XIX. THE PARSON IN REFERENCE.

The country Parson is sincere and upright in all his relations. And first, he is just to his country; as when he is set at an armour, or horse, he borrows them not to serve the turn, nor provides slight and unuseful, but such as are every way fitting to do his country true and laudable service, when occasion requires. To do otherwise is deceit, and therefore not for him who is hearty and true in all his ways, as being the servant of Him in whom there was no guile. Likewise in any other country duty, he considers what is the end of any command, and then he suits things faithfully according to that end. Secondly, he carries himself very respectfully as to all the Fathers of the Church, so especially to his diocesan, honouring him both in word and behaviour, and resorting unto him in any difficulty, either in his studies or in his parish. He observes visitations, and being there, makes due use of them, as of clergy councils, for the benefit of the diocese. And therefore before he comes, having observed some defects in the ministry, he then either in sermon, if he preach, or at some other time of the day, propounds among his brethren what were fitting to be done. Thirdly, he keeps good correspondence with all the neighbouring pastors round about him, performing for them any ministerial office, which is not to the prejudice of his own parish. Likewise he welcomes to his house any minister, how poor or mean soever, with as joyful a countenance as if he were to entertain some great lord. Fourthly, he fulfils the duty and debt of neighbourhood to all the parishes which are near him. For the apostle's rule (Philip. iv.) being admirable and large, that "we should do whatsoever things are honest, or just, or pure, or lovely, or of good report, if there be any virtue, or any praise;" and neighbourhood being ever reputed, even among the heathen, as an obligation to do good, rather than to those that are further, where things are otherwise equal, therefore he satisfies this duty also. Especially if God have sent any calamity either by fire or famine, to any neighbouring parish, then he expects no brief, but taking his parish together the next Sunday, or holy-day, and exposing to them the uncertainty of human affairs, none knowing whose turn may be next; and then when he hath affrighted them with this, exposing the obligation of charity, and neighbourhood, he first gives himself liberally, and then incites them to give; making together a sum either to be sent, or, which were more comfortable, all together choosing some fit day to carry it themselves, and cheer the afflicted. So, if any neighbouring village be overburdened with poor, and his own less charged, he finds some way of relieving it, and reducing the manna and bread of charity to some equality, representing to his people, that the blessing of God to them ought to make them the more charitable, and not the less, lest he cast their neighbours' poverty on them also.

---

[10] As in water face answereth to face, so the heart of man to man."—Proverbs xxvii. 17.

CHAPTER XX. THE PARSON IN GOD'S STEAD.

The country Parson is in God's stead to his parish, and dischargeth God what he can of his promises, wherefore there is nothing done, either well or ill, whereof he is not the rewarder or punisher. If he chance to find any reading in another's Bible, he provides him one of his own. If he find another giving a poor man a penny, he gives him a tester[11] for it, if the giver be fit to receive it; or if he be of a condition above such gifts, he sends him a good book, or easeth him in his tithes, telling him, when he hath forgotten it, This I do, because at such and such a time you were charitable. This is in some sort a discharging of God; as concerning this life, who hath promised, that godliness shall be gainful: but in the other, God is his own immediate paymaster, rewarding all good deeds to their full proportion. "The Parson's punishing of sin and vice is rather by withdrawing his bounty and courtesy from the parties offending, or by private or public reproof, as the case requires, than by causing them to be presented, or otherwise complained of. And yet, as the malice of the person, or heinousness of the crime may be, he is careful to see condign punishment inflicted, and with truly godly zeal, without hatred to the person, hungreth and thirsteth after righteous punishment of unrighteousness. Thus both in rewarding virtue, and in punishing vice, the Parson endeavoureth to be in God's stead, knowing that country people are drawn or led by sense, more than by faith; by present rewards or punishments, more than by future."

CHAPTER XXI. THE PARSON'S CATECHISING.[12]

The country Parson values catechising highly: For there being three points of his duty; the one, to infuse a competent knowledge of salvation in every one of his flock; the other, to multiply and build up this knowledge to a spiritual temple; the third, to inflame this knowledge, to press, and drive it to practice, turning it to reformation of life, by pithy and lively exhortations; catechising is the first point, and but by catechising, the other cannot be attained. Besides, whereas in sermons there is a kind of state, in catechising there is an humbleness very suitable to Christian regeneration; which exceedingly delights him as by way of exercise upon himself, and by way of preaching to himself, for the advancing of his own mortification: For in preaching to others, he forgets not himself, but is first a sermon to himself, and then to others; growing with the growth of his parish. He useth and preferreth the ordinary Church Catechism, partly for obedience to authority, partly for uniformity sake, that the same common truths may be everywhere professed, especially since many remove from parish to parish, who, like Christian soldiers, are to give the word, and to satisfy the congregation by their catholic answers. He exacts of all the doctrine of the Catechism; of the younger sort, the very words; of the elder, the substance.[13] Those he catechiseth publicly, these privately, giving age honour, according

---

[11] The value of a "tester" or 'testorne' was sixpence. The word is of frequent occurrence in old authors, from the days of Latimer to those of Bunyan. Shakespeare often uses it.

[12] And he (Herbert) then made it his humble request that they (his parishioners at Bemerton) would be constant to the afternoon's sermon and catechising, and shewed them convincing reasons why he desired it; and his obliging example and persuasions brought them to a willing conformity to his desires."—WALTON'S Life of HERBERT.

[13] "It is a great error to think that the Catechism was made for children only: for all Christians are equally concerned in those saving truths which are there taught; and the doctrine delivered in the Catechism is as proper for the study, and as necessary for the salvation of a great doctor, as of a weak Christian, or a young child."—

to the apostle's rule, 1 Tim. v. 1. He requires all to be present at catechising: First, for the authority of the work; secondly, that parents and masters, as they hear the answers prove, may, when they come home, either commend or reprove, either reward or punish. Thirdly, that those of the elder sort, who are not well grounded, may then, by an honourable way, take occasion to be better instructed. Fourthly, that those who are well grounded in the knowledge of religion may examine their grounds, renew their vows, and by occasion of both, enlarge their meditations. When once all have learned the words of the Catechism, he thinks it the most useful way that a pastor can take, to go over the same, but in other words: for many say the Catechism by rote, as parrots, without ever piercing into the sense of it. In this course the order of the Catechism would be kept, but the rest varied: as thus, in the Creed: How came this world to be as it is? Was it made, or came it by chance? Who made it? Did you see God make it? Then are there some things to be believed that are not seen? Is this the nature of belief? Is not Christianity full of such things, as are not to be seen, but believed? You said, God made the world; Who is God? And so forward, requiring answers to all these, and helping and cherishing the answerer, by making the questions very plain with comparisons, and making much even of a word of truth from him. This order being used to one, would be a little varied to another. And this is an admirable way of teaching, wherein the catechised will at length find delight, and by which the catechizer, if he once get the skill of it, will draw out of ignorant and silly souls, even the dark and deep points of religion. Socrates did thus in philosophy, who held that the seeds of all truth lay in every body, and accordingly, by questions well ordered, he found philosophy in silly tradesmen. That position will not hold in Christianity, because it contains things above nature: but after that the Catechism is once learned, that which nature is towards philosophy, the Catechism is towards divinity. To this purpose, some dialogues in Plato were worth the reading, where the singular dexterity of Socrates in this kind may be observed and imitated. Yet the skill consists but in these three points: First, an aim and mark of the whole discourse, whither to drive the answerer, which the questionist must have in his mind before any question be propounded, upon which and to which the questions are to be chained. Secondly, a most plain and easy framing the question, even containing, in virtue, the answer also, especially to the more ignorant. Thirdly, when the answerer sticks, an illustrating the thing by something else, which he knows, making what he knows to serve him in that which he knows not: as, when the parson once demanded, after other questions about man's misery; since man is so miserable, what is to be done? And the answerer could not tell; he asked him again, what he would do if he were in a ditch? This familiar illustration made the answer so plain, that he was even ashamed of his ignorance; for he could not but say, he would haste out of it as fast as he could. Then he proceeded to ask, whether he could get out of the ditch alone, or whether he needed a helper, and who was that helper. This is the skill, and doubtless the holy Scripture intends thus much, when it condescends to the naming of a plough, a hatchet, a bushel, leaven, boys piping and dancing; shewing that things of ordinary use are not only to serve in the way of drudgery, but to be washed and cleansed, and serve for lights even of heavenly truths. This is the practice which, the Parson so much commends to all his fellow-labourers; the secret of whose good consists in this, that at sermons and prayers men may sleep or wander, but when one is asked a question, he must discover what he is. This practice exceeds even sermons in teaching: But there being two things in sermons, the one informing, the other inflaming; as sermons

---

Bishop Ken's Exposition, Prose Works (Round), p. 339 (quoted by Mr. Wilmott in his edition of Herbert.)

come short of questions in the one, so they far exceed them in the other. For questions cannot inflame or ravish; that must be done by a set, and laboured, and continued speech.

CHAPTER XXII. THE PARSON IN SACRAMENTS.

The country Parson being to administer the Sacraments, is at a stand with himself, how or what behaviour to assume for so holy things. Especially at communion times he is in a great confusion, as being not only to receive God, but to break and administer him. Neither finds he any issue in this, but to throw himself down at the throne of grace, saying, "Lord, thou knowest what thou didst, when thou appointedst it to be done thus; therefore do thou fulfil what thou didst appoint; for thou art not only the feast, but the way to it." At baptism, being himself in white, he requires the presence of all, and baptizeth not willingly, but on Sundays, or great days. He admits no vain or idle names, but such as are usual and accustomed.[14] He says that prayer with great devotion, where God is thanked for calling us to the knowledge of his grace, baptism being a blessing that the world hath not the like. He willingly and cheerfully crosseth the child, and thinketh the ceremony not only innocent but reverend. He instructeth the godfathers and godmothers, that it is no complimental or light thing to sustain that place, but a great honour, and no less burden, as being done both in the presence of God and his saints, and by way of undertaking for a Christian soul. He adviseth all to call to mind their baptism often; for if wise men have thought it the best way of preserving a state to reduce it to its principles by which it grew great; certainly it is the safest course for Christians also to meditate on their baptism often (being the first step into their great and glorious calling) and upon what terms and with what vows they were baptized. At the times of the holy communion, he first takes order with the church-wardens, that the elements be of the best, not cheap, or coarse, much less ill-tasted or unwholesome. Secondly, he considers and looks into the ignorance or carelessness of his flock, and accordingly applies himself with catechizings and lively exhortations, not on the Sunday of the communion only (for then it is too late), but the Sunday or Sundays before the communion, or on the eves of all those days. If there be any who having not received yet, is to enter into this great work, he takes the more pains with them, that he may lay the foundation of future blessings. The time of every one's first receiving is not so much by years as by understanding; particularly the rule may be this: When any one can distinguish the sacramental from common bread, knowing the institution, and the difference, he ought to receive, of what age soever. Children and youths are usually deferred too long, under pretence of devotion to the sacrament, but it is for want of instruction; their understandings being ripe enough for ill things, and why not then for better? But parents and masters should make haste in this, as to a great purchase for their children and servants; which while they defer, both sides suffer; the one, in wanting many excitings of grace, the other, in being worse served and obeyed. The saying of the catechism is necessary, but not enough; because to answer

---

[14] "Pride lives with all; strange names our rustics give
To helpless infants, that their own may live;
Pleased to be known, they'll some attention claim,
And find some by-way to the house of fame.
'Why Lonicera, wilt thou name thy child?'
I asked the gardener's wife in accents mild;
We have a right,' replied the sturdy dame;
And Lonicera was the infant's name."
Crabbe, quoted by Wilmott.

in form may still admit ignorance: but the questions must be propounded loosely and wildly, and then the answerer will discover what he is. Thirdly, for the manner of receiving, as the Parson useth all reverence himself, so he administers to none but to the reverent. The feast indeed requires sitting, because it is a feast; but man's unpreparedness asks kneeling. He that comes to the sacrament, hath the confidence of a guest, and he that kneels, confesseth himself an unworthy one, and therefore differs from other feasters; but he that sits or lies, puts up to an apostle: Contentiousness in a feast of charity is more scandal than any posture. Fourthly, touching the frequency of the communion, the Parson celebrates it, if not duly once a month, yet at least five or six times in the year; as at Easter, Christmas, Whitsuntide, before and after harvest, and the beginning of Lent. And this he doth, not only for the benefit of the work, but also for the discharge of the church-wardens, who being to present all that receive not thrice a year; if there be but three communions, neither can all the people so order their affairs as to receive just at those times, nor the church-wardens so well take notice who receive thrice, and who not.

CHAPTER XXIII. THE PARSON'S COMPLETENESS.

The country Parson desires to be all to his parish, and not only a pastor, but a lawyer also, and a physician. Therefore he endures not that any of his flock should go to law; but in any controversy, that they should resort to him as their judge. To this end, he hath gotten to himself some insight in things ordinarily incident and controverted, by experience, and by reading some initiatory treatises in the law, with Dalton's[15] Justice of Peace, and the Abridgments of the Statutes, as also by discourse with men of that profession, whom he hath ever some cases to ask, when he meets with them; holding that rule, that to put men to discourse of that, wherein they are most eminent, is the most gainful way of conversation. Yet whenever any controversy is brought to him, he never decides it alone; but sends for three or four of the ablest of the parish to hear the cause with him, whom he makes to deliver their opinion first; out of which he gathers, in case he be ignorant himself, what to hold; and so the thing passeth with more authority, and less envy; in judging he follows that which is altogether right: so that if the poorest man of the parish detain but a pin unjustly from the richest, he absolutely restores it as a judge; but when he hath so done, then he assumes the Parson, and exhorts to charity. Nevertheless, there may happen sometimes some cases, wherein he chooseth to permit his parishioners rather to make use of the law than himself: as in cases of an obscure and dark nature, not easily determinable by lawyers themselves; or in cases of high consequence, as establishing of inheritances: or lastly, when the persons are of a contentious disposition, and cannot be gained, but that they still fall from all compromises that have been made. But then he shews them how to go to law, even as brethren, and not as enemies, neither avoiding therefore one another's company, much less defaming one another. Now, as the Parson is in law, so is he in sickness also: if there be any of his flock sick, he is their physician, or at least his wife, of whom, instead of the qualities of the world, he asks no other, but to have the skill of healing a wound, or helping the sick. But if neither himself nor his wife have the skill, and his means serve, he keeps some young practitioner in his house for the benefit of his parish, whom yet he ever exhorts not to exceed his bounds, but in difficult cases to call in help. If all fail, then he keeps good correspondence with some neighbour physician, and entertains him for the

---

[15] Dalton, the compiler, nere referred to, was Dora 1554, and died about the breaking out of the Civil War.

cure of his parish. Yet it is easy for any scholar to attain to such a measure of physic, as may be of much use to him, both for himself and others. This is done by seeing one anatomy, reading one book of physic, having one herbal by him. And let Fernelius[16] be the physic author, for he writes briefly, neatly, and judiciously: especially let his method of physic be diligently perused, as being the practical part, and of most use. Now both the reading of him and the knowing of herbs may be done at such times as they may be a help and a recreation to more divine studies, nature serving grace both in comfort of diversion, and the benefit of application, when need requires: as also, by way of illustration, even as our Saviour made plants and seeds to teach the people: for he was the true householder, who bringeth out of his treasure things new and old; the old things of philosophy and the new of grace, and maketh the one serve the other. And I conceive our Saviour did this for three reasons: First, that by familiar things he might make his doctrine slip the more easily into the hearts even of the meanest. Secondly, that labouring people (whom he chiefly considered) might have every where monuments of his doctrine, remembering in gardens his mustard-seed and lilies; in the field his seed-corn and tares; and so not be drowned altogether in the works of their vocation, but sometimes lift up their minds to better things, even in the midst of their pains. Thirdly, that he might set a copy for Parsons. In the knowledge of simples, wherein the manifold wisdom of God is wonderfully to be seen, one thing should be carefully observed; which is to know what herbs may be used instead of drugs of the same nature, and to make the garden the shop: for home-bred medicines are both more easy for the Parson's purse, and more familiar for all men's bodies. So, where the apothecary useth either for loosing, rhubarb; or for binding, bolearmena, the Parson useth damask or white roses for the one, and plaintain, shepherd's purse, knot-grass, for the other, and that with better success. As for spices, he doth not only prefer home-bred things before them, but condemns them for vanities, and so shuts them out of his family, esteeming that there is no spice comparable for herbs, to rosemary, thyme, savory, mints; and for seeds, to fennel and carraway seeds. Accordingly for salves, his wife seeks not the city, but prefers her garden and fields, before all outlandish gums. And surely hyssop, valerian, mercury, adder's tongue, verrow, melilot, and St John's-wort, made into a salve; and elder, camomile, mallows, comphrey and smallage, made into a poultice, have done great and rare cures. In curing of any, the Parson and his family use to premise prayers, for this is to cure like a Parson, and this raiseth the action from the shop to the church. But though the parson sets forward all charitable deeds, yet he looks not in this point of curing beyond his own parish, except the person be so poor that he is not able to reward the physician: for as he is charitable, so he is just also. Now it is a justice and debt to the commonwealth he lives in, not to encroach on others professions, but to live on his own. And justice is the ground of charity.

CHAPTER XXIV. THE PARSON'S ARGUING.

The country Parson, if there be any of his parish that hold strange doctrines, useth all possible diligence to reduce them to the common faith. The first means he useth is prayer, beseeching the Father of lights to open their eyes, and to give him power so to fit his discourse to them, that it may effectually pierce their hearts and convert them. The second means is a very loving and sweet usage of them, both in going to and sending for

---

[16] John Francis Fernel, a famous physician, who flourished in France in the reign of Henry II.

them often, and in finding out courtesies to place on them; as in their tithes or otherwise. The third means is the observation, what is the main foundation and pillar of their cause, whereon they rely; as if he be a Papist, the church is the hinge he turns on; if a schismatic, scandal.[17] Wherefore the parson hath diligently examined these two with himself, as "What the church is; how it began; how it proceeded; whether it be a rule to itself; whether it hath a rule; whether having a rule, it ought not to be guided by it; whether any rule in the world be obscure; and how then should the best be so, at least in fundamental things; the obscurity in some points being the exercise of the church, the light in the foundations being the guide; the church needing both an evidence and an exercise. So for scandal: What scandal is; when given or taken; whether there being two precepts, one of obeying authority, the other of not giving scandal, that ought not to be preferred, especially since in disobeying there is scandal also: whether things once indifferent, being made by the precept of authority more than indifferent, it be in our power to omit or refuse them." These and the like points he hath accurately digested, having ever besides two great helps and powerful persuaders on his side; the one a strict religious life; the other an humble and ingenuous search of truth, being unmoved in arguing, and void of all contentiousness: which are two great lights able to dazzle the eyes of the misled, while they consider that God cannot be wanting to them in doctrine, to whom he is so gracious in life.

CHAPTER XXV. THE PARSON PUNISHING.

Whensoever the country Parson proceeds so far as to call in authority, and to do such things of legal opposition either in the presenting or punishing of any, as the vulgar ever construes for signs of ill-will: he forbears not in any wise to use the delinquent as before, in his behaviour and carriage towards him, not avoiding his company, or doing anything of averseness, save in the very act of punishment: neither doth he esteem him for an enemy, but as a brother still, except some small and temporary estrangeing may corroborate the punishment to a better subduing and humbling of the delinquent; which, if it happily take effect, he then comes on the faster, and makes so much the more of him, as before he alienated himself; doubling his regards, and shewing, by all means, that the delinquent's return is to his advantage.

CHAPTER XXVI. THE PARSON'S EYE.

The country Parson, at spare times from action, standing on a hill, and considering his flock, discovers two sorts of vices, and two sorts of vicious persons. There are some vices, whose natures are always clear and evident, as adultery, murder, hatred, lying, &c. There are other vices, whose natures, at least in the beginning, are dark and obscure; as covetousness and gluttony. So likewise there are some persons, who abstain not even from known sins; there are others who, when they know a sin evidently, they commit it not. It is true, indeed, they are long a knowing it, being partial to themselves, and witty to others who shall reprove them for it. A man may be both covetous and intemperate, and yet hear sermons against both, and himself condemn both in good earnest: and the reason hereof is, because the natures of these vices being not evidently discussed or known commonly, the beginnings of them are not easily observable: and the beginnings of them

---

[17] "Scandal" in its original sense signifies a "stumbling-block."

are not observed, because of the sudden passing from that which was just now lawful, to that which is presently unlawful, even in one continued action. So a man dining, eats at first lawfully; but proceeding on, comes to do unlawfully, even before he is aware; not knowing the bounds of the action, nor when his eating begins to be unlawful. So a man storing up money for his necessary provisions, both in present for his family and in future for his children, hardly perceives when his storing becomes unlawful: yet is there a period for his storing, and a point, or centre, when his storing, which was even now good, passeth from good to bad. Wherefore the Parson being true to his business, hath exactly sifted the definitions of all virtues and vices; especially canvassing those whose natures are most stealing, and beginnings uncertain. Particularly, concerning these two vices, not because they are all that are of this dark and creeping disposition, but for example sake, and because they are most common, he thus thinks: First, for Covetousness, he lays this ground: Whosoever, when a just occasion calls, either spends not at all, or not in some proportion to God's blessing upon him, is covetous. The reason of the ground is manifest, because wealth is given to that end, to supply our occasions. Now, if I do not give every thing its end, I abuse the creature; I am false to my reason which should guide me; I offend the supreme Judge, in perverting that order which he hath set both to things and to reason. The application of the ground would be infinite; but, in brief, a poor man is an occasion, my country is an occasion, my friend is an occasion, my table is an occasion, my apparel is an occasion: if in all these, and those more which concern me, I either do nothing, or pinch and scrape, and squeeze blood indecently to the station wherein God hath placed me, I am covetous. More particularly, and to give one instance for all, if God have given me servants, and I either provide too little for them, or that which is unwholesome, being sometimes baned meat, sometimes too salt, and so not competent nourishment, I am covetous. I bring this example, because men usually think, that servants for their money are as other things that they buy, even as a piece of wood, which they may cut, or hack, or throw into the fire; and so they pay them their wages, all is well. Nay, to descend yet more particularly, if a man have wherewithal to buy a spade, and yet he chooseth rather to use his neighbour's, and wear out that, he is covetous. Nevertheless, few bring covetousness thus low, or consider it so narrowly, which yet ought to be done, since "there is a justice in the least things, and for the least there shall be a judgment." Country people are full of these petty injustices, being cunning to make use of another and spare themselves: And scholars ought to be diligent in the observation of these, and driving of their general school-rules ever to the smallest actions of life; which while they dwell in their books, they will never find; but being seated in the country, and doing their duty faithfully, they will soon discover: especially if they carry their eyes ever open, and fix them on their charge, and not on their preferment. Secondly, for gluttony, the Parson lays this ground: he that either for quantity eats more than his health or employments will bear, or for quality is lickerish after dainties, is a glutton; as he that eats more than his estate will bear, is a prodigal: and he that eats offensively to the company, either in his order, or length of eating, is scandalous and uncharitable. These three rules generally comprehend the faults of "eating, and the truth of them needs no proof: so that men must eat, neither to the disturbance of their health nor of their affairs, which, being overburdened or studying dainties too much, they cannot well dispatch), nor of their estate, nor of their brethren." One act in these things is bad, but it is the custom and habit that names a glutton. Many think they are more at liberty than they are, as if they were masters of their health, and so they will stand to the pain, all is well. But to eat to one's hurt comprehends, besides the hurt, an act against reason, because it is unnatural to hurt oneself; and this they are not masters of. Yet of hurtful things, I am more bound to abstain from those which by my own experience I have found hurtful, than from those which by a common tradition and vulgar knowledge are reputed to be so. That which is said of hurtful meats extends to hurtful drinks also. As for the quantity, touching our employments, none must eat so as to disable themselves from a fit discharging either of Divine duties, or duties of their calling. So that if after dinner they are not fit (or unwieldy) either to pray, or work, they are gluttons. Not that all must presently work after dinner, for they rather must not work (especially students, and those that are weakly); but that they must rise so, as that it is not meat or drink that hinders them from working. To guide them in this, there are three rules: First, the custom and knowledge of their own body, and what it can well digest: the second, the feeling of themselves in time of eating, which, because it is deceitful (for one thinks in eating, that he can eat more than afterwards he finds true): the third is the observation with what appetite they sit down. This last rule, joined with the first, never fails. For knowing what one usually can well digest, and feeling when I go to meat in what disposition I am, either hungry or not, according as I feel myself, either I take my wonted proportion or diminish of it. Yet physicians bid those that would live in health, not keep a uniform diet, but to feed variously, now more, now less: and Gerson,[18] a spiritual man, wisheth all to incline rather to too much than to too little; his reason is, because diseases of exinanition are more dangerous than diseases of repletion. But the Parson distinguisheth according to his double aim, either of abstinence a moral virtue, or mortification a divine. When he deals with any that is heavy and carnal, he gives him those freer rules; but when he meets with a refined and heavenly disposition, he carries them higher, even sometimes to a forgetting of themselves, knowing that there is one who, when they forget, remembers for them; as when the people hungered and thirsted after our Saviour's doctrine, and tarried so long at it, that they would have fainted had they returned empty, he suffered it not; but rather made food miraculously, than suffered so good desires to miscarry.

CHAPTER XXVII. THE PARSON IN MIRTH.

The country Parson is generally sad, because he knows nothing but the Cross of Christ, his mind being defixed on it, with those nails wherewith his Master was: or if he have any leisure to look off from thence, he meets continually with two most sad spectacles, sin and misery; God dishonoured every day, and man affiicted. Nevertheless, he sometimes refresheth himself, as knowing that nature will not bear everlasting droopings, and that pleasantness of disposition is a great key to do good; not only because all men shun the company of perpetual severity, but also for that when they are in company, instructions seasoned with pleasantness both enter sooner and root deeper. Where-fore he condescends to human frailties both in himself and others; and intermingles some mirth in his discourses occasionally, according to the pulse of the hearer.

---

[18] Surnamed "The Most Christian Doctor." His works were edited by Du Pin, in five volumes.

CHAPTER XXVIII. THE PARSON IN CONTEMPT.

The country Parson knows well, that both for the general ignominy which is cast upon the profession, and much more for those rules which, out of his choicest judgment, he hath resolved to observe, and which are described in this book, he must be despised; because this has been the portion of God his Master, and of God's saints his brethren, and this is foretold, that it shall be so, until things be no more. Nevertheless, according to the apostle's rule, he endeavours that none shall despise him; especially in his own parish, he suffers it not to his utmost power; for that, where contempt is, there is no room for instruction. This he procures, first, by his holy and unblameable life; which carries a reverence with it, even above contempt. Secondly, by a courteous carriage and winning behaviour: he that will be respected, must respect; doing kindnesses, but receiving none; at least of those who are apt to despise: for this argues a height and eminency of mind, which is not easily despised, except it degenerate to pride. Thirdly, by a bold and impartial reproof, even of the best in the parish, when occasion requires: for this may produce hatred in those that are reproved, but never contempt either in them or others.[1] Lastly, if the contempt shall proceed so far as to do any thing punishable by law, as contempt is apt to do, if it be not thwarted, the Parson having a due respect both to the person and to the cause, referreth the whole matter to the examination and punishment of those which are in authority; that so the sentence lighting upon one, the example may reach to all. But if the contempt be not punishable by law, or being so, the parson think it in his discretion either unfit or bootless to contend, then when any despises him he takes it either in an humble way, saying nothing at all, or else in a slighting way, shewing that reproaches touch him no more than a stone thrown against heaven, where he is, and lives; or in a sad way, grieved at his own and others' sins, which continually break God's laws, and dishonour him with those mouths which he continually fills and feeds: or else, in a doctrinal way, saying to the contemner, Alas, why do you thus? you hurt yourself, not me; he that throws a stone at another, hits himself; and so, between gentle reasoning and pitying, he overcomes the evil: or lastly, in a triumphant way, being glad and joyful that he is made conformable to his Master; and being in the world as he was, hath this undoubted pledge of his salvation. These are the five shields wherewith the godly receive the darts of the wicked; leaving anger, and retorting, and revenge, to the children of the world, whom another's ill mastereth, and leadeth captive without any resistance, even in resistance to the same destruction. For while they resist the person that reviles, they resist not the evil which takes hold of them, and is far the worst enemy.

CHAPTER XXIX. THE PARSON WITH HIS CHURCH WARDENS.

The country Parson doth often, both publickly and privately, instruct his church-wardens what a great charge lies upon them, and that indeed the whole order and discipline of the parish is put into their hands. If himself reform any thing, it is out of the overflowing of his conscience, whereas they are to do it by command and by oath. Neither hath the place its dignity from the ecclesiastical laws only, since even by the common statute-law they are taken for a kind of corporation, as being persons enabled by that name to take moveable goods or chattels, and to sue and to be sued at law concerning such goods, for the use and profit of their parish: and by the same law they are to levy penalties for negligence in resorting to church, or for disorderly carriage in time of divine service. Wherefore the parson suffers not the place to be vilified or debased, by being cast on the lower rank of people; but invites and urges the best unto it, shewing that they do not lose or go less, but gain by it; it being the greatest honour of this world to do God and his chosen service; or as David says, to be even a door-keeper in the house of God. Now the canons being the church-warden's rule, the Parson adviseth them to read or hear them often, as also the visitation articles, which are grounded upon the canons, that so they may know their duty and keep their oath the better; in which regard, considering the great consequence of their place, and more of their oath, he wisheth them by no means to spare any, though never so great; but if after gentle and neighbourly admonitions, they still persist in ill, to present them; yea though they be tenants, or otherwise engaged to the delinquent: for their obligation to God and their own soul is above any temporal tie. Do well and right, and let the world sink.

CHAPTER XXX. THE PARSON'S CONSIDERATION OF PROVIDENCE.

The country Parson, considering the great aptness country people have to think that all things come by a kind of natural course, and that if they sow and soil their grounds, they must have corn, if they keep and fodder well their cattle, they must have milk and calves, labours to reduce them to see God's hand in all things, and to believe that things are not set in such an inevitable order, but that God often changeth it according as he sees fit, either for reward or punishment. To this end he represents to his flock that God hath and exerciseth a threefold power in every thing which concerns man. The first is a sustaining power; the second a governing power; the third a spiritual power. By his sustaining power he preserves and actuates every thing in his being; so that corn doth not grow by any other virtue than by that which he continually supplies, as the corn needs it; without which supply the corn would instantly dry up, as a river would if the fountain were stopped. And it is observable that if any thing could presume of an inevitable course and constancy in their operations, certainly it should be either the sun in heaven or the fire on earth, by reason of their fierce, strong, and violent natures; yet when God pleased the sun stood still, the fire burned not. By God's governing power he preserves and orders the references of things one to the other, so that though the corn do grow and be preserved in that act by his sustaining power, yet if he suit not other things to the growth, as seasons and weather, and other accidents, by his governing power, the fairest harvests come to nothing. And it is observable that God delights to have men feel and acknowledge and reverence his power, and therefore he often overturns things when they are thought past danger; that is his time of interposing: as when a merchant hath a ship come home after many a storm, which it hath escaped, he destroys it sometimes in the very haven; or if the goods be housed, a fire hath broken forth, and suddenly consumed them. Now this he doth that men should perpetuate and not break off their acts of dependence, how fair soever the opportunities present themselves. So that if a farmer should depend upon God all the year, and being ready to put hand to sickle, shall then secure himself, and think all cock sure; then God sends such weather as lays the corn and destroys it: or if he depend on God further, even till he inbarn his corn, and then think all sure, God sends a fire and consumes all that he hath: for that he ought not to break off, but to continue his dependence on God, not only before the corn is inned, but after also; and, indeed, to depend and fear continually. The third power is spiritual, by which God turns all outward blessings to inward advantages. So that if a farmer hath both a fair harvest, and that also well inned and inbarned, and continuing safe there; yet if God give him not the grace to use and utter this well, all his advantages are to his loss. Better were his corn burnt than not spiritually improved. And it is observable in this, how God's goodness strives with man's refractoriness. Man would sit down at this world; God bids him sell it, and purchase a better. Just as a father who hath in his hand an apple, and a piece of gold under it; the child comes, and with pulling, gets the apple out of his father's hand: his father bids him throw it away, and he will give him the gold for it, which the child utterly refusing, eats it, and is troubled with worms: so is the carnal and wilful man with the worm of the grave in this world, and the worm of conscience in the next.

CHAPTER XXXI. THE PARSON IN LIBERTY.

The country Parson observing the manifold wiles of Satan (who plays his part sometimes in drawing God's servants from him, sometimes in perplexing them in the service of God) stands fast in the liberty wherewith Christ hath made us free. This liberty he compasseth by one distinction, and that is, of what is necessary, and what is additionary. As, for example, it is necessary that all Christians should pray twice a day, every day of the week, and four times on Sunday, if they be well. This is so necessary and essential to a Christian, that he cannot without this maintain himself in a Christian state. Besides this, the godly have ever added some hours of prayer, as at nine, or at three, or at midnight, or as they think fit and see cause, or rather as God's Spirit leads them. But these prayers are not necessary, but additionary. Now it so happens, that the godly petitioner, upon some emergent interruption in the day, or by oversleeping himself at night, omits his additionary prayer. Upon this his mind begins to be perplexed and troubled, and Satan, who knows the exigent, blows the fire, endeavouring to disorder the Christian, and put him out of his station, and to enlarge the perplexity, until it spread and taint his other duties of piety, which none can perform so well in trouble as in calmness. Here the Parson interposeth with his distinction, and shews the perplexed Christian, that this prayer being additionary, not necessary, taken in, not commanded, the omission thereof upon just occasion ought by no means to trouble him. God knows the occasion as well as he, and he is a gracious Father, who more accepte a common course of devotion than dislikes an occasional interruption. And of this he is so to assure himself as to admit no scruple, but to go on as cheerfully as if he had not been interrupted. By this it is evident that the distinction is of singular use and comfort, especially to pious minds, which are ever tender and delicate. But here there are two cautions to be added. First, that this interruption proceed not out of slackness or coldness, which will appear if the pious soul foresee and prevent such interruptions, what he may, before they come, and when for all that they do come, he be a little affected therewith, but not afflicted or troubled; if he resent it to a mislike, but not a grief. Secondly, that this interruption proceed not out of shame. As, for example, a godly man, not out of superstition but of reverence to God's house, resolves whenever he enters into a church to kneel down and pray, either blessing God that he will be pleased to dwell among men, or beseeching him, that whenever he repairs to his house, he may behave himself so as befits so great a presence; and this briefly. But it happens that near the place where he is to pray, he spies some scoffing ruffian, who is likely to deride him for his pains: if he now shall, either for fear or shame, break his custom, he shall do passing ill; so much the rather ought he to proceed, as that by this he may take into his prayer humiliation also. On the other side, if I am to visit the sick in haste, and my nearest way lie through the church, I will not doubt to go without staying to pray there (but only, as I pass, in my heart) because this kind of prayer is additionary, not necessary, and the other duty overweighs it: so that if any scruple arise, I will throw it away, and be most confident that God is not displeased. This distinction may run through all Christian duties, and it is a great stay and settling to religious souls.

CHAPTER XXXII. THE PARSON'S SURVEYS.

The country Parson hath not only taken a particular survey of the faults of his own parish, but a general also of the diseases of the time, that so, when his occasions carry him abroad, or bring strangers to him, he may be the better armed to encounter them. The great and national sin of this land he esteems to be idleness; great in itself, and great in consequence: for when men have nothing to do, then they fall to drink, to steal, to whore, to scoff, to revile, to all sorts of gamings. "Come," say they, "we have nothing to do, let's go to the tavern, or to the stews," or what not. Wherefore the Parson strongly opposeth this sin, wheresoever he goes. And because idleness is twofold, the one in having no calling, the other in walking carelessly in our calling, he first represents to every body the necessity of a vocation. The reason of this assertion is taken from the nature of man, wherein God hath placed two great instruments, reason in the soul, and a hand in the body, as engagements of working, so that even in Paradise man had a calling; and how much more out of Paradise, when the evils which he is now subject unto may be prevented or diverted by reasonable employment? Besides, every gift or ability is a talent to be accounted for, and to be improved to our Master's advantage. Yet it is also a debt to our country to have a calling; and it concerns the commonwealth that none should be idle, but all busied. Lastly, riches are the blessing of God, and the great instrument of doing admirable good; therefore all are to procure them honestly and seasonably when they are not better employed. Now this reason crosseth not our Saviour's precept of selling what we have, because when we have sold all, and given it to the poor, we must not be idle, but labour to get more, that we may give more; according to St Paul's rule, Ephesians iv. 28, 1 Thessalonians iv. 11, 12. So that our Saviour's selling is so far from crossing Saint Paul's working, that it rather establisheth it, since they that have nothing are fittest to work. Now because the only opposer to this doctrine is the gallant, who is witty enough to abuse both others and himself, and who is ready to ask if he shall mend shoes, or what he shall do; therefore the Parson, unmoved, sheweth that ingenuous and fit employment is never wanting to those that seek it. But if it should be, the assertion stands thus: all are either to have a calling, or prepare for it: he that hath or can have yet no employment, if he truly and seriously prepare for it, he is safe and within bounds. Wherefore all are either presently to enter into a calling, if they be fit for it and it for them, or else to examine with care and advice what they are fittest for, and to prepare for that with all diligence. But it will not be amiss in this exceeding useful point to descend to particulars; for exactness lies in particulars. Men are either single or married; the married and housekeeper hath his hands full, if he do what he ought to do. For there are two branches of his affairs; first, the improvement of his family, by bringing them up in the fear and nurture of the Lord; and secondly, the improvement of his grounds, by drowning, or amning, or stocking, or fencing, and ordering his land to the best advantage both of himself and his neighbours. The Italians say, None fouls his hand in his own business; and it is an honest and just care, so it exceed not bounds, for every one to employ himself to the advancement of his affairs, that he may have wherewithal to do good. But his family is his best care, to labour Christian souls, and raise them to their height, even to heaven: to dress and prune them, and take as much joy in a straight-growing child, or servant, as a gardener doth in a choice tree. Could men find out this delight, they would seldom be from home; whereas now, of any place they are least there. But if after all this care well dispatched, the housekeeper's family be so small, and his dexterity so great, that he have leisure to look out, the village or parish which either he lives in or is near unto it is his employment. He considers every one there, and either helps them in particular, or hath general propositions to the whole town or hamlet, of advancing the public stock, and managing commons or woods, according as the place suggests. But if he may be of the commission of peace, there is nothing to that: no commonwealth in the world hath a braver institution than that of justices of the peace: for it is both a security to the king, who hath so many dispersed officers at his beck throughout the kingdom, accountable for the public good, and also an honourable employment of a gentle or nobleman in the country he lives in, enabling him with power to do good, and to restrain all those who else might both trouble him and the whole state. Wherefore it behoves all who are come to the gravity and ripeness of judgment for so excellent a place, not to refuse, but rather to procure it. And whereas there are usually three objections made against the place; the one, the abuse of it, by taking petty country bribes; the other, the casting of it on mean persons, especially in some shires; and lastly, the trouble of it. These are so far from deterring any good men from the place, that they kindle them rather to redeem the dignity either from true faults or unjust aspersions. Now, for single men, they are either heirs, or younger brothers: the heirs are to prepare in all the fore-mentioned points against the time of their practice. Therefore they are to mark their father's discretion in ordering his house and affairs; and also elsewhere, when they see any remarkable point of education or good husbandry, and to transplant it in time to his own home, with the same care as others, when they meet with good fruit, get a graft of the tree, enriching their orchard, and neglecting their house. Besides, they are to read books of law and justice; especially the Statutes at large. As for better books of divinity, they are not in this consideration, because we are about a calling and a preparation thereunto. But chiefly, and above all things, they are to frequent sessions and assizes; for it is both an honour which they owe to the reverend judges and magistrates to attend them at least in their shire, and it is a great advantage to know the practice of the land, for our law is practice. Sometimes he may go to court, as the eminent place both of good and ill. At other times he is to travel over the king's dominions, cutting out the kingdom into portions, which every year he surveys piece-meal. When there is a parliament, he is to endeavour by all means to be a knight or burgess there; for there is no school to a parliament. And when he is there, he must not only be a morning man, but at committees also; for there the particulars are exactly discussed, which are brought from thence to the house but in general. When none of these occasions call him abroad, every morning that he is at home he must either ride the great horse, or exercise some of his military postures. For all gentlemen that are now weakened, and disarmed with sedentary lives, are to know the use of their arms: and as the husbandman labours for them, so must they fight for and defend them when occasion calls. This is the duty of each to other, which they ought to fulfil: and the Parson is a lover and exciter to justice in all things, even as John the Baptist squared out to every one (even to soldiers) what to do. As for younger brothers, those whom the Parson finds loose, and not engaged in some profession by their parents, whose neglect in this point is intolerable, and a shameful wrong both to the commonwealth and their own house; to them, after he hath shewed the unlawfulness of spending the day in dressing, complimenting, visiting, and sporting, he first commends the study of the civil law, as a brave and wise knowledge, the professors whereof were much employed by Queen

Elizabeth, because it is the key of commerce, and discovers the rules of foreign nations. Secondly, he commends the mathematics as the only wonder-working knowledge, and therefore requiring the best spirits. After the several knowledge of these, he adviseth to insist and dwell chiefly on the two noble branches thereof, of fortification and navigation; the one being useful to all countries, and the other especially to islands. But if the young gallant think these courses dull and phlegmatic, where can he busy himself better than in those new plantations and discoveries, which are not only a noble, but also, as they may be handled, a religious employment? or let him travel into Germany and France, and observing the artifices and manufacturers there, transplant them hither, as divers have done lately, to our country's advantage.

CHAPTER XXXIII. THE PARSON'S LIBRARY.

The country Parson's library is a holy life: for besides the blessing that that brings upon it, there being a promise, that if the kingdom of God be first sought, all other things shall be added, even itself is a sermon. For the temptations with which a good man is beset, and the ways which he used to overcome them, being told to another, whether in private conference or in the church, are a sermon. He that hath considered how to carry himself at table about his appetite, if he tell this to another, preacheth, and much more feelingly and judiciously than he writes his rules of temperance out of books. So that the Parson having studied and mastered all his lusts and affections within, and the whole army of temptations without, hath ever so many sermons ready penned as he hath victories. And it fares in this as it doth in physic: he that hath been sick of a consumption, and knows what recovered him, is a physician, so far as he meets with the same disease and temper: and can much better and particularly do it than he that it is generally learned, and was never sick. And if the same person had been sick of all diseases, and were recovered of all, by things that he knew, there were no such physician as he, both for skill and tenderness. Just so it is in divinity, and that not without manifest reason: for though the temptations may be diverse in divers Christians, yet the victory is alike in all, being by the self-same spirit. Neither is this true only in the military state of a Christian life, but even in the peaceable also; when the servant of God, freed for a while from temptation, in a quiet sweetness seeks how to please his God. Thus the Parson considering that repentance is the great virtue of the Gosoel, and one of the first steps of pleasing God, having for his own use examined the nature of it, is able to explain it after to others. And particularly, having doubted sometimes whether his repentance were true, or at least in that degree it ought to be, since he found himself sometimes to weep more for the loss of some temporal things than for offending God, he came at length to this resolution, that repentance is an act of the mind, not of the body, even as the original signifies; and that the chief thing which God in Scripture requires, is the heart and the spirit, and to worship him in truth and spirit. Wherefore in case a Christian endeavour to weep, and cannot, since we are not masters of our bodies, this sufficeth. And consequently he found that the essence of repentance, that it may be alike in all God's children (which as concerning weeping it cannot be, some being of a more melting temper than others), consisteth in a true detestation of the soul abhorring and renouncing sin, and turning unto God in truth of heart and newness of life: which acts of repentance are and must be found in all God's servants. Not that weeping is not useful, where it can be, that so the body may join in the grief, as it did in the sin; but that, so the other acts be, that is not necessary: so that he as truly repents who performs the other acts of repentance, when he cannot more, as he that weeps a flood of tears. This instruction and comfort the Parson getting for himself, when he tells it to others, becomes a sermon. The like he doth in other Christian virtues, as of faith and love, and the cases of conscience belonging thereunto, wherein (as St Paul implies that he ought, Romans ii.) he first preacheth to himself, and then to others.

CHAPTER XXXIV. THE PARSON'S DEXTERITY IN APPLYING OF REMEDIES.

The country Parson knows that there is a double state of a Christian, even in this life: the one military, the other peaceable. The military is, when we are assaulted with temptations either from within or from without. The peaceable is, when the devil for a time leaves us, as he did our Saviour, and the angels minister to us their own food, even joy, and peace, and comfort in the Holy Ghost. These two states were in our Saviour, not only in the beginning of his preaching, but afterwards also, as Matth. xxii. 35, He was tempted: And Luke x. 21, He rejoiced in spirit: And they must be likewise in all that are his. Now the Parson having a spiritual judgment, according as he discovers any of his flock to be in one or the other state, so he applies himself to them. Those that he finds in the peaceable state, he adviseth to be very vigilant, and not to let go the reins as soon as the horse goes easy. Particularly, he counselleth them to two things: First, to take heed lest their quiet betray them (as it is apt to do) to a coldness and carelessness in their devotions, but to labour still to be as fervent in Christian duties as they remember themselves were, when affliction did blow the coals. Secondly, not to take the full compass and liberty of their peace: not to eat of all those dishes at table, which even their present health otherwise admits; nor to store their house with all those furnitures, which even their present plenty of wealth otherwise admits; nor when they are among them that are merry, to extend themselves to all that mirth, which the present occasion of wit and company otherwise admits; but to put bounds and hoops to their joys: so will they last the longer, and when they depart, return the sooner. If we would judge ourselves, we should not be judged; and if we would bound ourselves, we should not be bounded. But if they shall fear that at such or such a time their peace and mirth have carried them further than this moderation, then to take Job's admirable course, who sacrificed lest his children should have transgressed in their mirth: so let them go and find some poor afflicted soul, and there be bountiful and liberal; for with such sacrifices God is well pleased. Those that the Parson finds in the military state, he fortifies and strengthens with his utmost skill. Now in those that are tempted, whatsoever is unruly, falls upon two heads; either they think that there is none that can or will look after things, but all goes by chance or wit; or else, though there be a great Governor of all things, yet to them he is lost, as if they said, God doth forsake and persecute them, and there is none to deliver them. If the Parson suspect the first, and find sparks of such thoughts now and then to break forth, then without opposing directly (for disputation is no cure for atheism), he scatters in his discourse three sorts of arguments. The first taken from nature, the second from the law, the third from grace. For nature, he sees not how a house could be either built without a builder, or kept in repair without a housekeeper. He conceives not possibly how the winds should blow so much as they can, and the sea rage as much as it can, and all things do what they can, and all, not only without dissolution of the whole, but also of any part, by taking away so much as the usual seasons of summer and winter, earing and harvest. Let the weather be what it will, still we have bread, though sometimes more, sometimes less; wherewith also a careful Joseph might meet. He conceives not possibly how he that would believe a divinity, if he had been at the creation of all things, should less believe it, seeing the preservation of all things; for preservation is a creation; and more, it is a continued creation, and a creation every moment. Secondly, for the law, there may be so evident though unused a proof of divinity taken from thence, that the atheist or epicurean can have nothing to contradict. The Jews yet live and are known: they have their law and language bearing witness to them, and they to it: they are circumcised to this day, and expect the promises of the Scripture; their country also is known, the places and rivers travelled unto and frequented by others, but to them an unpenetrable rock, an inaccessible desert. Wherefore if the Jews live, all the great wonders of old live in them, and then who can deny the stretched-out arm of a mighty God? especially since it may be a just doubt, whether considering the stubbornness of the nation, their living then in their country, under so many miracles, were a stranger thing than their present exile, and disability to live in their country. And it is observable, that this very thing was intended by God, that the Jews should be his proof and witnesses, as he calls them, Isaiah xliii. 12. And their very dispersion in all lands, was intended not only for a punishment to them, but for an exciting to others by their sight to the acknowledging of God and his power, Psalm lix. 11. And therefore this kind of punishment was chosen rather than any other. Thirdly, for grace. Besides the continual succession (since the Gospel) of holy men who have borne witness to the truth (there being no reason why any should distrust St Luke, or Tertullian, or Chrysostom, more than Tully, Virgil, or Livy), there are two prophecies in the Gospel, which evidently argue Christ's divinity by their success: the one concerning the woman that spent the ointment on our Saviour, for which he told, that it should never be forgotten, but with the Gospel itself be preached to all ages, Matthew xxvi. 13. The other concerning the destruction of Jerusalem, of which our Saviour said that that generation should not pass till all were fulfilled, Luke xxi. 32; which Josephus's history confirmeth, and the continuance of which verdict is yet evident. To these might be added the preaching of the Gospel in all nations, Matthew xxiv. 14, which we see even miraculously effected in these new discoveries, God turning men's covetousness and ambitions to the effecting of his word. Now a prophecy is a wonder sent to posterity, lest they complain of want of wonders. It is a letter sealed and sent, which to the bearer is but paper, but to the receiver and opener is full of power. He that saw Christ open a blind man's eyes, saw not more divinity than he that reads of the woman's ointment in the Gospel, or sees Jerusalem destroyed. With some of these heads enlarged and woven into this discourse, at several times and occasions, the Parson settleth wavering minds. But if he sees them nearer desperation than atheism, not so much doubting a God as that he is theirs, then he dives into the boundless ocean of God's love, and the unspeakable riches of his loving-kindness. He hath one argument unanswerable. If God hate them, either he doth it as they are creatures, dust and ashes, or as they are sinful. As creatures, he must needs love them; for no perfect artist ever yet hated his own work. As sinful, he must much more love them; because notwithstanding his infinite hate of sin, his love overcame that hate; and with an exceeding great victory, which in the creation needed not, gave them love for love, even the Son of his love out of his bosom of love; so that man, which way soever he turns, hath two pledges of God's love, that in the mouth of two or three witnesses every word may be established; the one in his being, the other in his sinful being; and this is the more faulty in him, so the more glorious in God. And all may certainly conclude, that God loves them, till either they despise that love, or despair of his mercy; not any sin else but is within his love; but the despising of love must needs be without it. The thrusting away of his arm makes us only not embraced.

CHAPTER XXXV. THE PARSON'S CONDESCENDING.

The country Parson is a lover of old customs, if they be good and harmless; and the rather, because country people are much addicted to them, so that to favour them therein is to win their hearts, and to oppose them therein is to deject them. If there be any ill in the custom that may be severed from the good, he pares the apple, and gives them the clean to feed on. Particularly he loves procession, and maintains it, because there are contained therein four manifest advantages: First, A blessing of God for the fruits of the field: Secondly, Justice in the preservation of bounds: Thirdly, Charity in loving walking, and neighbourly accompanying one another, with reconciling of differences at that time, if there be any: Fourthly, Mercy in relieving the poor by a liberal distribution and largess, which at that time is or ought to be used. Wherefore he exacts of all to be present at the perambulation, and those that withdraw, and sever themselves from it, he mislikes, and reproves as uncharitable and unneighbourly; and if they will not reform, presents them. Nay, he is so far from condemning such assemblies, that he rather procures them to be often, as knowing that absence breeds strangeness, but presence love. Now love is his business and aim; wherefore he likes well that his parish at good times invite one another to their houses, and he urgeth them to it: and sometimes, where he knows there hath been or is a little difference, he takes one of the parties, and goes with him to the other, and all dine or sup together. There is much preaching in this friendliness. Another old custom there is of saying, when light is brought in, God sends us the light of heaven; and the Parson likes this very well: neither is he afraid of praising or praying to God at all times, but is rather glad of catching opportunities to do them. Light is a great blessing, and as great as food, for which we give thanks; and those that think this superstitious, neither know superstition nor themselves. As for those that are ashamed to use this form as being old and obsolete, and not the fashion, he reforms and teaches them that at baptism they professed not to be ashamed of Christ's cross, or for any shame to leave that which is good. He that is ashamed in small things, will extend his-pusillanimity to greater. Bather should a Christian soldier take such occasions to harden himself and to further his exercises of mortification.

CHAPTER XXXVI. THE PARSON BLESSING.

The country Parson wonders that blessing the people is in so little use with his brethren; whereas he thinks it not only a grave and reverend thing, but a beneficial also. Those who use it not, do so either out of niceness, because they like the salutations and compliments and forms of worldly language better; which conformity and fashionableness is so exceedingly unbefitting a minister, that it deserves reproof, not refutation, or else because they think it empty and superfluous. But that which the apostles used so diligently in their writings, nay, which our Saviour himself used (Mark x. 16), cannot be vain and superfluous. But this was not proper to Christ, or the apostles only, no more than to be a spiritual father was appropriated to them. And if temporal fathers bless their children, how much more may and ought spiritual fathers? Besides, the priests of the Old Testament were commanded to bless the people, and the form thereof is prescribed, Numbers vi. Now, as the Apostle argues in another case, if the ministration of condemnation did bless, how shall not the ministration of the Spirit exceed in blessing? The fruit of this blessing good Hannah found, and received with great joy (1 Samuel i.

18), though it came from a man disallowed by God: for it was not the person but priesthood that blessed; so that even ill priests may bless. Neither have the ministers power of blessing only, but also of cursing. So in the Old Testament, Elisha cursed the children (2 Kings ii. 24), which, though our Saviour reproved as unfitting for his particular, who was to show all humility before his passion, yet he allows it in his apostles. And therefore St Peter used that fearful imprecation to Simon Magus (Acts viii.), Thy money perish with thee: and the event confirmed it. So did St Paul, 2 Timothy iv. 14, and 1 Timothy i. 20. Speaking of Alexander the coppersmith, who had withstood his preaching, The Lord (saith he) reward him according to his works. And again of Hymeneus and Alexander, he saith he had delivered them to Satan, that they might learn not to blaspheme. The forms both of blessing and cursing are expounded in the Common Prayer Book: the one in the grace of our Lord Jesus Christ, &c. and the peace of God, &c.; the other in general in the Commination. Now, blessing differs from prayer in assurance, because it is not performed by way of request, but of confidence and power, effectually applying God's favour to the blessed by the interesting of that dignity wherewith God hath invested the priest, and engaging of God's own power and institution for a blessing. The neglect of this duty in ministers themselves hath made the people also neglect it; so that they are so iar from craving this benefit from their ghostly father, that they oftentimes go out of church before he hath blessed them. In the time of Popery, the priest's benedicite and his holy water were over highly valued; and now we are fallen to the clean contrary, even from superstition to coldness and atheism. But the Parson first values the gift in himself, and then teacheth his parish to value it. And it is observable, that if a minister talk with a great man in the ordinary course of complimenting language, he shall be esteemed as ordinary complimentera; but if he often interpose a blessing, when the other gives him just opportunity, by speaking any good, this unusual form begets a reverence, and makes him esteemed according to his profession. The same is to be observed in writing letters also. To conclude, if all men are to bless upon occasion, as appears Romans xii. 14, how much more those who are spiritual fathers?

CHAPTER XXXVII. CONCERNING DETRACTION.

The country Parson perceiving that most, when they are at leisure, make others' faults their entertainment and discourse, and that even some good men think, so they speak truth, they may disclose another's faults, finds it somewhat difficult how to proceed in this point. For if he absolutely shut up men's mouths, and forbid all disclosing of faults, many an evil may not only be, but also spread in his parish, without any remedy (which cannot be applied without notice) to the dishonour of God and the infection of his flock, and the discomfort, discredit, and hindrance of the pastor. On the other side, if it be unlawful to open faults, no benefit or advantage can make it lawful; for we must not do evil that good may come of it. Now the Parson taking this point to task, which is so exceeding userai, and hath taken so deep root, that it seems the very life and substance of conversation, hath proceeded thus far in the discussing of it. Faults are either notorious or private. Again, notorious faults are either such as are made known by common fame (and of these, those that know them may talk, so they do it not with sport, but commiseration); or else such as have passed judgment, and been corrected either by whipping, or imprisoning, or the like. Of these also men may talk, and more, they may discover them to those that know them not; because infamy is a part of the sentence against malefactors which the law intends, as is evident by those which are branded for rogues that they may be known, or put into the stocks that they may be looked upon. But some may say, though the law allow this, the Gospel doth not, which hath so much advanced charity, and ranked backbiters among the generation of the wicked, Bomans i. 80. But this is easily answered: as the executioner is not uncharitable that takes away the life of the condemned, except, besides his office, he had a tincture of private malice in the joy and haste of acting his part; so neither is he that defames him whom the law would have defamed, except he also do it out of rancour. For in infamy all are executioners, and the law gives the malefactor to all to be defamed. And as malefactors may lose and forfeit their goods or life, so may they their good name, and the possession thereof, which before their offence and judgment they had in all men's breasts; for all are honest till the contrary be proved. Besides, it concerns the commonwealth that rogues should be known, and charity to the public hath the precedence of private charity. So that it is so far from being a fault to discover such offenders, that it is a duty rather, which may do much good, and save much harm. Nevertheless, if the punished delinquent shall be much troubled for his sins, and turn quite another man, doubtless then also men's affections and words must turn, and forbear to speak of that which even God himself hath forgotten.

THE AUTHOR'S PRAYER BEFORE SERMON.

O Almighty and ever living Lord God! Majesty and Power, and Brightness and Glory! How shall we dare to appear before thy face, who are contrary to thee in all we call thee? for we are darkness, and weakness, and filthiness, and shame. Misery and sin fill our days; yet art thou our Creator, and we thy work. Thy hands both made us, and also made us lords of all thy creatures; giving us one world in ourselves, and another to serve us: then didst thou place us in Paradise, and wert proceeding still on in thy favours, until we interrupted thy counsels, disappointed thy purposes, and sold our God, our glorious, our gracious God, for an apple. O write it! O brand it in our foreheads for ever: for an apple once we lost our God, and still lose him for no more; for money, for meat, for diet! But thou, Lord, art patience, and pity, and sweetness, and love; therefore we sons of men are not consumed. Thou hast exalted thy mercy above all things, and hast made our salvation, not our punishment, thy glory: so that then where sin abounded, not death but grace superabounded; accordingly, when we had sinned beyond any help in heaven or earth, then thou saidst, Lo, I come! then did the Lord of life, unable of himself to die, contrive to do it. He took flesh, he wept, he died; for his enemies he died; even for those that derided him then, and still despise him. Blessed Saviour! many waters could not quench thy love, nor no pit overwhelm it! But though the streams of thy blood were current through darkness, grave, and hell, yet by these thy conflicts, and seemingly hazards, didst thou arise triumphant, and therein madest us victorious.

Neither doth thy love yet stay here! for this word of thy rich peace and reconciliation thou has committed, not to thunder or angels, but to silly and sinful men; even to me, pardoning my sins, and bidding me go feed the people of thy love.

Blessed be the God of heaven and earth, who only doth wondrous things. Awake, therefore, my lute and my viol! awake all my powers to glorify thee! We praise thee, we bless thee, we magnify thee forever! And now, O Lord, in the power of thy victories, and in the ways of thy ordinances, and in the truth of thy love, Lo, we stand here, beseeching thee to bless thy word, wherever spoken this day throughout the universal Church. O make it a word of power and peace to convert those who are not yet thine, and to confirm those that are; particularly bless it in this thy own kingdom, which thou hast made a land of light, a storehouse of thy treasures and mercies: O let not our foolish and unworthy hearts rob us of the continuance of this thy sweet love, but pardon our sins, and perfect what thou hast begun. Ride on, Lord, because of the word of truth and meekness and righteousness, and thy right hand shall teach thee terrible things. Especially, bless this portion here assembled together, with thy unworthy servant speaking unto them. Lord Jesu! teach thou me, that I may teach them. Sanctify and enable all my powers, that in their full strength they may deliver thy message reverently, readily, faithfully, and fruitfully! O make thy word a swift word, passing from the ear to the heart, from the heart to the life and conversation, that as the rain returns not empty, so neither may thy word, but accomplish that for which it is given! O Lord, hear! O Lord, forgive! O Lord, hearken and do so for thy blessed Son's sake! in whose sweet and pleasing words, we say, Our Father, &c.

PRAYER AFTER SERMON.

Blessed be God and the Father of all mercy, who continueth to pour his benefits upon us! Thou hast elected us, thou hast called us, thou hast justified us, sanctified, and glorified us. Thou wast born for us, and thou livedst and diedst for us. Thou hast given us the blessings of this life, and of a better. O Lord, thy blessings hang in clusters, they come trooping upon us! they break forth like mighty waters on every side. And now, Lord, thou hast fed us with the bread of life; so man did eat angel's food. O Lord, bless it; O Lord, make it health and strength unto us, still striving and prospering so long within us, until our obedience reach thy measure of thy love, who hast done for us as much as may be. Grant this, dear Father, for thy Son's sake, our only Saviour; to whom with thee and the Holy Ghost, three persons but one most glorious incomprehensible God, be ascribed all honour, and glory, and praise, for ever! Amen.

LETTERS OF GEORGE HERBERT.

From George Herbert to Mr H. Herbert.[19]

Brother,

1618.

The disease which I am troubled with now is the short ness of time, for it hath been my fortune of late to have such sudden warning, that I have not leisure to impart unto you some of those observations which I have framed to myself in conversation, and whereof I would not have you ignorant. As I shall find occasion, you shall receive them by pieces; and if there be any such which you have found useful to yourself, communicate them to me. Tou live in a brave nation, where, except you wink, you cannot but see many brave examples. Be covetous, then, of all good which you see in Frenchmen, whether it be in knowledge, or in fashion, or in words; for I would have you,

P.S. My brother is somewhat of the same temper, and perhaps a little more mild, but you will hardly perceive it.

To my dear Brother,
Mr Henry Herbert, at Paris.

To Sir Henry Herbert.

Dear Brother,

It is so long since I heard from you, that I long to hear both how you and yours do: and also what becomes of you this summer. It is the whole amount of this letter, and therefore entertain it accordingly from your very affectionate brother, G. Herbert.

7th June, Bemerton.
My wife's and nieces' service to you.

Dear Brother,

I was glad of your Cambridge news, but you joyed me exceedingly with your relation of my lady duchess's forwardness in our church building. I am glad I used you in it, and you have no cause to be sorry, since it is God's business. If there fall out yet any

---

[19] "Henry, after he had been brought up in learning, as the other brothers were, was sent by his friends into France, where he attained the language of that country in perfection, after which he came to court, and was made Gentleman of the King's Privy Chamber and Master of the Revels; by which means, as also by a good marriage, he attained to great fortunes, for himself and his posterity to enjoy. He also hath given several proofs of his courage in duels, and otherwise, being no less dexterous in the ways of the Court, as having gotten much by it."—Life of himself, by Lord Herbert of Cherbury even in speeches to observe so much, as when you meet with a witty French speech, try to speak the like in English: So shall you play a good merchant, by transporting French commodities to your own country. Let there be no kind of excellency which it is possible for you to attain to, which you seek not, and have a good conceit of your wit, mark what I say, have a good conceit of your wit; that is, be proud, not with a foolish vaunting of yourself when there is no cause, but by setting a just price of your qualities: And it is the part of a poor spirit to undervalue himself and blush. But I am out of my time: When I have more time, you shall hear more; and write you freely to me in your letters, for I am your ever loving brother, G. Herbert.

rub, you shall hear of me; and your offering of yourself to move my Lords of Manchester and Bolingbroke is very welcome to me. To show a forwardness in religious works is a good testimony of a good spirit. The Lord bless you, and make you abound in every good work, to the joy of your ever loving brother,

G. Herbert.

March 21, Bemerton.
    To my dear Brother,
Sir Henry Herbert, at Court.

    Dear Brother,

That you did not only entertain my proposals, but advance them, was lovingly done, and like a good brother. Yet truly it was none of my meaning, when I wrote, to put one of our nieces into your hands, but barely what I wrote I meant, and no more, and am glad that, although you offer more, yet you will do, as you write, that also. I was desirous to put a good mind into the way of charity, and that was all I intended. For concerning your offer of receiving one, I will tell you what I wrote to our eldest brother, when he urged one upon me, and but one, and that at my choice. I wrote to him that I would have both or neither; and that upon this ground, because they were to come into an unknown country, tender in knowledge, sense, and age, and knew none but one who could be no company to them. Therefore I considered that if one only came, the comfort intended would prove a discomfort. Since that I have seen the fruit of my observation, for they have lived so lovingly, lying, eating, walking, praying, working, still together, that I take a comfort therein; and would not have to part them yet, till I take some opportunity to let them know your love, for which both they shall, and I do thank you. It is true there is a third sister, whom to receive were the greatest charity of all, for she is youngest, and least looked unto; having none to do it but her school-mistress, and you know what those mercenary creatures are. Neither hath she any to repair unto at good times, as Christmas, &c. which you know is the encouragement of learning all the year after, except my cousin Bett take pity of her, which yet at that distance is some difficulty. If you could think of taking her, as once you did, surely it were a great good deed, and I would have her conveyed to you. But I judge you not: do that which God shall put into your heart, and the Lord bless all your purposes to his glory. Yet, truly, if you take her not, I am thinking to do it, even beyond my strength; especially at this time, being more beggarly now than I have been these many years, as having spent two hundred pounds in building; which to me that have nothing yet, is very much. But though I both consider this, and your observation, also, of the unthankfulness of kindred bred up (which generally is very true), yet I care not; I forget all things, so I may do them good who want it. So I do my part to them, let them think of me what they will or can. I have another Judge, to whom *i* stand or fall. If I should regard such things, it were in another's power to defeat my charity, and evil should be stronger than good: but difficulties are so far from cooling Christians, that they whet them. Truly it grieves me to think of the child, how destitute she is, and that in this necessary time of education. For the time of breeding is the time of doing children good: and not as many who think they have done fairly, if they leave them a good portion after their decease. But take this rule, and it is an outlandish one, which I commend to you as being now a father, the best bred child hath the best portion. Well, the good God bless you more and more, and all yours, and make your family a houseful of God's servants. So prays your ever loving brother,

G. Herbert.

My wife's and nieces' service.

To my very dear Brother,
  Sir Henry Herbert, at Court.

LETTERS WRITTEN AT CAMBRIDGE.

For my dear sick Sister.[20]

Most dear Sister,
Think not my silence forgetfulness, or that my love is as dumb as my papers; though business may stop my hand, yet my heart, a much better member, is always with you: and which is more, with our good and gracious God, incessantly begging some ease of your pains, with that earnestness that becomes your griefs, and my love. God who knows and sees this writing, knows also that my soliciting him has been much, and my tears many for you; judge me then by those waters, and not by my ink, and then you shall justly value your most truly, most heartily, affectionate brother and servant,

George Herbert.

Trinity College, December 6, 1620.

To Sir J. D.[21]

Sir,
Though I had the best wit in the world, yet it would easily tire me to find out variety of thanks for the diversity of your favours, if I sought to do so; but I profess it not: And therefore let it be sufficient for me, that the same heart, which you have won long since, is still true to you, and hath nothing else to answer your infinite kindnesses, but a constancy of obedience; only hereafter I will take heed how I propose my desires unto you, since I find you so willing to yield to my requests; for, since your favours come a-horseback, there is reason that my desires should go a-foot; neither do I make any question, but that you have performed your kindness to the full, and that the horse is every way fit for me, and I will strive to imitate the completeness of your love, with being in some proportion, and after my manner, your most obedient servant,

George Herbert.

Sir,
I dare no longer be silent, lest while I think I am modest, I wrong both myself, and also the confidence my friends have in me; wherefore I will open my case unto you, which I think deserves the reading at the least; and it is this, I want books extremely. You know, sir, how I am now setting foot into divinity, to lay the platform of my future life, and shall I then be fain always to borrow books, and build on another's foundation? What tradesman is there who will set up without his tools? Pardon my boldness, sir, it is a most serious case, nor can I write coldly in that, wherein consisteth the making good of my former education, of obeying that Spirit which hath guided me hitherto, and of achieving

---

[20] Wife of Sir Henry Jones. She died in London, after a sickness of fourteen years.
[21] Sir John Danvers, the second husband of Herbert's mother.

my (I dare say) holy ends. This also is aggravated, in that I apprehend what my friends would have been forward to say, if I had taken ill courses, Follow your book, and you shall want nothing. You know, sir, it is their ordinary speech, and now let them make it good; for since I hope I have not deceived their expectations, let not them deceive mine; but perhaps they will say, You are sickly, you must not study too hard; it is true (God knows) I am weak, yet not so, but that everyday, I may step one step towards my journey's end; and I love my friends so well, that if all things proved not well, I had rather the fault should lie on me than on them; but they will object again, what becomes of your annuity? Sir, if there be any truth in me, I find it little enough to keep me in health. You know I was sick last vacation, neither am I yet recovered, so that I am lain ever and anon, to buy somewhat tending towards my health; for infirmities are both painful and costly. Now this Lent I am forbid utterly to eat any fish, so that I am fain to diet in my chamber at mine own cost; for in our public halls, you know, is nothing but fish and white-meats; out of Lent, also twice a-week, on Fridays and Saturdays, I must do so, which yet sometimes I fast. Sometimes also I ride to Newmarket, and there lie a day or two for fresh air; all which tend to avoiding of costlier matters, if I should fall absolutely sick: I protest and vow I even study thrift, and yet I am scarce able with much ado to make one half year's allowance shake hands with the other. And yet if a book of four or five shillings come in my way, I buy it, though I fast for it; yea, sometimes of ten shillings: but, alas! sir, what is that to those infinite volumes of divinity, which yet every day swell and grow bigger? Noble sir, pardon my boldness, and consider but these three things. First, the bulk of divinity; secondly, the time when I desire this (which is now, when I must lay the foundation of my whole life); thirdly, what I desire, and to what end, not vain pleasures, nor to a vain end. If then, sir, there be any course, either by engaging my future annuity, or any other way, I desire you, sir, to be my mediator to them in my behalf.

Now I write to you, sir, because to you I have ever opened my heart; and have reason, by the patents of your perpetual favour to do so still, for I am sure you love your faithfullest servant,

George Herbert.

Trinity College, March 18, 1617.

Sir,

This week hath loaded me with your favours; I wish I could have come in person to thank you, but it is not possible. Presently after Michaelmas I am to make an oration to the whole University of an hour long in Latin, and my Lincoln journey hath set me much behind hand; neither can I so much as go to Bugden, and deliver your letter, yet I have sent it thither by a faithful messenger this day. I beseech you all, you and my dear mother and sister, to pardon me, for my Cambridge necessities are stronger to tie me here, than yours to London. If I could possibly have come, none should have done my message to Sir Fr. Nethersole for me. He and I are ancient acquaintance, and I have a strong opinion of him, that if he can do me a courtesy, he will of himself; yet your appearing in it affects me strangely. I have sent you here enclosed a letter from our master on my behalf, which if you can send to Sir Francis before his departure, it will do well, for it expresseth the University's inclination to me; yet if you cannot send it with much convenience, it is no matter, for the gentleman needs no incitation to love me.

The orator's place (that you may understand what it is) is the finest place in the University, though not the gain-fullest; yet that will be about L.30 per annum, but the commodiousness is beyond the revenue; for the orator writes all the university letters, makes all the orations, be it to king, prince, or whatever comes to the University; to requite these pains, he takes place next the doctors, is at all their assemblies and meetings, and sits above the proctors, is regent, or non-regent at his pleasure, and such like gaynesses, which will please a young man well.

I long to hear from Sir Francis. I pray, sir, send the letter you receive from him to me as soon as you can, that I may work the heads to my purpose. I hope I shall get this place without all your London helps, of which I am very proud, not but that I joy in your favours, but that you may see that if all fail, yet I am able to stand on mine own legs. Noble sir, I thank you for your infinite favours; I fear only that I have omitted some fitting circumstance, yet you will pardon my haste, which is very great, though never so, but that I have both time and work to be your extreme servant,

George Herbert.

Sir,

I have received the things you sent me safe, and now the only thing I long for is to hear of my dear sick sister: first, how her health fares; next, whether my peace be yet made with her concerning my unkind departure. Can I be so happy as to hear of both these that they succeed well? Is it not too much for me? Good sir, make it plain to her that I loved her even in my departure, in looking to her son, and my charge. I suppose she is not disposed to spend her eyesight on a piece of paper, or else I had wrote to her. When I shall understand that a letter will be seasonable, my pen is ready. Concerning the orator's place, all goes well yet; the next Friday it is tried, and accordingly you shall hear. I have forty businesses in my hands: your courtesy will pardon the haste of your humblest servant,

George Hebert.

Trinity College, January 19, 1619.

Sir,

I understand, by Sir Francis Nethersole's letter, that he fears I have not folly resolved of the matter, since this place being civil may divert me too much from divinity, at which, not without canse, he thinks I aim; but I have wrote him back, that this dignity hath no such earthiness in it, but it may very well be joined with Heaven; or if it had to others, yet to me it should not, for aught I yet knew; and therefore I desire him to send me a direct answer in his next letter. I pray, sir, therefore, cause this inclosed to be carried to his brother's house of his own name (as I think) at the sign of the Pedler and the Pack on London Bridge, for there he assigns me. I cannot yet find leisure to write to my lord, or Sir Benjamin Ruddyard; but I hope I shall shortly, though for the reckoning of your favours, I shall never find time and paper enough, yet am I your readiest servant,

George Herbert.

Trinity College, October 6, 1619.

I remember my most humble duty to my mother, who cannot think me lazy, since I rode 200 miles to see a sister, in a way I knew not, and in the midst of much business, and all in a fortnight, not long since.

To the truly noble Sir J. D.

Sir,

 I understand, by a letter from my brother Henry, that he hath bought a parcel of books for me, and that they are coming over. Now, though they have hitherto travelled upon your charge, yet if my sister were acquainted that they are ready, I dare say she would make good her promise of taking five or six pounds upon her, which she hath hitherto deferred to do, not of herself, but upon the want of those books which were not to be got in England; for that which surmounts, though your noble disposition is infinitely free, yet I had rather fly to my old ward, that if any course could be taken of doubling my annuity now, upon condition that I should surcease from all title to it, after I entered into a benefice, I should be most glad to entertain it, and both pay for the surplusage of these books, and for ever after cease my clamorous and greedy bookish requests. It is high time now that I should be no more a burden to you, since I can never answer what I have already received; for your favours are so ancient, that they prevent my memory, and yet still grow upon your humblest servant,

George Herbert.

 I remember my most humble duty to my mother. I have wrote to my dear sick sister this week already, and therefore now I hope may be excused.

 I pray, sir, pardon my boldness of enclosing my brother's letter in yours, for it was because I know your lodging, but not his.

To the Right Hon. the Lady Anne, Countess of Pembroke and Montgomery, at Court.

Madam,

What a trouble hath your goodness brought on you, by admitting our poor services! now they creep in a vessel of metheglin, and still they will be presenting or wishing to see if atlength they may find out something not unworthy of those hands at which they aim. In the meantime a priest's blessing, though it be none of the court style, yet, doubtless, Madam, can do you no hurt: Wherefore the Lord make good the blessing of your mother upon you, and cause all her wishes, diligence, prayers and tears, to bud, blow, and bear fruit in your soul, to his glory, your own good, and the great joy of, Madam, your most faithful servant in Christ Jesus,

George Herbert.

Dec. 10, 1631. Bemerton.

 Madam, your poor colony of servants present their humble duties.

THE ORATION OF MASTER GEORGE HERBERT

Orator of the University of Cambridge, when the Ambassadors were made Masters of Arts. 27th Feb. 1622.

MOST EXCELLENT AND MOST MAGNIFICENT LORDS,

After many singular honours, remarkable commands, most noble ambassages, and other titles most pleasing, as well to us remembering, as to you deserving them, we at last salute you masters of arts; yea, indeed of all, both courtly, military, academical. The accession of which new title to your excellencies, all the muses and graces congratulate; entreating that you would awhile lay aside those warlike looks, with which you used to conquer your enemies, and assume more mild and gracious aspects; and we also putting off that countenance and gravity, by which we well know how to convince the stern, and more austere sort of philosophy, for respect to you, embrace all that is cheerful, joyous, pleasing. For, what could have happened more pleasing to us, than the access of the officers of the Catholic King? whose exceeding glory is equally round with the world itself: who tying, as with a knot, both Indies to his Spain, knows no limits of his praise, no, not, as in past ages, those pillars of Hercules. Long since, all we and our whole kingdom exult with joy, to be united with that blood which useth to infuse so great and worthy spirits. And that which first deserveth our observation, to the end we might the more by love grow on, both the Spanish and British nation serve and worship James. James is the protecting saint unto us both, that you may well conceive your excellencies to be more dear unto us, in that you are of the same order and habit, of which we all in this kingdom glory to be. The praises also and virtues of the most renowned Princess Isabel, passing daily our neighbouring sea, wondrously sound through all our coasts and ears. And necessarily must the felicity of so great princes redound also to those servants, in the choice of whom their judgment doth even now appear. Wherefore most excellent, most illustrious lords, since you are so great both in your princes and yourselves, we justly fear that there is nothing here answerable to the greatness of your presence. For amongst us, what glorious shew is there, either of garments or of any thing else? what splendour? surely, since there is a twofold brightness which dazzleth the eyes of men, we have as much failed as your excellencies do excel in both. But yet the arts in quietness and silence here are reverenced: here is tranquillity, repose, peace with all but bookworms, perpetual poverty, but when your excellencies appear. Yet do not ye contemn these our slight glories, which we raise from books, and painful industry; how could you be like great Alexander, unless history delivered his actions? Fame is sown in this age, that it may be reaped in the following; let the first be the care of your excellencies; we for your gracious acceptance of these poor duties wish, and vow unto you of the last a plenteous harvest.

PREFACE AND NOTES TO THE DIVINE CONSIDERATIONS OF JOHN VALDESSO.

PRINTED AT CAMBRIDGE, 1646.

[The "Considerations" of John Valdesso, a Spanish gentleman, were translated by Nicholas Ferrar, who had become acquainted with the author at the court of Charles V. "Before it was made public," says Walton, "he sent it to be examined and censured by Mr. Herbert," who read and returned it "with many marginal notes, as they be now printed with it; and with them Mr. Herbert's affectionate letter to Mr. Ferrar."]

My dear and deserving brother, your Valdesso I now return with many thanks and some notes, in which, perhaps, you will discover some care which I forbear not in the midst of my griefs: first, for your sake, because I would do nothing negligently that you commit unto me: secondly, for the author's sake, whom I have conceived to have been a true servant of God, and to such, and all that is theirs, I owe diligence: thirdly, for the Church's sake, to whom by printing it, I would have you consecrate it. You owe the Church a debt, and God hath put this into your hands (as he sent the fish with money to Saint Peter) to discharge it; happily also with this (as his thoughts are fruitful), intending the honour of his servant the author, who being obscured in his own country, he would have to flourish in this land of light and region of the Gospel, among his chosen. It is true there are some things which I like not in him, as my fragments will express, when you read them; nevertheless I wish you by all means to publish it, for these three eminent things observable therein: first, that God in the midst of popery should open the eyes of one to understand and express so clearly and excellently the intent of the Gospel, in the acceptation of Christ's righteousness (as he sheweth through all his considerations), a thing strangely buried and darkened by the adversaries and their great stumbling-block. Secondly, the great honour and reverence which he everywhere bears towards our dear Master and Lord, concluding every consideration almost with his holy Name, and setting his merit forth so piously; for which I do so love him, that were there nothing eke I would print it, that with it the honour of my Lord might be published. Thirdly, the many pious rules of ordering our life, about mortification, and observation of God's kingdom within us, and the working thereof, of which he was a very diligent observer. These three things are very eminent in the author, and overweigh the defects, as I conceive, towards the publishing thereof.

From Bemerton, near Salisbury.
September 29, 1632.

NOTES TO THE DIVINE CONSIDERATIONS.

Page 33.

He often useth this manner of speech, believing by revelation, whereby I understand he meaneth only the effectual operation or illumination of the Holy Spirit, testifying and applying the revealed truth of the Gospel, and not any private enthusiasms or revelations: as if he should say, a general apprehension or assent to the promises of the Gospel, by hearsay or relation from others, is not that which filleth the heart with joy and peace in believing, but the Spirit's bearing witness with our spirit, revealing and applying the general promises to every one in particular, with such sincerity and efficacy, that it makes him godly, righteous, and sober all his life long. This I call believing by revelation, and not by relation.

Page 107.

I much mislike the comparison of images and Holy Scriptures, as if they were both but alphabets, and after a time to be left. The Holy Scriptures have not only an elementary use, but a use of perfection; neither can they ever be exhausted (as pictures may be by a plenary circumspection), but still, even to the most learned and perfect in them, there is somewhat to be learned more; therefore David desireth God, in the 119th Psalm, to open his eyes, that he might see the wondrous things of his law, and that he would make them his study; although, by other words of the same psalm, it is evident that he was not meanly conversant in them. Indeed, he that shall so attend to the back of the letter as to neglect the consideration of God's work in his heart through the word, doth amiss; both are to be done: the Scriptures still used, and God's work within us still observed, who works by his word, and ever in the reading of it. As for that text, They shall be all taught of God, it being Scripture, cannot be spoken to the disparagement of Scripture; but the meaning is this, that God in the days of the Gospel will not give an outward law of ceremonies as of old, but such a one as shall still have the assistance of the Holy Spirit applying it to our hearts, and ever outrunning the teacher, as it did when Peter taught Cornelius. There the case is plain: Cornelius had revelation, yet Peter was to be sent for: and those that have inspirations must still use Peter, God's word: if we make another sense of the text, we shall overthrow all means save catechizing, and set up enthusiasms.

In the Scriptures are
Doctrines, these ever teach more and more.
Promises, these ever comfort more and more.
Rom. xv. 4.

Page 109.

The doctrine of this consideration cleareth that of the former; for as the servant leaves not the letter when he hath read it, but keeps it by him, and reads it again and again, and the more the promise is delayed the more he reads it, and fortifies himself with it, so are we to do with the Scriptures, and this is the use of the promises of the Scriptures. But the use of the doctrinal part is more, in regard it presents us not with the same thing only when it is read, as the promises do, but enlightens us with new considerations the more we read it. Much more might be said, but this sufficeth. He himself allows it for a holy conversation and refreshment in the 32nd consideration; and amongst all divine and spiritual exercises and duties, he nameth the reading and meditation of Holy Scripture for the first and principal, as Consid. 47, and others; so that it is plain the author had a very reverend esteem of the Holy Scripture, especially considering the time and place where he lived.

Page 122.

All the discourse from this place to the end of the chapter may seem strange, but it is suitable to what the author holds elsewhere; for he maintains that it is faith and infidelity that shall judge us now since the Gospel, and that no other sin or virtue hath any thing to do with us; if we believe, no sin shall hurt us; if we believe not, no virtue shall help us. Therefore he saith here, we shall not be punished for evil doing, nor rewarded for well doing or living, for all the point lies in believing or not believing. And with this exposition the chapter is clear enough; but the truth of the doctrine would be examined, however it may pass for his opinion, in the Church of God there is one fundamental, but else variety. The author's good meaning in this will better appear by his 98th Consideration of faith and good works.

Page 155.

He meaneth (I suppose) that a man presume not to merit, that is, to oblige God, or justify himself before God, by any acts or exercises of religion; but that he ought to pray God affectionately and fervently, to send him the light of his Spirit, which may be unto him as the sun to a traveller in his journey; he in the meanwhile applying himself to the unquestioned duties of true piety and sincere religion, such as are prayer, fasting, alms-deeds, &c. after the example of devout Cornelius. Or thus: There are two sorts of acts in religion, acts of humiliation and acts of confidence and joy: the person here described to be in the dark ought to use the first, and to forbear the second. Of the first sort are repentance, prayers, fasting, alms, mortifications, &c.; of the second, receiving of the communion, praises, psalms, &c. These in divers cases ought, and were of old forborne for a time.

Page 174.

In indifferent things there is room for motions, and expecting of them; but in things good, as to relieve my neighbour, God hath already revealed his will about it; therefore we ought to proceed, except there be a restraining motion, (as St Paul had) when he would have preached in Asia. And I conceive that restraining motions are much more frequent to the godly than inviting motions, because the Scripture invites enough, for it invites us to all good. According to that singular place, Phil. iv. 8, a man is to embrace all good; but because ho cannot do all, God often chooseth which he shall do, and that by restraining him from what he would not have him do.

Page 177.

This doctrine, howsoever it is true in substance, yet it requireth discreet and wary explaining.

Page 199.

By renouncing the help of human learning in the studying to understand Holy Scripture, he meaneth that we should not use it as the only or as the principal means, because the anointing which we have received and abideth in us teacheth us. 1 John ii. 27.

Page 217.

This chapter is considerable. The intent of it, that the world pierceth not only godly men's actions no more than God's, is in some sort true, because they are spiritually discerned; 1 Cor. ii. 14. So likewise are the godly in some sort exempt from laws, for the law is not made for a righteous man; 1 Tim. i. 9. But when he enlargeth he goes too far: for first, concerning Abraham and Sarah, I ever took that for a weakness in the great patriarch, and that the best of God's servants should have weaknesses, is no way repugnant to the way of God's Spirit in them, or to the Scriptures, or to themselves, being still men, though godly men. Nay, they are purposely recorded in Holy Writ. Wherefore, as David's adultery cannot be excused, so need not Abraham's equivocation, nor Paul's neither, when he professed himself a pharisee, which strictly he was not, though in the point of resurrection he agreed with them and they with him. The reviling also of Ananias seems by his own recalling, an oversight; yet I remember the Father forbids us to judge of the doubtful actions of saints in Scripture, which is a modest admonition. But it is one thing not to judge, another to defend them. Secondly, when he useth the word jurisdiction, allowing no jurisdiction over the godly, this cannot stand, and it is ill doctrine in a commonwealth. The godly are punishable as others when they do amiss, and they are to be judged according to the outward fact, unless it be evident to others as well as to themselves that God moved them; for otherwise any malefactor may pretend motions which is insufferable in a commonwealth. Neither do I doubt but if Abraham had lived in our kingdom under government, and had killed his son Isaac, but he might justly have been put to death for it by the magistrate, unless he could have made it appear that it was done by God's immediate precept. He had done justly, and yet had been punished justly, that is, In humano foro, &c. secundum præsumptionem legalem: according to the common and legal proceedings among men. So may a war be just on both sides, and was just in the Canaanites and Israelites both. How the godly are exempt from laws is a known point among divines; but when he says they are equally exempt with God, that is dangerous and too far. The best salve for the whole chapter is to distinguish judgment. There is a judgment of authority (upon a fact), and there is a judgment of the learned; for as a magistrate judgeth in his tribunal, so a scholar judgeth in his study, and censureth this or that; whence come so many books of several men's opinions: perhaps he meant all of this latter, not of the former. Worldly learned men cannot judge spiritual men's actions; but the magistrate may, and surely this the author meant by the word jurisdiction, for so he useth the same word in Consideration 68 ad finem.

Page 220.

The author doth still discover too slight a regard of the Scripture, as if it were but children's meat, whereas there is not only milk there, but strong meat also, Heb. v. 14; things hard to be understood, 2 Pet. iii. 16; things needing great consideration, Matt. xxiv. 15. Besides, he opposeth the teaching of the Spirit to the teaching of Scripture which the Holy Spirit wrote. Although the Holy Spirit apply the Scripture, yet what the Scripture teacheth the Spirit teacheth; the Holy Spirit, indeed, some time doubly teaching, both in penning and in applying. I wonder how this opinion could befall so good a man as it seems Valdesso was, since the saints of God in all ages have ever held in so precious esteem the word of God, as their joy and crown, and their treasure on earth. Yet his own practice seems to confute his opinion; for the most of his Considerations, being grounded upon some text of Scripture, shows that he was continually conversant in it, and not used it for a time only, and then cast it away, as he says, strangely. There is no more to be said of this chapter, especially of the fifth thing in it, but that this his opinion of the Scripture is insufferable. As for the text of St Peter, 2 Pet. i. 19, which he makes the ground of this consideration, building it all upon the word, "Until the day-star arise;" it is nothing. How many places do the Fathers bring about "until" against the heretics who disputed against the virginity of the blessed virgin, out of the text, Matt. I, 25; where it is said, Joseph knew her not "until" she had brought forth her firstborn son, as if afterwards he had known her; and indeed, in common sense, if I bid a man stay in a place until I come, I do not then bid him go away, but rather stay longer, that I may speak with him or do something else when I come. So St Peter bidding the dispersed Hebrews attend to the word till the day dawn, doth not bid them then cast away the word, or leave it off; but, however, he would have them attend to it till that time, and then afterward they will of themselves attend it without his exhortation. Nay, it is observable that in that very place he prefers the word before the sight of the transfiguration of Christ. So that the word hath the precedence even of revelation and visions.

Page 239.

Divines hold that justifying faith and the faith of miracles are divers gifts, and of a different nature; the one being *gratia gratis data,* the other *gratia gratum faciens,* this being given only to the godly, and the other sometimes to the wicked: yet doubtless the best faith in us is defective, and arrives not to the point it should, which if it did, it would do more than it does. And miracle-working, as it may be severed from justifying faith, so it may be a fruit of it, and an exaltation. 1 John, v. 14.

Page 247.

Though this were the author's opinion, yet the truth of it would be examined. The 98th Consideration, about being justified by faith or by good works, or condemned for unbelief or evil works, make plain the author's meaning.

Page 270.

By the saints of the world he everywhere understands the cunning hypocrite, who by the world is counted a very saint for his outward show of holiness; and we meet with two sorts of these saints of the world: one whose holiness consists in a few ceremonies and superstitious observations; the others in a zeal against these, and in a strict performance of a few cheap and easy duties of religion with no less superstition; both of them having forms or vizors of godliness, but denying the power thereof.

Page 354.

Though this be the author's opinion, yet the truth of it would be examined. The 98th Consideration, about being justified by faith or by good works, or condemned for unbelief or evil works, make plain the author's meaning.

By Hebrew piety he meaneth not the very ceremonies of the Jews, which no Christian observes now, but an analogate observation of ecclesiastical and canonical laws superinduced to the Scriptures, like to that of the Jews, which they added to their divine law; this being well weighed will make the Consideration easy and very observable: for at least some of the Papists are come now to what the Pharisees were come to in our Saviour's time.

Page 355.

This is true only of the Popish cases of conscience, which depend almost wholly on their canon law and decretals, knots of their own tying and untying; but there are other cases of conscience, grounded on piety and morality, and the difficulty of applying their general rules to particular actions, which are a most noble study.

A TREATISE OF TEMPERANCE AND SOBRIETY.

Translated from the Italian of Ludovicus Cornarus.

Having observed in my time many of my friends, of excellent wit and noble disposition, overthrown and undone by intemperance; who, if they had lived, would have been an ornament to the world, and a comfort to their friends; I thought fit to discover, in a short treatise, that intemperance was not such an evil but it might easily be remedied; which I undertake the more willingly, because divers worthy young men have obliged me unto it. For when they saw their parents and kindred snatched away in the midst of their days, and me, contrariwise, at the age of eighty and one, strong and lusty; they had a great desire to know the way of my life, and how I came to be so. Wherefore, that I may satisfy their honest desire, and withal help many others, who will take this into consideration, I will declare the causes which moved me to forsake intemperance, and live a sober life, expressing also the means which I have used therein. I say therefore, that the infirmities, which did not only begin, but had already gone far in me, first caused me to leave intemperance, to which I was mach addicted: for by it, and my ill constitution (having a most cold and moist stomach), I fell into divers diseases, to wit, into the pain of the stomach, and often of the side, and the beginning of the gout, with almost a continual fever and thirst.

From this ill temper there remained little else to be expected of me, than that after many troubles and griefs I should quickly come to an end; whereas my life seemed as far from it by nature, as it was near it by intemperance. When therefore I was thus afflicted from the thirty-fifth year of my age to the fortieth, having tried all remedies fruitlessly, the physicians told me that yet there was one help for me, if I could constantly pursue it, to wit, a sober and orderly life: for this had every way great force for the recovering and preserving of health, as a disorderly life to the overthrowing of it: as I too well by experience found. For temperance preserves even old men and sickly men sound: But intemperance destroys most healthy and flourishing constitutions: for contrary causes have contrary effects, and the faults of nature are often amended by art, as barren grounds are made fruitful by good husbandry. They added withal, that unless I speedily used that remedy, within a few months I should be driven to that exigent, that there would be no help for me, but death shortly to be expected.

Upon this, weighing their reasons with myself, and abhorring from so sudden an end, and finding myself continually oppressed with pain and sickness, I grew fully persuaded, that all my griefs arose out of intemperance: and therefore out of a hope of avoiding death and pain, I resolved to live a temperate life.

Whereupon, being directed by them in the way I ought to hold, I understood, that the food I was to use was such as belonged to sickly constitutions, and that in a small quantity. This they had told me before: but I then not liking that kind of diet, followed ray appetite, and did eat meats pleasing to my taste; and when I felt inward heats, drank delightful wines, and that in great quantity; telling my physicians nothing thereof, as is the custom of sick people. But after I had resolved to follow temperance and reason, and saw that it was no hard thing to do so, but the proper duty of man, I so addicted myself to this course of life, that I never went a foot out of the way. Upon this, I found within a few days, that I was exceedingly helped, and by continuance thereof, within less than one year (although it may seem to some incredible), I was perfectly cured of all my infirmities.

Being now sound and well, I began to consider the force of temperance, and to think thus with myself: If temperance had so much power as to bring me health, how much more to preserve it? Wherefore I began to search out most diligently what meats were agreeable unto me, and what disagreeable: and I purposed to try, whether those that pleased my taste brought me commodity or discommodity; and whether that proverb, wherewith gluttons used to defend themselves, to wit, That which savours is good and nourisheth, be consonant to truth. This upon trial I found most false: for strong and very cool wines pleased my taste best, as also melons, and other fruit; in like manner, raw lettuce, fish, pork, sausages, pulse, and cake and piecrust, and the like: and yet all these I found hurtful.

Therefore trusting on experience, I forsook all these kind of meats and drinks, and chose that wine that fitted my stomach, and in such measure as easily might be digested: above all, taking care never to rise with a full stomach, but so as I might well both eat and drink more. By this means, within less than a year I was not only freed from all those evils which had so long beset me, and were almost become incurable; but also afterwards I fell not into that yearly disease, whereinto I was wont, when I pleased my sense and appetite. Which benefits also still continue, because from the time that I was made whole, I never since departed from my settled course of sobriety, whose admirable power causeth that the meat and drink that is taken in fit measure, gives true strength to the body, all superfluities passing away without difficulty, and no ill humours being engendered in the body.

Yet with this diet I avoided other hurtful things also, as too much heat and cold, weariness, watching, ill air, overmuch use of the benefit of marriage. For although the power of health consists most in the proportion of meat and drink, yet these forenamed things have also their force. I preserved me also, as much as I could, from hatred and melancholy, and other perturbations of the mind, which have a great power over our constitutions. Yet could I not so avoid all these, but that now and then I fell into them, which gained me this experience, that I perceived that they had no great power to hurt those bodies which were kept in good order by moderate diet: so that I can truly say, that they who in these two things that enter in at the month keep a fit proportion, shall receive little hurt from other excesses.

This Galen confirms, when he says, that immoderate heats and colds, and winds and labours, did little hurt him, because in his meats and drinks he kept a due moderation, and therefore never was sick by any of these inconveniences, except it were for one only day. But mine own experience confirmeth this more, as all that know me can testify: for having endured many heats and colds, and other like discommodities of the body and troubles of the mind, all these did hurt me little, whereas they hurt them very much who live intemperately. For when my brother and others of my kindred saw some great powerful men pick quarrels against me, fearing lest I should be overthrown, they were possessed with a deep melancholy (a thing usual to disorderly lives), which increased so much in them, that it brought them to a sudden end; but I, whom that matter ought to have affected most, received no inconvenience thereby, because that humour abounded not in me.

Nay, I began to persuade myself, that this suit and contention was raised by the Divine Providence, that I might know what great power a sober and temperate life hath over our bodies and minds, and that at length I should be a conqueror; as also a little after it came to pass: for in the end I got the victory, to my great honour and no less profit, whereupon also I joyed exceedingly, which excess of joy neither could do me any hurt: by which it is manifest, that neither melancholy nor any other passion can hurt a temperate life.

Moreover, I say, that even bruises, and squats, and falls, which often kill others, can bring little grief or hurt to those that are temperate. This I found by experience when I was seventy years old; for riding in a coach in a great haste, it happened that the coach was overturned, and then was dragged for a good space by the fury of the horses, whereby my head and whole body was sore hurt, and also one of my arms and legs put out of joint. Being carried home, when the physicians saw in what case I was, they concluded that I would die within three days; nevertheless, at a venture, two remedies might be used, letting of blood and purging, that the store of humours and inflammation and fever (which was certainly expected) might be hindered.

But I, considering what an orderly life I had led for many years together, which must needs so temper the humours of the body, that they could not be much troubled, or make a great concourse, refused both remedies, and only commanded that my arm and leg should be set, and my whole body anointed with oil; and so without other remedy or inconvenience I recovered, which seemed as a miracle to the physicians; whence I conclude, that they that live a temperate life can receive little hurt from other inconveniences.

But my experience taught me another thing also, to wit, than an orderly and regular life can hardly be altered without exceeding great danger.

About four years since, I was led, by the advice of physicians, and the daily importunity of my friends, to add something to my usual stint and measure. Divers reasons they brought, as that old age could not be sustained with so little meat and drink; which yet needs not only to be sustained, but also to gather strength, which could not be but by meat and drink. On the other side, I argued that nature was contented with a little, and that I had for many years continued in good health with that little measure; that custom was turned into nature, and therefore it was agreeable to reason, that my years increasing and strength decreasing, my stint of meat and drink should be diminished rather than increased, that the patient might be proportionable to the agent, and especially since the power of my stomach every day decreased. To this agreed two Italian proverbs, the one whereof was,[22] He that will eat much, let him eat little; because by eating little he prolongs his life. The other proberb was,[23] The meat which remaineth profits more than that which is eaten; by which it is intimated, that the hurt of too much meat is greater than the commodity of meat taken in a moderate proportion.

But all these things could not defend me against their importunities. Therefore to avoid obstinacy and gratify ray friends, at length I yielded, and permitted the quantity of meat to be increased, yet but two ounces only; for whereas before, the measure of my whole day's meat, viz. of my bread, and eggs, and flesh, and broth, was twelve ounces exactly weighed, I increased it to the quantity of two ounces more; and the measure of my drink, which before was fourteen ounces, I made now sixteen.

---

[22] Mangiera piu chi manco mangia. Ed e' contrario,
   Chi piu mangia, manco mangia. Il senso e
   Poco vive chi trodpo sparechia.
[23] Fa piu pro quel' che si lafcia ful' tondo, che
   Quel' che si mette nel ventre.

This addition, after ten days, wrought so much upon me, that of a cheerful and merry man I became melancholy and choleric, so that all things were troublesome to me; neither did I know well what I did or said. On the twelfth day, a pain of the side took me, which held me two and twenty hours. Upon the neck of it came a terrible fever, which continued thirty-five days and nights, although after the fifteenth day it grew less and less; besides all this I could not sleep, no, not a quarter of an hour, whereupon all gave me up for dead.

Nevertheless I, by the grace of God, cured myself only with returning to my former course of diet, although I was now seventy-eight years old, and my body spent with extreme leanness, and the season of the year was winter, and most cold air; and I am confident that, under God, nothing holp me, but that exact rule which I had so long continued; in all which time I felt no grief, save now and then a little indisposition for a day or two.

For the temperance of so many years spent all ill humours, and suffered not any new of that kind to arise, neither the good humours to be corrupted or contract any ill quality, as usually happens in old men's bodies, which live without rule; for there is no malignity of old age in the humours of my body which commonly kills men, and that new one which I contracted by breaking my diet, although it was a sore evil, yet had no power to kill me.

By this it may clearly be perceived how great is the power of order and disorder; whereof the one kept me well for many years, the other, though it was but a little excess, in a few days had so soon overthrown me. If the world consist of order, if our corporal life depend on the harmony of humours and elements, it is no wonder that order should preserve, and disorder destroy. Order makes arts easy, and armies victorious, and retains and confirms kingdoms, cities, and families in peace. Whence I conclude, than an orderly life is the most sure way and ground of health and long days, and the true and only medicine of many diseases.

Neither can any man deny this who will narrowly consider it. Hence it comes, that a physician, when he cometh to visit his patient, prescribes this physic first, that he use a moderate diet; and when he hath cured him, commends this also to him, if he will live in health. Neither is it to be doubted, but that he shall ever after live free from diseases, if he will keep such a course of life, because this will cut of all causes of diseases, so that he shall need neither physic nor physician: yea, if he will give his mind to those things which he should, he will prove himself a physician, and that a very complete one; for indeed no man can be a perfect physician to another, but to himself only. The reason whereof is this: Every one by long experience may know the qualities of his own nature, and what hidden properties it hath, what meat and drink agrees best with it; which things in others cannot be known without such observation as is not easily to be made upon others, especially since there is a greater diversity of tempers than of faces. Who would believe that old wine should hurt my stomach, and new should help it, or that cinnamon should heat me more than pepper? What physician could have discovered these hidden qualities to me, if I had not found them out by long experience? Wherefore one to another cannot be a perfect physician. Whereupon I conclude, since none can have a better physician than himself, nor better physic than a temperate life, temperance by all means is to be embraced.

Nevertheless, I deny not but that physicians are necessary, and greatly to be esteemed for the knowing and curing of diseases, into which they often fall who live disorderly: for if a friend who visits thee in thy sickness, and only comforts and condoles, doth perform an acceptable thing to thee, how much more dearly should a physician be esteemed, who not only as a friend doth visit thee, but help thee!

But that a man may preserve himself in health, I advise, that instead of a physician a regular life is to be embraced, which, as is manifest by experience, is a natural physic most agreeable to us, and also doth preserve even ill tempers in good health, and procure that they prolong their life even to a hundred years and more, and that at length they shut up their days like a lamp, only by a pure consumption of the radical moisture, without grief or perturbation of humours. Many have thought that this could be done by aurum potabile, or the philosopher's stone, sought of many, and found of few; but surely there is no such matter, if temperance be wanting.

But sensual men (as most are), desiring to satisfy their appetite and pamper their belly, although they see themselves ill handled by their intemperance, yet shun a sober life; because they say it is better to please the appetite (though they live ten years less than otherwise they should do) than always to live under bit and bridle. But they consider not of how great moment ten years are in mature age, wherein wisdom and all kind of virtues is most vigorous; which, but in that age, can hardly be perfected. And that I may say nothing of other things, are not almost all the learned books that we have, written by their authors in that age, and those ten years which they set at nought in regard of their belly?

Besides, these belly-gods say that an orderly life is so hard a thing that it cannot be kept. To this I answer that Galen kept it, and held it for the best physic; so did Plato also, and Isocrates and Tully, and many others of the ancients; and in our age, Paul the third, and Cardinal Bembo, who therefore lived so long; and among our Dukes, Laudus and Donatus, and many others of inferior condition, not only in the city, but also in villages and hamlets.

Wherefore, since many have observed a regular life, both of old times and later years, it is no such thing which may not be performed; especially since in observing it there needs not many and curious things, but only that a man should begin, and by little and little accustom himself unto it.

Neither doth it hinder, that Plato says, that they who are employed in the commonwealth cannot live regularly, because they must often endure heats, and colds, and winds, and showers, and divers labours, which suit not with an orderly life: for I answer, that those inconveniences are of no great moment (as I showed before) if a man be temperate in meat and drink, which is both easy for commonweal's men, and very convenient, both that they may preserve themselves from diseases, which hinder public employment; as also that their mind, in all things wherein they deal, may be more lively and vigorous.

But some may say, he which lives a regular life, eating always light meats and in a little quantity, what diet shall he use in diseases, which, being in health, he hath anticipated? I answer first, Nature, which endeavours to preserve a man as much as she can, teacheth us how to govern ourselves in sickness: for suddenly it takes away our appetite, so that we can eat but a very little, wherewith she is very well contented; so that a sick man, whether he hath lived heretofore orderly or disorderly, when he is sick, ought not to eat but such meats as are agreeable to his disease, and that in much smaller quantity than when he was well. For if he should keep his former proportion, nature, which is already burdened with a disease, would be wholly oppressed. Secondly, I answer better, that he which lives a temperate life, cannot fall into diseases, and but very seldom into indispositions, because temperance takes away the causes of diseases; and the cause being taken away, there is no place for the effect.

Wherefore, since an orderly life is so profitable, so virtuous, so decent, and so holy, it is worthy by all means to be embraced; especially since it is easy and most agreeable to the nature of man. No man that follows it, is bound to eat and drink so little as I: no man is forbidden to eat fruit or fish, which I eat not: for I eat little, because a little sufficeth my weak stomach; and I abstain from fruit and fish, and the like, because they hurt me. But they who find benefit in these meats may, yea ought to use them; yet all must needs take heed lest they take a greater quantity of any meat or drink (though most agreeable to them) than their stomach can easily digest: so that he which is offended with no kind of meat and drink, hath the quantity, and not the quality for his rule, which is very easy to be observed.

Let no man here object unto me, that there are many, who though they live disorderly, yet continue in health to their lives' end: because since this is at the best but uncertain, dangerous, and very rare, the presuming upon it ought not to lead us to a disorderly life.

It is not the part of a wise man to expose himself to so many dangers of diseases and death, only upon a hope of a happy issue, which yet befalls very few. An old man of an ill constitution, but living orderly, is more sure of his life than the most strong young man who lives disorderly.

But some, too mach given to appetite, object, that a long life is no each desirable thing, because that after one is once sixty-five years old, all the time we live after is rather death than life: but these err greatly, as I will show by myself recounting the delights and pleasures in this age of eighty-three, which now I take, and which are such as that men generally account me happy.

I am continually in health, and I am so nimble, that I can easily get on horseback without the advantage of the ground, and sometimes I go up high stairs and hills on foot. Then, I am ever cheerful, merry, and well-contented, free from all troubles and troublesome thoughts; in whose place joy and peace have taken up their standing in my heart. I am not weary of life, which I pass with great delight. I confer often with worthy men, excelling in wit, learning, behaviour, and other virtues. When I cannot have their company, I give myself to the reading of some learned book, and afterwards to writing; making it my aim in all things, how I may help others to the furthest of my power.

All these things I do at my ease, and at fit seasons, and in mine own houses; which, besides that they are in the fairest place of this learned city of Padua, are very beautiful and convenient above most in this age, being so built by me according to the rules of architecture, that they are cool in summer, and warm in winter.

I enjoy also my gardens, and those divers, parted with rills of running water, which truly is very delightful. Sometimes of the year I enjoy the pleasure of the Euganean hills, where also I have fountains and gardens, and a very convenient house. At other times, I repair to a village of mine, seated in the valley; which is therefore very pleasant, because many ways thither are so ordered, that they all meet, and end in a fair plot of ground; in the midst whereof is a church suitable to the condition of the place. This place is washed with the river Brenta; on both sides whereof are great and fruitful fields, well manured and adorned with many habitations. In former time it was not so, because the place was moorish and unhealthy, fitter for beasts than men. But I drained the ground, and made the air good: whereupon men flocked thither and built houses with happy success. By this means the place is come to that perfection we now see it is; so that I can truly say, that I have both given God a temple, and men to worship him in it: the memory whereof is exceeding delightful to me.

Sometimes I ride to some of the neighbour cities, that I may enjoy the sight and the communication of my friends, as also of excellent artificers in architecture, painting, stone-cutting, music, and husbandry, whereof in this age there is great plenty. I view their pieces, I compare them with those of antiquity; and ever I learn somewhat which is worthy of my knowledge. I survey palaces, gardens, and antiquities, public fabrics, temples, and fortifications; neither omit I anything that may either teach or delight me. I am much pleased also in my travels, with the beauty of situation. Neither is this my pleasure made less by the decaying dulness of my senses, which are all in their perfect vigour, but especially my taste; so that any simple fare is more savoury to me now than heretofore, when I was given to disorder and all the delights that could be.

To change my bed, troubles me not; I sleep well and quietly any where, and my dreams are fair and pleasant. But this chiefly delights me, that my advice hath taken effect in the reducing of many rude and untoiled places in my country, to cultivation and good husbandry. I was one of those that was deputed for the managing of that work, and abode in those fenny places two whole months in the heat of summer (which in Italy is very great), receiving not any hurt or inconvenience thereby: so great is the power and efficacy of that temperance which ever accompanied me.

These are the delights and solaces of my old age, which is altogether to be preferred before others' youth: because that by temperance and the grace of God I reel not those perturbations of body and mind, wherewith infinite both young and old are afflicted.

Moreover, by this also, in what estate I am, may be discovered, because at these years (viz. eighty-three) I have made a most pleasant comedy, full of honest wit and merriment: which kind of poems useth to be the child of youth, which it most suits withal for variety and pleasantness; as a tragedy with old age, by reason of the sad events which it contains. And if a Greek poet of old was praised, that at the age of seventy-three years he writ a tragedy, why should I be accounted less happy, or less myself, who being ten years older, have made a comedy?

Now lest there should be any delight wanting to my old age, I daily behold a kind of immortality in the succession of my posterity. For when I come home, I find eleven grand-children of mine, all the sons of one father and mother, all in perfect health; all, as far as I can conjecture, very apt and well given both for learning and behaviour. I am delighted with their music and fashion, and I myself also sing often; because I have now a clearer voice than ever I had in my life.

By which it is evident, that the life which I live at this age, is not a dead, dumpish, and sour life; but cheerful, lively, and pleasant: neither if I had my wish, would I change age and constitution with them who follow their youthful appetites, although they be of a most strong temper: because such are daily exposed to a thousand dangers and deaths, as daily experience showeth, and I also, when I was a young man, too well found. I know how inconsiderate that age is, and, though subject to death, yet continually afraid of it: for death to all young men is a terrible thing, as also to those that live in sin, and follow their appetites; whereas I by the experience of so many years have learned to give way to reason: whence it seems to me, not only a shameful thing to fear that which cannot be avoided; but also I hope, when I shall come to that point, I shall find no little comfort in the favour of Jesus Christ. Yet I am sure that my end is far from me: for I know that (setting casualties aside) I shall not die but by a pure resolution: because that by the regularity of my life I have shut out death all other ways; and that is a fair and desirable death, which nature brings by way of resolution.

Since, therefore, a temperate life is so happy and pleasant a thing, what remains, but that I should wish all who have the care of themselves, to embrace it with open arms?

Many things more might be said in commendation hereof: but lest in anything I forsake that temperance which I have found so good, I here make an end.

THE END

Printed by BoD in Norderstedt, Germany